THE

UNOFFICIAL
HARRY
POTTER
COOKBOOK

THE
UNOFFICIAL
HARRY
POTTER
COOKBOOK

From Cauldron Cakes to Knickerbocker Glory—More Than 150 Magical Recipes for Wizards and Non-Wizards Alike

DINAH BUCHOLZ

Adams Media
New York   London   Toronto   Sydney   New Delhi

Adams Media
An Imprint of Simon & Schuster, Inc.
57 Littlefield Street
Avon, Massachusetts 02322

For information about special discounts for bulk purchases, please contact Simon & Schuster Special Sales at 1-866-506-1949 or business@simonandschuster.com.

The Simon & Schuster Speakers Bureau can bring authors to your live event. For more information or to book an event contact the Simon & Schuster Speakers Bureau at 1-866-248-3049 or visit our website at www.simonspeakers.com.

Printed by LSC Harrisonburg, Virginia
50 49 48 47 46 45 44 43
October 2019

Library of Congress Cataloging-in-Publication Data
Bucholz, Dinah.
The unofficial Harry Potter cookbook / Dinah Bucholz.
p. cm.
Includes index.
ISBN 978-1-4405-0325-2
1. Cookery, English. 2. Potter, Harry (Fictitious character) 3. Rowling, J. K.—Characters—Harry Potter. 4. Potter, Harry I. Title. II. Title: Harry Potter cookbook.
TX717.B87 2010
641.5942—dc22
2010019544

ISBN 978-1-4405-0325-2
ISBN 978-1-4405-0852-3 (ebook)

Always follow safety and commonsense cooking protocols while using kitchen utensils, operating ovens and stoves, and handling uncooked food. If children are assisting in the preparation of any recipe, they should always be supervised by an adult.

The following recipes were created for this book by Chef Chris Koch. Chef Chris, a classically French–trained chef, is the culinary director of a Philadelphia cooking school, kitchen director for a number of TV shows, and author of *Learning the Basics: A Home Cook's Guide to the Kitchen*.

English Fried Eggs and a Gammon of Bacon
Tender Roast Loin of Pork with Variations
French Onion Soup
Melton Mowbray Pork Pies
English Farmhouse Scrambled Eggs and Bacon
Breaded Pork Chops
Queen Victoria's Soup
Chicken and Ham Pie
Bouillabaisse
Stewed Tripe and Onions

Also thanks to Abe Polatsek for contributing the recipe for The Roast Beef of Old England.

Acknowledgments

First I thank God, who is the source of all blessing. Second, I thank my husband, Heshy, who insisted I put him next to God in my acknowledgments, for more reasons than this book has space for.

George Beahm, author of *Fact, Fiction, and Folklore in Harry Potter's World* and *Muggles and Magic*, generously gave of his time to advise me on how to sell my book to an agent.

Mary Sue Seymour is probably the fastest, most efficient, and most professional agent out there. I am fortunate and blessed that she offered to represent this book.

Thanks to my editor at Adams Media, Andrea Norville, who saw the potential for this book and whose enthusiasm turned it from an idea into a reality.

Thanks to Kate Petrella for her thorough copyediting of the manuscript.

Thanks to Chef Chris Koch for his contribution to this book. Chef Chris developed those recipes that I could not due to my kosher diet.

Thanks to Chevi Schainbaum, Cheryl Albert, Yaffa Yermish, Ayala Tarshish, Israel Tarshish, Abe Polatsek, Naomi Polatsek, Batsheva Polatsek, Atara Eiss, and Goldy Joseph. And my friends, neighbors, and the engineers at L-3 for taste-testing (they were more than happy to oblige). So many people offered help and advice that it's inevitable I should leave someone out. If you are that someone, please forgive me.

I thank my mother, Esther (Amsel) Polatsek, who taught me how to cook, and my father, Alex Polatsek, who taught me that in a moral dilemma, the harder choice is often the right choice.

Thanks to my parents-in-law, Frimmy and Meyer Bucholz, for their love and support.

Finally, but no less dearly, thanks to my kids, Elisheva, Sarah, Eliyahu, and Toby, for their honest opinions on the food.

Contents

Foreword: A Feast of Food and Words

Harry Potter's first taste of Hogwarts, as it were, is an eye-opener. While the Dursleys did not completely neglect to feed Harry, they never allowed him to eat as much as he wanted. So at his first Hogwarts feast, for the first time in his short life, he is allowed to eat as much as he likes (see *Harry Potter and the Sorcerer's Stone*, Chapter 7).

Each school year at Hogwarts begins with a celebratory meal in its cavernous Great Hall. No doubt those magnificent meals left an indelible impression on a young Harry, who hungered for more when living with his Muggle relatives: a feeling of kinship and of family that he clearly lacked; a desire to know his clouded past, which had been carefully and deliberately hidden from him at all costs by his duplicitous uncle and aunt, the detestable Dursleys; and most of all, a desire to realize who he truly is, living in two diametrically opposed worlds, the unimaginative Muggle world and the enchanting world of wizards, his true home.

Though we Muggles will never get to taste life in the wizarding world, we must console ourselves with sampling the food Rowling writes about so lovingly.

In her seven novels, food—breakfast, lunch, dinner, and snacks—plays an important part, an essential ingredient that helps complete our picture of life at Hogwarts. That's especially true for American readers who are largely more familiar with Big Macs and fries at McDonald's than with traditional British cuisine: Black Pudding, Crumpets, Spotted Dick, Kippers, Steak and Kidney Pie, trifles, and other dishes.

Fortunately, we Americans do share a commonality with some of the foods mentioned in Rowling's novels and this delightful cookbook. First on that list is ice cream, which of course is universally loved and needs no explanation to Americans. (We each consume 23.3 quarts annually, according to *www.makeicecream.com*.)

Candy, too, is a universal favorite, though wizards get to enjoy confections not available to Muggles: Jelly Slugs, Fizzing Whizbees, and Fudge Flies, to name a few (see *Harry Potter and the Prisoner of Azkaban*, Chapter 10).

Rowling's mouth-watering dishes, desserts, and candies are left to our imaginations, hungry for more information about their appearance and taste. The Muggle-created versions, to be sold at The Wizarding World of Harry Potter in Universal Orlando Resort, are the closest we'll get to actually enjoying them. But for those of us not lucky enough to travel to Florida, what's left to savor?

Traditional British cuisine, which is the subject of this marvelous book by Dinah Bucholz, who serves up an enticing selection of recipes for Muggles who hunger for a taste of England.

Dishing out recipes that all Muggle readers ought to try at least once in their lives, this cookbook deserves a place in every Muggle kitchen. A brave new world of gustatory delights awaits, if only we Americans have the stomach to try something other than our favorite dishes of pizza, burgers, and sandwiches.

I raise my foaming mug of butterbeer—the most frequently mentioned beverage in the Harry Potter novels—in salute to Dinah, who serves up more than 150 recipes that will satisfy the appetites of hungry Muggles everywhere. Anyone for Toad in the Hole, Cock-a-Leekie, Haggis, or Goulash? Step right this way. Hey, where do you think *you're* going? Come back! Just try one bite!

For the gastronomically conservative reader who is willing to venture forth and broaden his palate with traditional British dishes, *The Unofficial Harry Potter Cookbook* will satisfy the appetite, no matter how persnickety.

Bon appétit!

—George Beahm, author of *Muggles and Magic* and *Fact, Fiction, and Folklore in Harry Potter's World*

Introduction

This book grants its reader great powers. It's true that a Muggle may twirl sticks and mutter incantations and the only thing that will happen is his or her mother will yell, "If you're not careful with that wand, you'll poke your brother's eye out." But despair not, dear Muggle. A branch of magic is still open to you—Curye, later known as Cookery, which combines elements of potions with transfiguration, and a bit of herbology and divination. According to Gamp's Law of Elemental Transfiguration (see *Harry Potter and the Deathly Hallows*, Chapter 15), good food cannot be created from nothing, but it can be created using this book. Within these pages you shall find directions for delightful dishes, exquisite elixirs, fabulous fare, tasty treats, and the ability to transform mundane ingredients into marvelous masterpieces.

If you're not from the British Isles you may not recognize the foods mentioned in the Harry Potter series. This book is your guide. Here you'll find more than just directions and recipes; you'll discover their long and fascinating history. Learn about the foods that are an integral part of British and Irish culture. Thrill to the stories of their discoveries and inventions. And then eat those foods. You'll never look at a crumpet the same way again.

Though you may be as clever as Hermione, blindly following recipes from a book will not guarantee success. Sometimes you don't have the best recipe; sometimes it's the technique that's wrong. Don't you wish you had a Half-Blood Prince looking over your shoulder, telling you, "I have a better way to concoct this potion?" Well, the recipes gathered here are a result of combining the best recipes out there, testing and retesting and retesting some more, until at last, the tastiest and easiest recipe that dish can have was created.

Helpful Hints

1. Always start with a clean work surface.

2. Read through the recipe carefully and make sure you have all the ingredients and equipment—and skills—to make that recipe. If you lack the necessary skills, you can give it a go anyway; just be sure to arm yourself with patience and humor and don't give up if it comes out wrong.

3. A word of caution: Some of the recipes in this book are dangerous. Any recipe involving boiling sugar (such as fudge or toffee) or deep-frying (such as doughnuts) should be attempted only by adults or children at least in their teens under very close adult supervision.

4. Substitutions: Some of the recipes in this book call for currants. If you can't find currants, dried cranberries can be used as a substitute. Where vegetable oil is specified, canola oil can be used instead. Also, in recipes calling for cocoa powder use Dutch cocoa powder if you can find it, as it's far superior to natural cocoa powder.

5. The ice cream and custard recipes call for tempering egg yolks. This is a process by which the yolks are brought up to a higher temperature slowly to prevent curdling.

6. When making cakes and cookies, make sure the butter, eggs, and milk are at room temperature (68°F to 72°F). The butter needs to be soft to be properly creamed, and cold eggs or milk added to a properly creamed mixture will curdle it. If you've done everything right and the mixture appears curdled anyway, don't worry. The addition of liquid can cause that appearance, which will smooth out when you add the flour.

7. To grease and flour a pan, you can use a flour-and-oil baking spray. It's much faster and yields better results than the old-fashioned method of buttering the pan and dusting the flour over it, then shaking out the excess flour. Make sure you also line your cake pans with parchment paper so that the layers come out in one piece.

8. It's important to measure ingredients precisely. You will need one liquid measuring cup and a set of dry measuring cups as well as a set of measuring spoons. To measure flour or sugar, dip the measuring cup into the container and level it with a straight edge, such as the flat side of a knife. Do not pack down the flour or shake the cup to even the top. To measure packed brown sugar, use your fingers, your fist, your knuckles, or a spoon to pack down the sugar as you fill the cup.

9. If you do not own a food processor, you can make pie or tart dough by hand. Rub the fat into the flour using your fingertips or cut it into the flour using two forks until the mixture resembles coarse yellow meal. Make sure to incorporate all the white powdery bits. Proceed as directed in the recipe.

10. Pie dough is easy to make once you master the technique. Make sure you use very cold ingredients and be careful to work the dough as little as possible. Mixing too much makes the crust hard to roll out (it will keep springing back) and yields a tough texture. When adding water, it's better to add too much than too little. You can always add extra flour when rolling out the dough to prevent sticking, but a dry dough will keep cracking and tearing when you roll it out, and you won't be able to save it.

11. Many recipes call for toasting nuts. To do this properly, spread the nuts in a single layer on a baking sheet and toast in a 350°F oven for 7 to 10 minutes until brown and fragrant.

12. Some recipes specify treacle or golden syrup. These sweeteners are produced during the sugar refining process and are similar to molasses. You can find treacle or golden syrup in a well-stocked supermarket or specialty food store, but if you can't find them, use the following substitutions:

    For black treacle, use dark molasses or blackstrap molasses. For golden syrup, use light or dark corn syrup, light molasses, or pure maple syrup. Maple syrup will impart a unique flavor to the finished product, so use it with discretion.

13. Turbinado sugar, also called demerara sugar, is raw cane sugar, which looks like large, pale brown, translucent crystals, and is great for sprinkling on cookies or muffins because it looks pretty and is a lot crunchier than granulated sugar. It's easy to find in the baking aisle of your supermarket. A common supermarket brand is Sugar in the Raw.

14. If you use glass pans such as Pyrex or dark metal pans to bake cakes, subtract 25 degrees from the temperature specified in the recipe, as these pans get hotter and retain heat for longer. Baking at the higher temperature will cause the cakes to overbake.

15. The food processor used for testing the recipes in this book was an old model. The number of pulses specified is simply a guideline; use the visual cues provided in the recipe to know when to stop pulsing. This is especially important in pie and tart doughs, as overprocessing can yield a tough rather than tender crust.

Chapter One

Good Food with Bad Relatives

The Dursleys might thank you to remember that they are as normal as can be, but their treatment of their own flesh-and-blood nephew Harry Potter is anything but. Determined to stamp out any vestiges of magic he might have inherited from his wizard parents, they keep him as downtrodden as possible. But they can't force him to avoid his destiny. On the stroke of midnight of his eleventh birthday, after years of fantasizing about a kind relative coming to claim him, Harry is visited by a half-giant called Hagrid, who tells him the truth about his heritage. Despite the best efforts of the Dursleys to prevent this, Harry finally escapes to Hogwarts to be trained as a wizard (see *Harry Potter and the Sorcerer's Stone*, Chapters 1–6).

Aunt Petunia has always hated her sister for being able to master potions, but she is no slouch around the cauldron either, at least when it comes to cooking. In *Harry Potter and the Chamber of Secrets* she whips up a three-course meal for a classy dinner party with the Masons, and in *Harry Potter and the Prisoner of Azkaban*, a fancy meal for Aunt Marge. To the disgust, shame, and horror of the Dursleys, Harry ruins both meals . . . and Uncle Vernon will never forgive him for losing the deal that would have bought him a summer home in Majorca.

English Fried Eggs and a Gammon of Bacon

Does Harry sometimes remind you of Cinderella? He has to cook, he has to clean . . . . Often he plays the role of breakfast chef at the Dursleys', and the morning of Dudley's birthday is no exception. Aunt Petunia darkly warns him not to burn breakfast (see *Harry Potter and the Sorcerer's Stone*, Chapter 2).

Eggs and bacon doesn't sound very posh, but some 400 years ago, it was the "Breakfast of Queens." Henrietta Maria, Queen Consort of England and wife of King Charles I, would finish off a fancy breakfast with a simple dish of poached eggs and bacon. In England, a "rasher" is used to refer to a slice of bacon.

2 rashers (slices) of bacon
1 tablespoon lard or bacon drippings reserved from frying
2 large eggs
Salt and freshly ground black pepper to taste

1. To pan-fry the bacon, heat a skillet or sauté pan over medium-high heat. Lay the bacon carefully in the pan. Let the bacon cook for 2 minutes; then, using a pair of tongs or a fork, turn the bacon and cook for 2 minutes more. Continue cooking and turning every 30 seconds until the bacon reaches desired crispness. Remove the bacon and let it drain on paper towels. Drain all but 1 tablespoon of fat from the pan.

2. Reduce the heat to medium low. Break the eggs into a small bowl. When the fat begins to sizzle, add the eggs and season with salt and pepper.

Serves 1

Fried eggs are served by a degree of doneness: sunny side up, over-easy, over-medium, or over-hard. For sunny side up, cook the eggs for 4 minutes or until the white is set and firm. For "over" eggs, add the eggs to the pan and let cook for 3 minutes. Carefully flip the eggs using a spatula and cook as follows: over-easy for 2 minutes on second side; over-medium, 2 minutes, 15 seconds; over-hard, 2 minutes, 30 seconds or until the yolk is completely firm. You can also break the yolk before turning for over-hard.

Double Chocolate Ice Cream Cones

When Harry goes with the Dursleys to the zoo, the day starts out like a dream come true. Harry has never been taken along on Dudley's birthday trips before and he can hardly believe his luck. Uncle Vernon buys chocolate ice creams for Dudley and his friend Piers to enjoy on their outing. There's none for Harry, of course (see *Harry Potter and the Sorcerer's Stone*, Chapter 2).

When the first ice cream recipe found its way to England in the 1600s, King Charles I wanted to keep it for himself. Ice cream was a treat reserved for royalty and the king wanted to make sure it stayed that way. According to legend, he swore his cook to keep the recipe a secret. But when the king died, the secret got out . . . and now you can enjoy this sumptuous ice cream recipe.

2 cups whole milk
2 cups heavy cream
¾ cup granulated sugar
2 tablespoons unsweetened cocoa
  powder

5 large egg yolks
8 ounces bittersweet chocolate,
  melted and cooled
1 teaspoon pure vanilla extract
Sugar cones for serving

1. Combine the milk, heavy cream, sugar, and cocoa powder in a medium saucepan and cook, stirring frequently, until hot but not simmering. Whisk the melted chocolate into the egg yolks (it will be thick and difficult to whisk). Temper the egg yolk mixture by slowly pouring 1 cup of the hot milk mixture into the yolks while whisking vigorously. Pour the yolk mixture into the saucepan containing the rest of the milk mixture and cook, stirring constantly, until very hot but not simmering. Do not boil.

2. Pour the mixture through a sieve. Stir in the vanilla extract. Cover the surface with plastic wrap to prevent a skin from forming and cool to room temperature, then chill until completely cold, about 6 hours. Freeze in your ice cream maker following the manufacturer's instructions. Transfer to an airtight container and freeze until firm, 8 hours or overnight.

3. To serve, scoop 2 balls of ice cream into each cone and top with your favorite toppings.

Makes about 5 cups

If the ice cream is rock hard after freezing, allow it to soften at room temperature for 15 minutes before serving. Homemade ice cream keeps for about a week. Also, to keep the cones from leaking, pour melted bittersweet chocolate into the bottom of each one before filling with the ice cream.

Triple Power Icy Lemon Pops

The Dursleys don't want to buy Harry chocolate ice cream when they take him to the zoo on Dudley's birthday, but when the lady asks him what he'll have, they at least have the decency to be embarrassed to not buy him anything. They compromise by buying him a lemon pop, which Harry enjoys anyway (see *Harry Potter and the Sorcerer's Stone*, Chapter 2).

Grated zest of 1 lemon

3 tablespoons lemon juice

7 tablespoons granulated sugar

1¾ cups water

½ teaspoon lemon extract

Who doesn't like a nice frozen pop on a hot day? Slushies and other frozen treats have been around for thousands of years. The famous conqueror Alexander the Great had fresh snow brought to him from the mountains to chill his wine, and the evil Roman emperor Nero used to mix snow with honey and fruit for dessert, which he had to eat right away before it melted. Fortunately, thanks to modern technology, we don't have to go to such lengths to enjoy these treats.

1. Place the lemon zest, lemon juice, sugar, and water in a saucepan and heat, stirring frequently, just until beginning to simmer. Remove from the heat and stir in the lemon extract. Pour into ice pop molds.
2. Freeze until solid, about 5 hours.

Makes approximately 4 (4-ounce) pops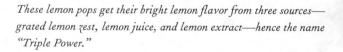

These lemon pops get their bright lemon flavor from three sources— grated lemon zest, lemon juice, and lemon extract—hence the name "Triple Power."

Knickerbocker Glory

Dudley pretends to cry when he discovers that Harry will have to come along with him on his birthday trip. Aunt Petunia, fooled by his antics, assures Dudley that she won't let Harry spoil his special day. Little does she know! But before the day ends in disaster, Harry enjoys the knickerbocker glory he has been allowed to finish when Dudley complains his doesn't have enough ice cream (see *Harry Potter and the Sorcerer's Stone*, Chapter 2).

This is a terrific summer treat and easy to prepare. It's time to revive the knickerbocker glory in America. This parfait-like dessert was first recorded in the United States in the 1930s, but instead of taking off here, it found its way across the ocean and became popular in England. How did it get its curious name? Some say from striped knickerbockers: the layers of ice cream, jelly, custard, fruit, and whipped cream look like striped knee breeches. However, "knickerbockers" was also a term used to refer to New Yorkers, so that might be a connection too.

2 cups custard (recipe follows)
Whipped cream (recipe follows)
2 cups any flavor Jell-O (prepared in advance)
Chopped toasted nuts, such as peanuts
2 cups chopped fresh fruit (such as peaches or berries)
1 pint vanilla ice cream
Chocolate syrup

1. Prepare the custard, whipped cream, and Jell-O in advance; chop and toast the nuts ahead as well.
2. Wash, and if necessary, peel and chop the fruit you are using.
3. Set out six tall sundae glasses. Divide ½ pint of the ice cream into the bottom of the six glasses. Evenly divide 1 cup of the fruit into the glasses. Then evenly divide 1 cup of the Jell-O over the fruit and 1 cup of the custard over the Jell-O. Repeat the layering once with the remaining ice cream, fruit, Jell-O, and custard.
4. Top with the whipped cream, toasted nuts, and chocolate syrup.

Serves 6

Custard

¼ cup granulated sugar, divided
3 tablespoons cornstarch
¼ teaspoon salt
1 cup whole milk and ½ cup heavy cream or 1½ cups whole milk
3 large egg yolks
1 teaspoon pure vanilla extract

1. Combine 2 tablespoons of the sugar with the cornstarch and salt in a small heavy-bottomed saucepan. Add the milk and cream and stir until the cornstarch dissolves. In a separate bowl, whisk the egg yolks with the remaining 2 tablespoons sugar.

2. Cook the milk mixture over medium-high heat until the mixture is just starting to bubble and thicken. Reduce the heat to low. Temper the yolks by slowly pouring ½ cup of the hot mixture into the yolks while whisking constantly. Pour the yolk mixture into the saucepan, stirring constantly.

3. Turn the heat back up to medium-high. Cook, stirring constantly but gently, until the mixture is thick. Once the mixture starts to thicken, it must be handled gently or the cornstarch will lose its thickening power. Remove the pan from the heat and stir in the vanilla.

4. Strain the custard through a sieve into another bowl. (You may need to push it through the sieve with a rubber spatula; this gets rid of lumps.) Cover the custard with plastic wrap to prevent a skin from forming, and chill until it is set.

Whipped Cream

1 cup heavy cream
3 tablespoons confectioners' sugar
1 teaspoon pure vanilla extract

Place the heavy cream, confectioners' sugar, and vanilla in a mixing bowl and whip until firm peaks form and stay in place when you lift up the beater and turn the bowl upside down.

Old-Fashioned Chocolate Buttermilk Sheet Cake

Harry hates going to his babysitter, Mrs. Figg, when the Dursleys need him out of the way. She has too many cats, her house smells like cabbages, and her chocolate cake tastes ancient (see *Harry Potter and the Sorcerer's Stone*, Chapters 2 and 3).

"Cake" comes from the Old Norse word *kaka* (what were the Vikings thinking?). But you can imagine that what the Vikings called *kaka* and we call *cake* are vastly different items. Not until the 1700s were eggs and sugar and even icings added to cakes to turn them into something we would recognize.

2 ounces chopped bittersweet chocolate
1 tablespoon instant coffee
1¼ cups boiling water
2¾ cups all-purpose flour
2¾ cups granulated sugar
¾ cup unsweetened cocoa powder
½ teaspoon salt
2 teaspoons baking soda
1 teaspoon baking powder
1 cup vegetable oil
1¼ cups buttermilk
4 large eggs
2 teaspoons pure vanilla extract

1. Preheat the oven to 350°F. Grease and flour a 9" × 13" cake pan.
2. Place the chocolate and coffee in a small bowl. Pour the boiling water over the chocolate and coffee and let it stand 5 minutes. Whisk until smooth.
3. Using an electric mixer, combine the flour, sugar, cocoa powder, salt, baking soda, and baking powder in a large bowl. Mix on low speed until well combined. Add the oil and buttermilk and mix well, scraping down the sides as needed. Add the eggs one at a time, beating after each until incorporated. Add the chocolate-coffee mixture very carefully, on the lowest speed, as it will slosh around the bowl. Add the vanilla. Finish by scraping the bowl down and mixing all the batter with a rubber spatula.
4. Scrape the batter into the prepared pan and bake for about 45 minutes, until the cake feels firm when touched lightly in the center or a toothpick inserted in the center comes out with a few moist crumbs attached. If the toothpick comes out clean, the cake is over baked.
5. Cool the cake completely in the pan on a wire rack. Dust with confectioners' sugar and serve right out of the pan.

Makes 24 pieces

Nutty Fruitcake for Kids

Uncle Vernon goes so nuts when letter after letter arrives addressed to Harry Potter that he hammers in a nail with a piece of fruitcake to seal the mail slot (see *Harry Potter and the Sorcerer's Stone*, Chapter 3).

How did Uncle Vernon get to such a state that he confused a piece of fruitcake for a hammer? It's not such a strange mistake to make when you consider that fruitcakes are made to last a year—it must have gotten as hard as forged steel and so could be used as a hammer! Queen Victoria, to show self-control, would wait one year before eating a fruitcake she received as a gift.

Traditionally, fruitcake is made with alcohol, which keeps the cake moist and fresh for an extended period of time. Adults who wish to make traditional fruitcake should replace the apple juice with brandy. After the cake cools, use a skewer to poke holes in the bottom of the cake. Pour another ½ cup brandy over the bottom of the cake, wrap the cake in a double layer of aluminum foil, and store upside down. If you want to make this cake months in advance, then once a month, unwrap the cake and pour ½ cup brandy over the bottom. The flavor improves with age.

2¼ cups all-purpose flour
½ cup finely ground almonds
1 teaspoon ground cinnamon
½ teaspoon ground allspice
¼ teaspoon ground nutmeg
⅛ teaspoon ground cloves
¼ teaspoon salt
2 sticks butter, at room temperature
1¼ cups packed dark brown sugar

Grated zest of 1 orange
Grated zest of 1 lemon
4 large eggs, at room temperature
¼ cup orange marmalade
½ cup dark raisins
½ cup golden raisins
½ cup dried currants or sweetened dried cranberries
¼ cup apple juice

1. Preheat the oven to 300°F. Grease and flour a 9-inch round cake pan that is at least 2 inches deep and line the bottom with parchment paper. In a large mixing bowl, whisk together the flour, ground almonds, spices, and salt.

2. In another large bowl, cream the butter, sugar, and zest of orange and lemon with an electric mixer, scraping down the sides as needed, until light and fluffy, about 5 minutes. Add the eggs one at time, beating well after each until incorporated. Beat in the marmalade. Stir in the flour mixture and then the dark raisins, golden raisins, and currants or cranberries. Stir in the apple juice. Using a spatula, give one final stir to make sure the batter is evenly mixed. Scrape the batter into the pan and bake for 2 hours.

3. Remove the cake from the oven and leave it in the pan to cool. Unmold the cake onto a sheet of aluminum foil and peel off the parchment paper, then reinvert the cake onto a platter or cardboard round. The cake should be eaten the day it is made or wrapped well in plastic wrap and frozen for up to 2 months. Serve with a nice cup of tea.

Serves 16

Tender Roast Loin of Pork with Variations

Aunt Petunia serves roast pork loin at the business dinner with the Masons, doomed by Dobby the house-elf, whose repeated efforts to help Harry end up almost killing him each time (see *Harry Potter and the Chamber of Secrets*, Chapter 1).

Unlike chickens and pheasants, this is one animal the Romans didn't bring with them to England. Pigs have been around in Europe for millions of years, and since we humans discovered them we've been using them for food.

1 teaspoon salt
¼ teaspoon freshly ground black pepper
¼ teaspoon ground thyme
¼ teaspoon dried rosemary
Pinch cayenne pepper
2 pounds pork loin

1. Preheat the oven to 325°F. In a small bowl, combine all the ingredients except the pork. Rub the mixture all over the pork and place the pork loin on a rack in a roasting pan.

2. Roast the pork for about 40 minutes until an instant-read thermometer inserted into the thickest part of the roast reads 145°F. Remove the roast from the oven and let it rest for 15 minutes before slicing.

Serves 6

Tender Roast Loin of Pork with Variations

(continued)

Apple Blossom Glazed Pork Loin

1 cup water

1 cup honey

½ cup apple butter or applesauce

1 teaspoon crushed red pepper

½ cup dried cranberries

½ cup pickled watermelon rind, diced

2 pounds pork loin

1. Preheat the oven to 325°F. In a saucepan, combine the water, honey, and apple butter or applesauce, and stir to blend. Add the crushed peppers, dried cranberries, and diced watermelon rind. Bring to a boil, cover, remove from the heat, and let stand for 10 minutes.
2. Pour half of the fruit sauce over the pork loin and place it in the preheated oven. Bake the pork for 30 minutes. Pour ¼ of the remaining sauce over the pork and continue cooking 10 minutes longer or until the internal temperature registers 145°F on an instant-read thermometer.
3. Rest the pork loin for 15 minutes before slicing. Drizzle the remaining fruit sauce over the sliced pork and serve.

Bourbon-Glazed Pork Loin with Peaches for Adults

¼ cup Kentucky bourbon

¼ cup soy sauce

¼ cup packed brown sugar

2 cloves garlic

¼ cup Dijon mustard

½ teaspoon ground ginger

2 tablespoons Worcestershire sauce

¼ cup vegetable oil

1 dash hot sauce

2 pounds pork loin

4 fresh or canned peaches, pitted and cut in quarters

1. Preheat the oven to 325°F. In a blender or food processor, combine the bourbon, soy sauce, brown sugar, garlic, mustard, ginger, Worcestershire sauce, oil, and hot sauce. Pulse until smooth.
2. Place the pork loin and peaches into a resealable plastic bag and pour in the marinade. Remove excess air and store in the refrigerator for 24 hours.
3. Remove the pork from the marinade and place it on a rack in a roasting pan. Roast the pork for about 40 minutes until an instant-read thermometer registers 145°F. Remove the roast from the oven and let it rest for 15 minutes before slicing. Bring the remaining marinade to a boil in a small saucepan and set aside.
4. Slice the pork and drizzle it with the marinade. Arrange the peaches around the sliced pork.

Petunia's Pudding (English Strawberry Trifle)

When Harry comes inside after completing his chores, he notices that the dessert Aunt Petunia prepared for the dinner party with the Masons is sitting on top of the refrigerator (see *Harry Potter and the Chamber of Secrets*, Chapter 1). The British call any dessert "pudding," as in "What's for pudding?" Since the classic trifle is covered in dollops of whipped cream and often decorated with sugared violets, this is probably what Petunia intended to serve the Masons (before Dobby destroyed it).

This is a beautiful and easy dessert you can make to impress your friends. English trifle started out as a simple custard made of cream and egg yolks, sweetened, and then flavored with ginger and rosewater. It grew into its more elegant form in the 1800s: cake layered with fruit and custard in a clear glass dish and topped with whipped cream. American-style trifle bowls are too deep for English trifle. Instead, use a round serving dish, about 9 inches in diameter and about 3 inches deep.

1 loaf yellow cake, sliced into
   ½-inch-thick slices (recipe follows)
½ cup strawberry jam
Custard (recipe follows)
1 pound fresh strawberries, washed,
  patted dry, and sliced into
  ⅛-inch-thick slices

Whipped cream
1 tablespoon toasted sliced almonds
  or sugared violets, if available

1. Place the cake slices on a cutting board and trim off the crusts. Spread half the slices with the jam and top with the remaining slices. Cut the sandwiches into 2-inch squares. Layer the sandwiches in the bottom of a round glass serving dish. Cut the remaining sandwiches into small pieces to fill any empty spaces.

2. Spread the custard over the cake layer. Line the pan around the perimeter with strawberry slices; then pile the remaining sliced strawberries in the center. Cover with plastic wrap and refrigerate 8 hours or overnight to allow the flavors to meld.

3. Prepare the whipped cream before serving. Remove the plastic wrap and spread the whipped cream on top of the trifle, completely covering all the strawberries with the cream. For a pretty effect, you can fill a pastry bag fitted with a ¾-inch star tip and pipe the cream over the strawberries. Decorate with the toasted almonds or sugared violets.

Serves 8 to 10

For quick and easy trifle, use store-bought sponge or pound cake and instant vanilla pudding instead of the homemade custard.

Petunia's Pudding (English Strawberry Trifle)

(continued)

Yellow Loaf Cake

1½ cups all-purpose flour
1½ teaspoons baking powder
¼ teaspoon salt
1 stick (8 tablespoons) butter, at room temperature
1 cup granulated sugar
2 large eggs, at room temperature
1½ teaspoons pure vanilla extract
½ cup whole milk, at room temperature

1. Preheat the oven to 350°F and grease and flour an 8½" × 4½" loaf pan. Whisk together the flour, baking powder, and salt. Set aside.
2. Using an electric mixer, cream the butter and sugar until light and fluffy, scraping down the sides of the bowl as needed, about 5 minutes. Add the eggs one at a time, beating after each to combine and scraping down as needed, about 30 seconds. Add the vanilla and beat until combined.
3. Add the flour mixture and milk alternately, beginning and ending with the flour and using the slowest speed on your mixer. Scrape down the sides of the bowl and gently fold the batter together with a rubber spatula, taking care not to over mix.
4. Scrape the batter into the prepared pan and bake about 1 hour, or until the cake feels firm when touched lightly in the center or a toothpick inserted in the center comes out clean. Remove the cake from the oven and let it cool in the pan.

Custard

1½ cups whole milk plus ½ cup heavy cream or 2 cups whole milk
½ cup granulated sugar (divided)
¼ cup cornstarch
¼ teaspoon salt
4 large egg yolks
1 teaspoon pure vanilla extract
¼ stick (2 tablespoons) butter (only if not using any heavy cream)

1. Combine the milk or milk and heavy cream, ¼ cup of the sugar, cornstarch, and salt in a small saucepan. In a medium bowl, whisk the yolks with the remaining ¼ cup of sugar until smooth.
2. Heat the milk mixture over medium-high heat, stirring constantly, until it is hot but not bubbling. Reduce the heat to low. Pour 1 cup of the hot mixture in a slow stream into the egg yolk mixture while whisking quickly to temper the egg yolks. Pour the egg yolk mixture slowly back into the saucepan while stirring constantly. Return to medium-high heat, stirring constantly, until the mixture thickens and begins to boil. (Once the mixture begins to thicken, it must be handled gently so the cornstarch won't lose its thickening power.)
3. Remove the pan from the heat and add the vanilla. Add the butter if you did not use heavy cream. Stir gently until the butter is melted and combined. Strain the custard through a sieve into a bowl to ensure a smooth custard. (Use a rubber spatula to push the custard through the sieve.) Cover with plastic wrap and refrigerate until cold.

Lemon Meringue Pie

They had the soup; they had the salmon; now they're listening to Uncle Vernon talk about his work while they eat lemon meringue pie. Soon Aunt Marge will have too much brandy and soon Harry will get into lots of trouble (see *Harry Potter and the Prisoner of Azkaban*, Chapter 2).

Lemon meringue pie is actually more American than apple pie. Apple pies were being made in England long before the colonists came over. Open pies, without a top crust, or pies topped with meringue tend to be American. Lemon meringue pie is a bit complex, but it's so worth it! Give yourself plenty of time to prepare this dessert, and you'll never want to buy the mass-produced kind again.

Pie Crust

1¼ cups all-purpose flour

2 tablespoons granulated sugar

½ teaspoon salt

½ stick (4 tablespoons) cold butter, cut into chunks

4 tablespoons vegetable shortening, chilled and cut into chunks

4–6 tablespoons ice water

Lemon Filling

1¼ cups granulated sugar

⅓ cup cornstarch

1½ cups water

4 large egg yolks, lightly beaten (save the egg whites for the meringue)

½ cup lemon juice

1 tablespoon grated lemon zest

¼ stick (2 tablespoons) butter

Meringue Topping

4 large egg whites, at room temperature

¼ teaspoon cream of tartar

¼ teaspoon salt

½ teaspoon pure vanilla extract

1 cup granulated sugar

Lemon Meringue Pie

(continued)

1. For the crust, combine the flour, sugar, and salt in the bowl of a food processor. Pulse 2 or 3 times to combine. Sprinkle the butter and shortening over the flour mixture and pulse about 15 times, until the mixture resembles coarse yellow meal. Turn the mixture out into a large mixing bowl. Sprinkle 4 tablespoons ice water over the flour mixture, and toss with a spatula until the dough starts to clump together. If the dough is dry, add more ice water 1 tablespoon at a time. Gather the dough together in a ball, pat it into a disk, wrap it in plastic wrap, and refrigerate it for 1 hour or up to 3 days.

2. On a floured surface, roll out the dough to an 11-inch circle. Fold the dough into quarters and brush off the excess flour after each fold. Unfold the dough into the pie pan, fitting it in carefully without pulling or stretching. Trim the dough, leaving 1 inch of overhang; fold the overhang under and crimp the edges, either by pressing down with the tines of a fork or by pinching with your fingers. Prick the bottom and sides with a fork. Place the crust in the freezer for about 30 minutes. While the crust is freezing, preheat the oven to 425°F.

3. Spread a sheet of aluminum foil inside the frozen pie crust; press the foil into the edges and be sure to cover the rim. Fill the crust with pie weights or beans and bake until the crust is dry and set, 15 to 20 minutes. Reduce the temperature to 350°F, remove the foil, and continue to bake until the crust is golden brown, about 8 more minutes. Remove from the oven and set aside.

4. For the filling, combine the sugar, cornstarch, and water in a small heavy-bottomed saucepan and stir until the cornstarch is dissolved. Cook over low heat, stirring constantly, until the mixture thickens. Whisk in the yolks and continue cooking and stirring until the mixture is thick and bubbling. Remove from the heat and add the lemon juice, lemon zest, and butter. Stir gently until fully incorporated.

5. For the meringue, beat the egg whites, cream of tartar, salt, and vanilla until soft mounds form. Add the sugar gradually while beating on medium speed. Increase speed to medium-high and beat until the egg whites are stiff and glossy but not dry.

6. To assemble and bake the pie, preheat the oven to 350°F. Pour the filling into the crust. Spread the meringue over the filling, taking care to seal the edges to prevent the meringue from shrinking. Make peaks and swirls in the meringue with the back of a spoon or fork.

7. Bake the pie until the meringue browns, about 15 minutes. Cool the pie before serving. Serve cold or at room temperature.

Serves 8

Save your baking of lemon meringue pie for dry weather. Humidity can cause your lovely meringue to weep, which means you'll find beads of caramel-colored moisture gathering atop your snowy mound.

For perfectly beaten egg whites, make sure the beaters and the bowl are squeaky clean and grease free; a tiny amount of grease can cause the whites not to beat properly. A tiny amount of yolk won't affect the outcome. Add the sugar slowly only when soft mounds begin to form.

Warm and Hearty Mulligatawny Soup

The last day of Aunt Marge's visit, Aunt Petunia serves soup, which Harry manages to get through uneventfully before finally losing it and blowing up Aunt Marge (see *Harry Potter and the Prisoner of Azkaban*, Chapter 2).

Only the British can take some Indian words and make it sound like a place in Ireland. Mulligatawny is actually a combination of two Tamil words (Tamil is one of many Indian languages) that means "pepper" and "water." British officers during colonial times fell in love with this dish and brought it back to England from India.

2 tablespoons vegetable oil

4 bone-in, skin-on chicken thighs, rinsed and patted dry

1 onion, finely chopped

2 carrots, sliced

2 celery ribs, finely chopped

6 cups water

1 tart apple, such as Granny Smith, peeled, cored, and diced

1 tablespoon curry

1 tablespoon salt

½ teaspoon freshly ground black pepper

2 cups cooked long grain white rice (½ cup dry rice will yield about 2 cups cooked)

Shredded sweetened coconut, optional, for serving

1. Heat the oil in a Dutch oven or wide pot. Sear the chicken over high heat on both sides until golden and crispy, about 4 minutes per side. Remove chicken from the pot and set aside.

2. Pour off the fat, leaving about 2 tablespoons in the pot. Add the onions, carrots, and celery, stirring and scraping over medium heat until the onions are softened, 3 to 5 minutes. Add the water, apple, curry, salt, and pepper.

3. Add the chicken back to the pot. Bring to a boil, then reduce the heat and simmer for 30 to 45 minutes, until the chicken is tender. Remove the chicken from the pot. Discard the skin and bones, cut the chicken into bite-size pieces, and return it to the pot. Using a wide spoon such as a serving spoon, skim the fat off the surface. Stir in the rice.

4. To serve, sprinkle a small handful of coconut, if using, over each bowl.

Serves 6

Four Scrumptious Cakes

Ah, sweet revenge! The summer that Uncle Vernon and Aunt Petunia put Dudley on a strict diet, Harry revels in his knowledge of the good food hidden upstairs in his room while Dudley starves in the kitchen. When Harry informs his friends of the severe diet imposed on the whole family, they loyally send him fabulous birthday cakes. The following four cakes are an imagining of what Ron, Hermione, Hagrid, and Sirius sent to Harry (see *Harry Potter and the Goblet of Fire*, Chapter 3).

This is the simplest of cakes, yet elegant and delicious. It's called Victoria Sponge because the famous queen of that name used to have a slice with her tea. The name "sponge" is misleading because it's actually a dense, rich cake, not an airy, fluffy sponge.

Victoria Sponge Sandwich Cake (from Ron)

1½ cups all-purpose flour
1 teaspoon baking powder
¼ teaspoon salt
1½ sticks (12 tablespoons) butter, at room temperature
1 cup granulated sugar

3 large eggs, at room temperature
½ cup raspberry jam
Confectioners' sugar, for dusting
Whipped cream, for serving, optional

1. Preheat the oven to 350°F. Grease two 8-inch round cake pans and line the bottoms with parchment paper. Whisk together the flour, baking powder, and salt in a mixing bowl and set aside.
2. Using an electric mixer, beat the butter and sugar in a large bowl until light and fluffy, scraping down the sides of the bowl as needed, about 5 minutes. Add the eggs one a time, beating after each until incorporated and scraping down the sides as needed. Add the flour mixture and mix on the slowest speed until combined. Finish by scraping down and folding the batter together with a rubber spatula.
3. Divide the batter evenly between the two pans and bake for about 20 minutes until the cakes are golden brown around the edges—the tops of the cakes will be pale—and the cakes feel soft but set when touched lightly in the center or a toothpick inserted in the center comes out clean. Let the cakes cool in the pans for 10 minutes, then invert onto a wire rack and cool completely.
4. To assemble the cake, place one cake on a cardboard round top-side down and spread with the raspberry jam all the way to the edges. Top with the second cake, top-side up, and dust generously with confectioners' sugar. Serve with whipped cream and have it with tea.

Serves 8

Four Scrumptious Cakes

(continued)

A lot of delicious foods were created by accident, and this might be one of them. According to legend, the cook of the White Horse Inn in Bakewell (a town in Derbyshire, in the center of England) was asked by the landlady to make a strawberry tart. The cook forgot to mix the jam into the almond custard and tried to cover it up by spreading the jam on the tart shell, creating a whole new dessert. This popular cake imitates the flavors of the famous Bakewell Tart.

Cherry Bakewell Cake (from Hermione)

Almond Cake

1½ cups all-purpose flour
½ cup finely ground almonds
1 teaspoon baking powder
¼ teaspoon salt
1½ sticks (12 tablespoons) butter, at room temperature
1 cup granulated sugar
3 large eggs, at room temperature
1 teaspoon almond extract
½ cup whole milk, at room temperature

Butter Frosting

2 sticks (16 tablespoons) butter, at room temperature
2 cups confectioners' sugar
1 teaspoon pure vanilla extract
2 tablespoons whole milk

To Finish the Cake

½ cup cherry preserves
Maraschino cherries, for decorating
Toasted sliced almonds, for decorating

Four Scrumptious Cakes

(continued)

1. Preheat the oven to 350°F. Grease two 8-inch round cake pans and line the bottoms with parchment paper. Whisk together the flour, ground almonds, baking powder, and salt in a mixing bowl and set aside.

2. Using an electric mixer, beat the butter and sugar in a large bowl until light and fluffy, scraping down the sides of the bowl as needed, about 5 minutes. Add the eggs one a time, beating after each until incorporated and scraping down the sides as needed. Add the almond extract and beat until combined. Add the flour mixture and milk alternately, beginning and ending with the flour and mixing on the lowest speed to combine. Finish by scraping down and folding the batter together with a rubber spatula.

3. Divide the batter evenly between the 2 pans and bake for about 25 minutes, until the cakes feel soft but firm when touched lightly in the center or a toothpick inserted in the center comes out clean. Let the cakes cool in the pans for 10 minutes, then invert onto a wire rack and cool completely.

4. For the frosting, beat all the frosting ingredients together until smooth, creamy, and fluffy, scraping down the sides as needed, about 7 minutes.

5. To assemble the cake, place 1 cake top-side down on a cardboard round. Spread the cherry preserves on top of the cake all the way to the edges. Top with the second cake, top-side up. Spread about 1 cup of the frosting on top of the cake. Place the remaining frosting in a pastry bag fitted with a star tip and pipe a border around the edges of the cake. Line the inside of the border with maraschino cherries placed about 1 inch apart. Sprinkle the middle space with the toasted sliced almonds. You can also pipe stars against the cherry filling, 1 inch apart, for a pretty touch.

Serves 8

Custard is very, very British. In the mid-1800s a British chemist whose wife was allergic to eggs invented a custard thickened with cornstarch instead of eggs, which he sold as a powder, and since then custard sauce appears with just about every dessert. True cooks prefer to make a rich egg custard rather than using the instant powder that's easier to make but doesn't taste as good. Also, the British often refer to layer cakes as "sandwich cakes." Like the Victoria Sponge, the layers are dense and rich rather than light and fluffy.

Custard Sponge Sandwich (from Hagrid)

Sponge Cake

1½ cups all-purpose flour

1 teaspoon baking powder

¼ teaspoon salt

1½ sticks (12 tablespoons) butter, at room temperature

1 cup granulated sugar

3 large eggs, at room temperature

Confectioners' sugar, for dusting

Custard Filling

1 cup whole milk plus ½ cup heavy cream or 1½ cups whole milk

¼ cup granulated sugar, divided

3 tablespoons cornstarch

Pinch salt

3 egg large yolks

½ teaspoon pure vanilla extract

1 tablespoon butter (if not using heavy cream)

Whipped cream, for serving, optional

Four Scrumptious Cakes

(continued)

1. Preheat the oven to 350°F. Grease two 8-inch cake pans and line the bottoms with parchment paper. Whisk together the flour, baking powder, and salt in a mixing bowl and set aside.

2. Using an electric mixer, beat the butter and sugar in a large bowl until light and fluffy, scraping down the sides of the bowl as needed, about 5 minutes. Add the eggs one at a time, beating after each until incorporated and scraping down the sides as needed. Add the flour mixture and mix on the slowest speed until combined. Finish by scraping down and folding the batter together with a rubber spatula.

3. Divide the batter evenly between the two pans and bake for about 20 minutes until the cakes are golden brown around the edges—the tops of the cakes will be pale—and the cakes feel soft but set when touched lightly in the center or a toothpick inserted in the center comes out clean. Let the cakes cool in the pans for 10 minutes, then invert onto a wire rack and cool completely.

4. To make the custard, combine the milk or milk and heavy cream, 2 tablespoons of the sugar, cornstarch, and salt in a small saucepan and mix until the cornstarch is dissolved. Whisk the yolks with the remaining 2 tablespoons of sugar in a medium bowl until smooth.

5. Heat the milk mixture over medium-high heat, stirring constantly, until it is hot but not bubbling. Reduce the heat to low. Pour ½ cup of the hot mixture in a slow stream into the egg yolk mixture while whisking quickly to temper the egg yolks. Pour the egg yolk mixture slowly back into the saucepan while stirring constantly. Return the pan to medium-high heat, stirring constantly, until the mixture thickens and begins to boil. (Once the mixture begins to thicken, it must be handled gently so the cornstarch won't lose its thickening power.)

6. Remove the pan from the heat and add the vanilla. Add butter if you did not use heavy cream. Stir gently until the butter is melted and combined. Strain the custard through a sieve into a bowl to ensure a smooth custard. (Use a rubber spatula to push the custard through the sieve.) Cover with plastic wrap and refrigerate until cold.

7. To assemble the cake, place one cake layer top-side down on a cardboard round. Spread the custard over the cake until within ½ inch of the border. Top with the other cake layer, top-side up. Dust the top of the cake generously with the confectioners' sugar. Keep refrigerated, but bring to room temperature before serving. Serve with whipped cream and have it with tea.

Serves 8

Four Scrumptious Cakes

(continued)

Being that Sirius was sending letters to Harry via tropical birds, it follows that the cake he sent him would contain tropical flavors, like citrus and mango.

Citrus Sandwich Cake with Mango Filling (from Sirius)

Citrus Cake

2 cups cake flour

1 cup granulated sugar, divided

1 teaspoon baking powder

¼ teaspoon salt

1½ sticks (12 tablespoons) butter, at room temperature

½ cup whole milk

3 large egg yolks, at room temperature

Grated zest and juice of 1 lemon

Grated zest and juice of 1 orange

1 teaspoon pure vanilla extract

3 large egg whites, at room temperature

Mango Filling

3 ripe mangoes, peeled and cut into chunks

½ cup granulated sugar

½ cup water

Pinch salt

2 tablespoons cornstarch

3 large egg yolks

¼ stick (2 tablespoons) butter

Juice of 1 lemon

Whipped Cream Frosting

2 cups heavy cream

⅔ cup confectioners' sugar

2 teaspoons pure vanilla extract

A few drops yellow food coloring

Four Scrumptious Cakes

(continued)

1. Preheat the oven to 350°F. Grease and flour two 8-inch round cake pans and line the bottoms with parchment paper.

2. To make the cake, whisk together the flour, ½ cup of the sugar, baking powder, and salt. Add the butter and beat until the mixture resembles yellow crumbs. Add the milk, yolks, grated zest and juice of lemon and orange, and vanilla and beat until smooth, using the whisk attachment.

3. In a separate clean bowl with clean whisk, beat the egg whites until soft mounds form. Continue beating while adding the remaining ½ cup sugar gradually. Beat until stiff but still glossy. Whisk ¼ of the beaten egg whites into the batter to lighten it, then fold in the rest of the egg whites using a rubber spatula. Divide the batter evenly between the two pans and bake for 20 to 25 minutes, until the cakes are spotty brown and feel firm when touched lightly in the center. Do not overbake or the cakes will be dry. Cool in the pans, then invert the pans to remove the layers. If desired, the layers can be wrapped in plastic and frozen until needed.

4. To make the filling, process the mangoes in a food processor or blender until smooth, then push through a sieve with a rubber spatula, pushing down to extract as much juice as possible. Discard the pulp. Transfer the sieved mango to a medium saucepan. Add the sugar, water, salt, and cornstarch and stir to dissolve. Cook over medium heat until warm, stirring constantly. Whisk in the egg yolks and cook, stirring constantly, until thickened and bubbling. Remove from the heat, add the butter and lemon juice, and stir until melted and combined. Transfer the filling to a bowl, cover the surface directly with plastic wrap, and cool to room temperature. Refrigerate until needed, up to 2 days.

5. Make the frosting just before you're ready to assemble the cake. Whip the frosting ingredients together until stiff peaks form.

6. To assemble the cake, split the cake layers in half. Place one cake layer on a cardboard round and spread ⅓ of the mango filling over it. Repeat with the next two layers, spreading ⅓ of the filling over each, and top with the remaining cake layer. Cover the top and sides with the whipped cream frosting. Tint the remaining whipped cream with the yellow food coloring. Scoop the yellow frosting into a pastry bag fitted with the star tip and pipe decorative borders and rosettes around the edges of the cake.

Serves 8

Poached Salmon in Honey and Dill Sauce

Aunt Petunia may be horrible to Harry, but she can create a decent menu. On the last evening of Aunt Marge's stay, shortly before Harry loses control of his temper and blows her up, Aunt Petunia serves salmon for dinner (see *Harry Potter and the Prisoner of Azkaban*, Chapter 2).

The salmon has magical ability in Celtic mythology, where it's revered for its ability to survive in both fresh water and salt water. The Celts believed that there was a Salmon of Knowledge that would grant its eater wisdom beyond measure. Talk about fish being brain food. In one legend of King Arthur, two heroes ride the back of a salmon on a quest. Even modern Irish coins depicted the salmon until the Irish switched to the euro in 2002.

3 tablespoons butter
1 onion, finely chopped
2 tablespoons all-purpose flour
1 cup dry white wine
1 tablespoon honey

1 tablespoon chopped fresh dill
1½ pounds salmon fillet, rinsed and patted dry, cut along the length into four pieces
Salt and freshly ground black pepper

1. Heat the butter in a saucepan wide enough to accommodate the salmon fillets. When the butter starts to foam, add the onions and cook until they are translucent, stirring frequently, about 5 minutes.
2. Add the flour and stir until it is well blended. Pour in the wine and honey and cook, stirring constantly, until the flour-butter mixture is blended in. Add the dill.
3. Sprinkle the salmon fillets with salt and pepper and lay them in the pan, skin side down. Bring the sauce to a simmer and continue simmering, covered, until the salmon flakes apart when pierced with a fork, about 20 minutes. Occasionally scrape the bottom of the pan to prevent the fish from sticking. Taste the sauce and adjust the seasonings, if necessary.

Serves 4

Chapter Two

Delights Down the Alley

Diagon Alley, one of J. K. Rowling's famously clever names, is the busy marketplace of the wizarding world. Shops selling anything the wizard could possibly need line this crowded and bustling street. Here Harry buys his schoolbooks, wand, robes, potion ingredients, other school supplies, and wizard delicacies.

Harry often meets up with Ron and Hermione in Diagon Alley to buy their new books and supplies before the start of the term. A popular place for them to gather (until You-Know-Who's return) is at Florean Fortescue's Ice Cream Parlor, where one summer Florean plies Harry with free sundaes as well as valuable help with his homework (see *Harry Potter and the Prisoner of Azkaban*, Chapter 4).

Harry also eats at the Leaky Cauldron, behind which lies the entrance to Diagon Alley. Tom, the old and toothless innkeeper, supplies excellent meals and teas to the odd characters who frequent the pub.

Chocolate and Raspberry Ice Cream Cones with Chopped Nuts

While Harry is having a very unpleasant conversation with a pale blond boy at Madam Malkin's (he reminds Harry of a skinny version of Dudley), Hagrid comes to the window and holds up this treat to show Harry. When Harry's done being measured, he's relieved to escape the shop and enjoy a delicious ice cream cone (see *Harry Potter and the Sorcerer's Stone*, Chapter 5).

A good reason to be glad you live in modern times is ice cream. True, ice cream has been around since the 1600s, but there are two big "buts": one, ice cream was a treat only for the rich, and two, ice cream today is much better quality.

1 recipe Silky Chocolate Chunk Ice Cream (recipe follows)
1 recipe Perfectly Smooth Raspberry Ice Cream (recipe follows)
Sugar cones for serving
Chopped toasted almonds, for topping

Place 1 scoop of each flavor ice cream into the sugar cones and dip into the chopped almonds to coat. To prevent leaking, pour melted bittersweet chocolate into the bottoms of the cones before adding the ice cream.

Silky Chocolate Chunk Ice Cream

2 cups whole milk
2 cups heavy cream
¾ cup granulated sugar
2 tablespoons unsweetened cocoa powder
8 ounces bittersweet chocolate, melted and cooled
5 large egg yolks
1 teaspoon pure vanilla extract
1 cup coarsely chopped bittersweet chocolate

1. Combine the milk, heavy cream, sugar, and cocoa powder in a medium saucepan and cook, stirring frequently, until hot but not simmering. Whisk the melted chocolate into the egg yolks (it will be thick and difficult to whisk). Temper the egg yolk mixture by slowly pouring 1 cup of the hot milk mixture into the yolks while whisking vigorously. Pour the yolk mixture into the saucepan and cook, stirring constantly, until very hot but not simmering. Do not boil.

2. Pour the mixture through a sieve. Stir in the vanilla extract. Cover the surface with plastic wrap to prevent a skin from forming; chill until completely cold. Freeze in your ice cream

Chocolate and Raspberry Ice Cream Cones with Chopped Nuts

(continued)

maker following the manufacturer's instructions. Toward the end of the churning time add the chopped chocolate. Transfer to an airtight container and freeze until firm, 6 hours or overnight. If the ice cream is hard, allow it to soften at room temperature for 10 to 15 minutes before serving.

Makes about 5 cups

Perfectly Smooth Raspberry Ice Cream

12 ounces fresh or frozen raspberries, thawed if frozen
¾ cup granulated sugar, divided
1 cup heavy cream
2 cups whole milk
4 large egg yolks

1. Process the raspberries with ¼ cup of the sugar in a blender or food processor until smooth. Push the mixture through a sieve with a rubber spatula into a bowl, pushing down on the solids to squeeze out as much juice as possible. Discard the solids.

2. Combine the heavy cream, milk, and remaining sugar in a medium saucepan and cook over medium heat, stirring frequently, until hot but not bubbling. Temper the egg yolks by slowly pouring 1 cup of the hot milk mixture into the egg yolks while whisking constantly. Pour the yolk mixture into the pot while whisking constantly. Continue whisking over medium-high heat until the mixture thickens slightly but before it begins to boil. Pour the mixture through a sieve into another bowl.

3. Whisk in the raspberry mixture and transfer it to an airtight container. Cool to room temperature, then chill in the refrigerator until very cold, about 6 hours or overnight.

4. Remove the cold mixture from the refrigerator and whisk in the raspberry mixture that settled to the bottom. Transfer to an ice cream maker and freeze according to the manufacturer's instructions. Transfer to an airtight container and freeze until firm, about 6 hours or overnight. If the ice cream is hard, allow it to soften at room temperature for 10 to 15 minutes before serving.

Makes about 4 cups

Paddington Burgers

Harry eats hamburgers with Hagrid at Paddington Station while trying to sort out everything that's been happening lately. He's just been told by a half-giant that he's a wizard, he's been whisked off to Diagon Alley by said giant to buy really strange school supplies, and to top it all off, he's just discovered that in this new world he's famous and he has no idea why. He really has a lot to chew over (see *Harry Potter and the Sorcerer's Stone*, Chapter 5).

Historians may not agree on who invented the hamburger, but one thing's for sure: It's named for the city of Hamburg in Germany. So it really has nothing to do with ham. As all the carnivores among us know, these patties typically are made from ground beef.

1½ pounds extra-lean ground beef
2 large eggs
1 onion, chopped and sautéed until well-browned
1 cup fresh bread crumbs
½ cup tomato sauce
1 tablespoon onion powder
½ teaspoon garlic powder
½ teaspoon salt
¼ teaspoon freshly ground black pepper
Sautéed sliced onions, for serving
English mustard, for serving
Lettuce, for serving
Tomato slices, for serving

1. Combine all the ingredients in a large mixing bowl and mix well.
2. Spray a skillet with cooking spray and heat the skillet. Form the mixture into patties and cook on both sides over medium-high heat until well-browned. Transfer to a paper-towel-lined plate and repeat until the beef mixture is used up. Or cook on a grill until well done.
3. Serve in toasted hamburger buns with sautéed sliced onions, English mustard, lettuce, and tomato.

Serves 6

Strawberry and Peanut Butter Ice Cream Cones

Locked in his room by a raging Uncle Vernon, Harry just barely manages to escape to the Burrow in Ron's father's flying car, where he spends the last bit of summer vacation. Harry, Ron, and Hermione join up in Diagon Alley to do their school shopping, and they enjoy a sunny day of friendship as well as peanut butter and strawberry ice cream cones—paid for by Harry (see *Harry Potter and the Chamber of Secrets*, Chapter 4).

Lots of people were involved in the discovery of peanut butter (including the famous Kellogg brothers), but George Washington Carver (an American, by the way) invented so many uses for peanuts that he is known, fairly or not, as the inventor of peanut butter.

1 recipe Strawberry Swirl Ice Cream (recipe follows)
1 recipe Chunky Peanut Butter Ice Cream (recipe follows)
Sugar cones for serving
Your favorite toppings or sauces

Place 1 scoop each of Strawberry Swirl Ice Cream and Chunky Peanut Butter Ice Cream into each cone. Dip into your favorite toppings to coat or drizzle with your favorite sauce. To prevent leaking, pour melted bittersweet chocolate into the bottoms of the cones before adding the ice cream.

Strawberry Swirl Ice Cream

1 pound strawberries, roughly chopped
¾ cup granulated sugar, divided
1 cup heavy cream
2 cups whole milk
3 large egg yolks
1 cup strawberry jam

1. Process the strawberries with ¼ cup of the sugar until smooth. Push the mixture through a sieve with a rubber spatula into a bowl, pushing down on the solids to squeeze out as much juice as possible. Discard the solids.
2. Transfer the strawberry mixture to a medium saucepan and cook over medium-high heat, stirring constantly, until the mixture is reduced and very thick. Set aside.
3. In a separate saucepan, heat the heavy cream, milk, and remaining sugar over medium-high heat, stirring frequently, until hot but not bubbling. Temper the egg yolks by slowly pouring 1 cup of the hot milk mixture into the egg yolks while whisking constantly. Pour the yolk mixture into the pot while whisking constantly. Continue whisking over medium-high heat until the mixture is hot but not bubbling. Pour the mixture through a sieve into another bowl.

Strawberry and Peanut Butter Ice Cream Cones

(continued)

4. Whisk in the strawberry mixture until smooth. Transfer the custard to an airtight container, cool to room temperature, and then chill in the refrigerator until very cold, about 6 hours or overnight.

5. Remove the cold mixture from the refrigerator and whisk in the strawberry mixture that settled to the bottom. Transfer to an ice cream maker and freeze according to the manufacturer's instructions.

6. Whisk the strawberry jam in a small bowl to loosen up the texture and slightly smooth it. Pour it into the ice cream canister and fold it in by hand to create a swirling effect. Be careful not to fold it in too much or it will become completely incorporated and you will lose the swirl. Transfer to an airtight container and freeze until firm, about 6 hours or overnight. If the ice cream is hard, allow it to soften at room temperature for 10 to 15 minutes before serving.

Makes about 4 cups

Chunky Peanut Butter Ice Cream

1 cup heavy cream
2 cups whole milk
¾ cup granulated sugar
5 large egg yolks
1 cup chunky peanut butter

1. In a medium saucepan, heat the heavy cream, milk, and sugar over medium-high heat, stirring frequently, until hot but not bubbling. Temper the egg yolks by slowly pouring 1 cup of the hot milk mixture into the egg yolks while whisking constantly. Pour the yolk mixture into the pot while whisking constantly. Continue whisking over medium-high heat until the mixture is hot but not bubbling. Pour the mixture through a sieve into another bowl. Cover the surface directly with plastic wrap to prevent a skin from forming. Cool to room temperature, transfer to an airtight container, and chill in the refrigerator until very cold, about 6 hours or overnight.

2. Remove the cold mixture from the refrigerator and freeze according to the manufacturer's instructions. Add the peanut butter to the canister and mix it in by hand with a rubber spatula or wooden spoon. Transfer to an airtight container and freeze until firm, about 6 hours or overnight. If the ice cream is hard, allow it to soften at room temperature for 10 to 15 minutes before serving.

Makes about 5 cups

Crumpets

Harry is a goner. He just blew up his Aunt Marge, used magic illegally, and ran away from home. He'll be expelled for sure. When he sees Minister Fudge at the Leaky Cauldron, he's terrified. But instead of chewing him out, Fudge cordially invites him in for tea and crumpets (see *Harry Potter and the Prisoner of Azkaban*, Chapter 3).

What's more stereotypically British than tea with crumpets? Crumpets hail from as far back as the 1300s, though you can imagine they were nothing like the crumpets of today, with their holey tops filled with melting butter.

1 cup all-purpose flour
1 tablespoon granulated sugar
1 teaspoon active dry yeast (½ packet)

¼ teaspoon salt
1 cup whole milk
¼ stick (2 tablespoons) butter, melted

1. Grease 4 crumpet rings (or 4 round 3¾-inch cookie cutters) and a skillet or griddle. Whisk together the flour, sugar, yeast, and salt until combined. Add the milk and melted butter and whisk until smooth. Cover with plastic wrap and leave in a warm place until puffy and risen, about 1 to 1½ hours.

2. Stir down the mixture. Heat the greased skillet or griddle and put the crumpet rings inside. Using a measuring cup, pour ⅓ cup batter into each ring. Cook over low heat until the tops fill with holes, about 5 minutes. Carefully remove the crumpet rings (they will be very hot; use tongs or oven mitts) and flip the crumpets over (they should be pale on the bottom). Cook until the other side is pale brown, about 5 minutes more. Repeat until all the batter is used up.

3. To serve, toast the crumpets until golden brown and serve with butter and jam. The crumpets can be refrigerated and toasted when needed.

Makes 8 crumpets

Because the crumpets are toasted after cooking them, it's important not to let them get too brown. Instead of crumpet rings or cookie cutters, you can use lobster rings.

Chocolate Pudding

Harry's having the time of his life, roaming Diagon Alley and buying and eating whatever he wants. And the fun heats up when he meets his best friends, Ron and Hermione. They all have dinner together with the Weasleys at the Leaky Cauldron, where toothless Tom outdoes himself serving a delicious meal topped off with a luxurious chocolate pudding (see *Harry Potter and the Prisoner of Azkaban*, Chapter 4).

In England chocolate pudding can be either a steamed or baked pudding, similar to chocolate cake, or a soft milk pudding thickened with cornstarch, as in the United States. Puddings go all the way back to the Romans. The milk pudding we know of today—the only kind in this country—wasn't invented until the 1800s. Since chocolate pudding can mean either kind, a recipe for each is included.

Rich, Smooth Chocolate Milk Pudding

½ cup granulated sugar
¼ cup cornstarch
2 tablespoons unsweetened cocoa powder, Dutch-process preferred
Pinch salt
2½ cups whole milk
1 cup heavy cream
6 ounces bittersweet chocolate, melted
¼ stick (2 tablespoons) butter
1 teaspoon pure vanilla extract

1. Combine the sugar, cornstarch, cocoa powder, and salt in a small heavy-bottomed saucepan and whisk until combined. Add the milk and cream and stir to combine. Cook over medium-high heat, stirring constantly, until the cocoa powder is dissolved. Turn off the heat and add the chocolate. Return to medium-high heat and continue to cook, stirring constantly, until the mixture is thickened and bubbling. Once it starts to thicken, stir gently or the cornstarch will lose its thickening power.
2. Remove the pan from the heat. Add the butter and vanilla and whisk gently until the butter is melted and combined. Strain the pudding into a bowl, cover with plastic wrap, and chill until set. Serve with whipped cream.

Serves 6

Chocolate Pudding

(continued)

(continued)

You know how some cookbooks call a recipe "Chocolate Indulgence"? Cliché or not, it totally applies to this pudding. It's so rich and chocolatey and moist that it doesn't need a sauce like most steamed puddings. Instead, serve it with whipped cream or vanilla ice cream.

Dense and Fudgy Steamed Chocolate Pudding

1 stick (8 tablespoons) butter

4 ounces bittersweet chocolate, chopped

1 cup all-purpose flour

½ cup unsweetened cocoa powder

¼ teaspoon salt

1¼ cups granulated sugar

1 teaspoon pure vanilla extract

2 large eggs, at room temperature

½ cup whole milk

1. Grease and flour a 1½-quart pudding bowl or a heatproof glass or ceramic bowl with a tight-fitting lid (grease and flour the lid as well). A similar size casserole dish with lid will work as well. Place a rack or overturned shallow bowl in the bottom of a large pot, fill a third of the way with water, and set it to boil. Melt the butter and chocolate in the microwave for 1 to 2 minutes and whisk until smooth. Set aside to cool. Whisk together the flour, cocoa powder, and salt in a separate bowl.

2. Whisk together the sugar, vanilla, eggs, and milk until smooth. Whisk in the chocolate mixture until smooth. Add the flour mixture and mix with a wooden spoon until combined. Scrape the batter into the prepared bowl and smooth the top with a rubber spatula. Cover the bowl with the lid, making sure it is secure.

3. Put the bowl in the pot, making sure the water reaches halfway up the sides of the bowl. Boil for 3 hours, checking the water level every so often and adding more water if necessary. Remove the pudding from the pot and uncover. Cool for 30 minutes, then turn it upside down onto a serving plate to unmold. If the pudding is stuck, shake it back and forth to loosen it. Serve warm with whipped cream or a scoop of vanilla ice cream.

Serves 6

Ice Cream Sundaes

How can Harry eat ice cream sundaes every half hour (supplied free by Florean Fortescue) while doing his homework and not get as fat as Dudley? No fair! (See *Harry Potter and the Prisoner of Azkaban*, Chapter 4.)

Necessity is the mother of invention. In the early 1900s, the blue laws (an old-fashioned set of laws that were passed to enforce Sabbath observance and other religious laws) forbade selling ice cream sodas on Sunday. So ice cream parlors took out the soda, which left the ice cream and syrup, and voilà! The Ice Cream Sunday was born. Too good to serve only on Sunday, the spelling was changed so it could be served every day. Following are ideas you can use to make your own delicious ice cream sundaes at home.

Lemon Meringue Pie Sundae

Place 1 scoop vanilla ice cream in a sundae glass. Add 2 tablespoons store-bought lemon curd or lemon pie filling and sprinkle broken meringue cookies on top. Repeat the layering once.

Triple Strawberry Burst Sundae

Place 1 scoop strawberry ice cream in a sundae glass. Cover with chopped fresh strawberries and strawberry syrup. Repeat layering once.

Nuts About Sundaes

Place a scoop of pistachio ice cream in a sundae glass. Sprinkle in a handful of chopped toasted nuts and squirt in some chocolate syrup. Repeat layering once.

Chocolate Fudge Brownie Sundae

Place a piece of warmed brownie in a sundae glass. Add 2 scoops of chocolate ice cream or vanilla fudge ice cream and top with chocolate syrup. Eat before the ice cream melts.

Serves as many as desired

Tea: How to Make a Proper Cuppa

Tea appears many times in the Harry Potter books, a testament to its importance in British life. A very significant tea is Harry's first one with Hagrid, the first of many and the beginning of a strong friendship (see *Harry Potter and the Sorcerer's Stone*, Chapter 8). The invitation to "come over and have a cuppa" comes from "have a cup o' tea." The way to prepare a proper cuppa is almost a ritual.

This most British of all drinks arrived in the 1600s from China and quickly replaced ale as the national drink. Tradition credits the Duchess of Bedford (1800s) with starting the tradition of afternoon tea. She got very hungry waiting from her noon dinner to her nine o'clock supper. So at around four in the afternoon, she would sneak some food and tea. Later on she came out in the open and invited some ladies for tea and sweet delicacies and gossip. This caught on quickly among the higher class, who began to have tea with scones and jam or with pastries and delicate sandwiches, such as the famous cucumber sandwiches.

1. First, boil water in a kettle.
2. After the water finishes boiling, warm the teapot by swirling some hot water inside and then pouring it out; this will ensure that the tea will stay boiling hot when you serve it.
3. Fill the teapot with as many cups of hot water as you have guests and put in 1 heaping teaspoon of tea for each cup, plus 1 more.
4. Let the tea steep for 3 or 4 minutes; then bring the teapot to the table. Make sure a sugar bowl is handy, as well as a pitcher of milk or cream.
5. Serve the tea with cookies or little cakes.

Chapter Three

Treats from the Train

Harry Potter is very worried. His ticket says he must board the eleven o'clock train to Hogwarts from Platform Nine and Three Quarters at King's Cross Station, but as his Uncle Vernon sneeringly points out before stomping away and leaving Harry alone, there is no such thing as Platform Nine and Three Quarters. Imagine Harry's surprise when he discovers that the platform is something you do: you lean against the barrier between Platforms Nine and Ten and fall through to see the shiny red steam engine called the Hogwarts Express belching smoke into the morning air.

Harry is one lucky chap to get to travel to school in a steam engine. The shiny red steam engines of the past had beautiful cars with carved wooden seats and handsome wooden paneling on the walls. But this particular one had something even better: a food cart that sold unusual sweets such as Cauldron Cakes and Pumpkin Pasties. Harry enjoys buying stacks of the Cauldron Cakes, piles of the Pumpkin Pasties, and mountains of the Chocolate Frogs to share with his friends (see *Harry Potter and the Sorcerer's Stone*, Chapter 6).

Pumpkin Pasties

To Harry's surprise, the snacks witch on the Hogwarts Express isn't selling Heath Bars or Doritos. For the first time in his life, Harry pulls out some money and buys as many treats as he wants, which include Pumpkin Pasties (see *Harry Potter and the Sorcerer's Stone*, Chapter 6).

*I*magine biting into a pasty only to discover you've just chomped down on a whole bird, skin and bones and all. Yuck! But in the Middle Ages, huge too-tough-to-eat pasties enclosed whole birds or whole beef roasts. Today the most common pasty is the Cornish pasty, but in Cyprus a pasty filled with pumpkin and crushed wheat is a popular treat.

Pasty Crust

1¼ cups all-purpose flour

1 tablespoon granulated sugar

¼ teaspoon salt

5 tablespoons cold butter, cut into chunks

3 tablespoons vegetable shortening, chilled and cut into chunks

4–6 tablespoons ice water

Filling

1 cup canned pumpkin, not pumpkin pie filling

¼ cup granulated sugar

⅛ teaspoon ground nutmeg

⅛ teaspoon ground cinnamon

1. Place the flour, sugar, and salt in the bowl of a food processor. Pulse a few times to combine. Scatter the butter and shortening over the flour mixture. Pulse about 15 times until the mixture resembles coarse yellow meal, with no white powdery bits remaining.

2. Transfer the mixture into a large mixing bowl. Sprinkle 4 tablespoons of cold water over the mixture. Toss the mixture together with a spatula until it starts clumping together. If it's too dry, add more water 1 tablespoon at a time (better too wet than too dry). Gather the dough into a ball and pat it into a disk. Wrap it in plastic wrap and refrigerate it for at least 1 hour.

3. Combine the pumpkin, sugar, nutmeg, and cinnamon in a mixing bowl. Mix well. Preheat the oven to 400°F. Roll out the dough ⅛-inch thick. Use a saucer to cut out 6-inch circles.

4. Put 2 to 3 tablespoons of filling in the center of each circle of dough. Moisten the edges with water, fold the dough over the filling, and crimp with a fork to seal the edges. Cut slits to make vents. Bake on an ungreased cookie sheet for 30 minutes or until browned.

Makes 6 pasties

Pumpkin Juice

What could be worse than missing the train and having to fly your father's car to school? Eating sweets for hours and then realizing you have nothing with which to wash it down, although crashing into a murderous tree probably ranks up there as well. After finishing the bag of toffees Harry and Ron find in the car, Harry is so thirsty he starts fantasizing about the pumpkin juice he could buy if he were on the Hogwarts Express (see *Harry Potter and the Chamber of Secrets*, Chapter 5).

It's unsurprising that witches—or wizards, in this case—would drink pumpkin juice. During the fall harvest, the Celts used to carve vegetable lanterns out of turnips and rutabagas to scare away evil spirits. Later, Americans started using pumpkins in the same tradition. The pumpkin lanterns eventually became associated with Halloween perhaps because of its connection with witches (and demons and vampires and such like).

1 small pumpkin, known as sugar
   pumpkin or pie pumpkin
2 cups apple juice

1 cup white grape juice
1 cup pineapple juice

1. Preheat the oven to 400°F. Slice the pumpkin in half pole to pole and scoop out the seeds. Don't worry about the stringy fibers; they are hard to remove and won't affect the results. Place the pumpkin halves face down on a baking sheet and roast 45 minutes to 1 hour until soft. Remove from the oven.

2. When the pumpkin is cool enough to handle, scoop out the flesh and discard the skin. Place the cooked pumpkin in a large fine-mesh sieve set over a bowl and push the pumpkin through using a rubber spatula. Scrape and mash as you push; it will take several minutes. Discard the pulpy mass left in the sieve. Stir the sieved pumpkin in the bowl to evenly distribute the juices, and then measure out 1 cup.

3. Place the cup of sieved pumpkin in a pitcher along with the apple juice, grape juice, and pineapple juice. Stir vigorously until the pumpkin is completely dispersed. Chill the juice until it's very cold.

4. Before serving, stir the juice well, as the pumpkin will settle to the bottom. Fill crystal goblets with ice cubes and pour the juice over the ice.

Makes 5 cups

Although this recipe was tested using freshly roasted pumpkin, it would probably work if you use canned pumpkin instead to save the bother of making it from scratch.

Big, Fluffy Pancakes

In the wizarding world this dish is called Cauldron Cakes. Harry sees them for the first time on the witch's trolley on board the Hogwarts Express in *Harry Potter and the Sorcerer's Stone.* He generously shares with Ron, who finds his dry corned beef sandwich unappealing (Chapter 6).

The humble pancake had an exciting birth. Frantically trying to use up all their butter, milk, and cream by Lent, housewives fried stacks and stacks of the stuff. One legend has a housewife flipping pancakes while running to church to be shriven (receive penance for her sins). So Shrove Tuesday became known as Pancake Day, a day when pancake-eating contests are still held. Women in some towns race to church while carrying frying pans filled with pancakes. The prize? A prayer book.

2 cups all-purpose flour
2 teaspoons baking powder
2 teaspoons baking soda
¼ teaspoon salt
2 large eggs, at room temperature
⅔ cup granulated sugar
Grated zest of 1 lemon
1 stick butter (8 tablespoons), melted

2½ cups whole milk mixed with juice of 1 lemon, left to sit at room temperature until thickened or microwaved for 30 seconds to 1 minute until thickened
Confectioners' sugar, for dusting
Marmalade, for serving

1. Whisk together the flour, baking powder, baking soda, and salt. In a separate bowl, whisk the eggs, sugar, and lemon zest together until light and fluffy, about 1 minute. Drizzle in the melted butter while whisking vigorously. Whisk in the milk.
2. Pour the milk mixture into the flour mixture. Whisk the two mixtures together briefly until just combined. The batter may be lumpy. Take care not to overmix or the pancakes will come out tough.
3. Spray an 8-inch skillet with cooking spray. Heat the skillet over medium-high heat. Pour ½ cup of batter into the skillet and cook until the surface bubbles and the bottom is golden brown (check by lifting gently with a fork). Cook on the other side for 1 to 2 minutes or until golden. Remove the cake from the pan and repeat until all the batter is used up, spraying the pan with cooking spray between each pancake.
4. Dust the pancakes with confectioners' sugar or serve with a dab of marmalade.

Makes about 11 large pancakes

Four Classically British Pies

Professor Slughorn likes his food. At his "Slug Club" gathering onboard the Hogwarts Express, he passes around a platter of assorted pies (see *Harry Potter and the Half-Blood Prince*, Chapter 7). Assuming some were savory and some were sweet, recipes for both types are included. The following four pie recipes are classically British.

Chicken and Mushroom Pies

Pie Crust

2½ cups all-purpose flour

1 teaspoon salt

1 stick (8 tablespoons) butter, chilled and cut into pieces

½ cup (8 tablespoons) vegetable shortening, chilled and cut into pieces

½ to ¾ cup cold water

Chicken and Mushroom Filling

2 tablespoons vegetable oil

1 small onion, finely chopped

5 ounces (half a package) white mushrooms, finely chopped

2 tablespoons all-purpose flour

1¼ cups chicken broth

8 ounces boneless, skinless chicken breast, diced into ¼-inch pieces

¼ teaspoon thyme

Salt and freshly ground black pepper to taste

1 egg beaten with 1 tablespoon water, for brushing the tops of the pies

Medieval pies were filled with all sorts of food thrown together, like a magpie's collection, hence the name pie. Today we try to stick to a theme, so we have "chicken and mushroom pie" and not "chicken and mushroom and apples and whipped cream and oats and raisins and cinnamon and black pepper pie."

Four Classically British Pies

(continued)

1. Place the flour and salt in the bowl of a food processor and pulse to combine. Scatter the pieces of butter and shortening over the flour mixture. Pulse until the mixture resembles coarse yellow meal without any white powdery bits remaining, about 15 pulses. Turn the mixture into a large mixing bowl. Sprinkle ½ cup water over the mixture and toss with a rubber spatula until the dough sticks together. Add more water 1 tablespoon at a time if the dough is dry (better too wet than too dry). Divide the dough in half, form into disks, wrap in plastic wrap, and chill for 2 hours or up to 3 days.

2. To make the Chicken and Mushroom Filling, heat the oil in a large skillet. Add the onions and mushrooms and sauté until well browned. Sprinkle the flour over and mix with a wooden spoon until combined. Slowly pour in the chicken broth while stirring. Cook until the mixture thickens. Add the chopped chicken breast, thyme, and salt and pepper. Stir until well combined. Bring back to a simmer and cook for about 5 minutes. Remove from the heat, transfer to another bowl, and cool to room temperature.

3. Preheat the oven to 350°F. Remove the chilled dough from the refrigerator. On a generously floured surface, roll out one of the disks very thin. Use a 6-inch saucer to cut out six circles. Fit the circles into a 6-cup muffin pan, leaving the overhang. Fill generously with the chicken and mushroom filling.

4. Roll out the second disk of dough. Use a 4-inch cookie cutter to cut out six circles. Brush the overhanging dough with water and lay the circles over the filling. For each pie, fold the overhang over the top circle of dough and press with your fingers to seal. Cut slits in the top of each pie to form vents, and brush the tops with the beaten egg. Bake for 1 hour until golden brown, rotating the pan midway through baking.

Makes 6 pies

A small town in West Yorkshire called Denby Dale makes the biggest meat and potato pies in the world to celebrate major events. The tradition started in 1788 to celebrate King George III's recovery from mental illness. In 1988, the pie that was baked to celebrate the 200th anniversary of this tradition made it into the *Guinness Book of World Records* at twenty feet by seven feet and eighteen inches deep. But the pie baked in 2000 to celebrate the millennium broke that record at forty feet by eight feet and forty-four inches deep.

Meat and Potato Pies

Pie Crust

2½ cups all-purpose flour

1 teaspoon salt

1 stick (8 tablespoons) butter, chilled and cut into pieces

½ cup (8 tablespoons) vegetable shortening, chilled and cut into pieces

½ to ¾ cup cold water

Meat and Potato Filling

2 tablespoons vegetable oil

6 ounces chuck steak, diced into ¼-inch pieces

1 small onion, finely chopped

2 tablespoons all-purpose flour

1½ cups chicken broth

1 medium red-skinned potato, peeled and diced into ¼-inch pieces

1 medium carrot, peeled and dieced into ¼-inch pieces

¼ teaspoon ground sage

Salt and freshly ground black pepper to taste

1 egg beaten with 1 tablespoon water, for brushing over the pie

Four Classically British Pies

(continued)

1. Place the flour and salt in the bowl of a food processor and pulse to combine. Scatter the pieces of butter and shortening over the flour mixture. Pulse until the mixture resembles coarse yellow meal without any white powdery bits remaining, about 15 pulses. Turn the mixture into a large mixing bowl. Sprinkle ½ cup water over the mixture and toss with a rubber spatula until the dough sticks together. Add more water 1 tablespoon at a time if the dough is dry (better too wet than too dry). Divide the dough in half, form into disks, wrap in plastic wrap, and chill for 2 hours or up to 3 days.

2. To make the Meat and Potato Filling, heat the oil in a large skillet. Add the meat and sear on both sides until crusty brown, about 4 minutes per side. Transfer to a bowl. Add the onions to the skillet and sauté until well browned. Return the meat to the pan, sprinkle the flour over, and mix with a wooden spoon until combined. Slowly pour in the chicken broth while stirring. Bring to a simmer and cook, stirring occasionally, for 1½ hours. Add the chopped potato and carrot, sage, salt, and pepper and cook for another 30 minutes. Remove from the heat, transfer to another bowl, and cool to room temperature.

3. Preheat the oven to 350°F. Remove the chilled dough from the refrigerator. On a generously floured surface, roll out one of the disks very thin. Use a 6-inch saucer to cut out six circles. Fit the circles into a 6-cup muffin pan, leaving the overhang. Fill generously with the meat and potato filling.

4. Roll out the second disk of dough. Use a 4-inch cookie cutter to cut out six circles. Brush the overhanging dough with water and lay the circles over the filling. For each pie, fold the overhang over the top dough circle and press with your fingers to seal. Cut slits in the top of each pie to form vents, and brush the tops with the beaten egg. Bake for 1 hour, rotating the pan midway through baking.

Makes 6 pies

Four Classically British Pies

(continued)

During World War II, home cooks simply didn't have enough flour to make a whole pie, so thrifty and resourceful English housewives came up with a way to make do with less. They dumped fruit in a pan and topped it with a mixture of flour, some kind of fat, and sugar—and the fruit crumble (generally called "crisp" in the United States) was born. The following recipe would have been too extravagant during the Second World War, as it calls for both a bottom crust and a crumble topping.

Apple Crumble Pies

Pie Crust

1¼ cups all-purpose flour

2 tablespoons granulated sugar

¼ teaspoon salt

1 stick (8 tablespoons) butter, chilled and cut into pieces

4–6 tablespoons cold water

Apple Filling

2 tablespoons butter

2 sweet apples (such as Gala or Braeburn), peeled, cored, and finely chopped

2 tart apples (such as Granny Smith), peeled, cored, and finely chopped

½ cup granulated sugar

½ teaspoon cinnamon

¼ teaspoon nutmeg

Zest and juice of half a lemon

Crumble Topping

½ cup all-purpose flour

¼ cup packed dark or light brown sugar

¼ teaspoon cinnamon

4 tablespoons (½ stick) butter, chilled and cut into pieces

⅓ cup chopped pecans

Four Classically British Pies

(continued)

1. Place the flour, sugar, and salt in the bowl of a food processor and pulse to combine. Scatter the pieces of butter over the flour mixture. Pulse until the mixture resembles coarse yellow meal without any white powdery bits remaining, about 15 pulses. Turn the mixture into a large mixing bowl. Sprinkle 4 tablespoons water over the mixture and toss with a rubber spatula until the dough sticks together. Add more water 1 tablespoon at a time if the dough is dry (better too wet than too dry). Form the dough into a disk, wrap in plastic wrap, and chill for 2 hours or up to 3 days.

2. To make the Apple Filling, heat the butter in a large skillet until it starts foaming. Add the apples, sugar, cinnamon, nutmeg, lemon zest, and lemon juice and mix with a wooden spoon. Cook over medium-high heat, stirring frequently, until the apples are soft and the juices have evaporated. Transfer to a bowl and cool to room temperature.

3. In a separate bowl, whisk together the flour, brown sugar, and cinnamon. Scatter the butter pieces on top and rub them into the flour mixture with your fingers until the mixture resembles the consistency of wet sand. Add the chopped pecans and toss to combine.

4. Preheat the oven to 350°F. Remove the chilled dough from the refrigerator. On a generously floured surface, roll out the dough very thin. Use a 4-inch cookie cutter to cut out twelve circles. Fit the circles into a 12-cup muffin pan. Fill each pie with a heaping tablespoon of filling. Generously sprinkle the flour and butter mixture on top.

5. Bake for 40 minutes, rotating the pan midway through baking, until the juices are bubbling over and the tops are browned. Remove from the oven and cool in the pans until cool enough to handle. To remove from the pans, run a knife around the edges to loosen the pies and lift out.

Makes 12 pies

Four Classically British Pies

(continued)

Banoffi Pies

Pie Crust

1¼ cups all-purpose flour

2 tablespoons granulated sugar

¼ teaspoon salt

8 tablespoons (1 stick) cold butter, cut into pieces

4–6 tablespoons ice water

Banoffi Filling

1 14-ounce can condensed milk

½ ripe but firm banana, cut into ⅛-inch slices (do not peel and slice until ready to assemble the pies)

Whipped Cream Topping

½ cup heavy cream

2 tablespoons confectioners' sugar

½ teaspoon instant coffee

Who invented Banoffi Pie? Nobody really knows. The Hungry Monk Café in Jevington takes credit for this banana and toffee-coffee pie created in the 1970s, but as it was never patented we'll never know for sure. This recipe contains one of the coolest discoveries out there. If you boil a can of condensed milk for a few hours, it turns into a lovely caramel-y goo.

Four Classically British Pies

(continued)

1. Place the flour, sugar, and salt in the bowl of a food processor and pulse to combine. Scatter the pieces of butter over the flour mixture. Pulse until the mixture resembles yellow meal without any white powdery bits remaining, about 15 pulses. Turn the mixture into a large mixing bowl. Sprinkle 4 tablespoons water over the mixture and toss with a rubber spatula until the dough sticks together. Add more water 1 tablespoon at a time if the dough is dry (better too wet than too dry). Form the dough into a disk, wrap in plastic wrap, and chill at least 1 hour or up to 3 days.

2. Preheat the oven to 425°F. Remove the chilled dough from the refrigerator. On a generously floured surface, roll out the dough ⅛-inch thick. Cut out six 5-inch circles. Fit the circles into a 6-cup muffin pan. Flute the edges for an attractive finish. Freeze the shells for 15 minutes.

3. Line the shells with aluminum foil, making sure to cover the edges. Fill with beans or pie weights. Bake until the dough is dry and set, about 20 minutes. Remove the foil and weights, reduce the temperature to 350°F, and bake until the shells are browned, another 8 minutes. Remove the shells from the oven and allow to cool.

4. Place the can of condensed milk in a pot and cover with water. Bring to a boil and boil for three hours, checking frequently to refill the pot if the water level drops. If the water level drops too low, the can may explode. Turn off the heat. When the can is cool enough to handle, remove it from the pot and chill in the refrigerator until cold.

5. To prepare the whipped cream, whisk together the cream, confectioners' sugar, and coffee in a mixing bowl until stiff peaks form.

6. To assemble the pies, lay two banana slices in the bottom of each shell. Spoon a tablespoon of toffee over the bananas in each shell. Snack on the remaining toffee while you work and reserve the rest for another use. Finish with a dollop of the whipped cream, or pipe it over the toffee for an attractive finish. Keep refrigerated until ready to serve. Serve within 24 hours.

Makes 6 pies

Do NOT attempt this recipe if you are absent-minded. If the water boils out, the can will explode. You need to keep an eye on the water level in the pot.

Roast Pheasant

Malfoy is feeling left out, but Harry would rather hang out with his friends, thank you very much, than accept the invitation to dine with Professor Slughorn aboard the Hogwarts Express, where Slughorn passes around pheasant to the select members of the "Slug Club" (see *Harry Potter and the Half-Blood Prince*, Chapter 7).

"Pheasant, peasant? What a pleasant present!" This famous line from William Steig's *Shrek* is terrific because "pheasant" is a hard word to rhyme. The Romans, of course, are the ones who introduced this pleasant present to England. But not for the peasants. In feudal times, the lord of the manor kept busy with hunting and falconry, but peasants also trapped birds, and on a lucky day, they might find a pheasant or a partridge in the traps.

1 onion, sliced into ¼-inch-thick slices
2 celery ribs, cut into chunks
2 carrots, cut into chunks
4 cloves garlic
1 pheasant
Olive oil for brushing on the pheasant
Salt and freshly ground black pepper
1 cup water

1. Preheat the oven to 375°F. Lay the onion slices in a roasting pan and scatter the celery, carrots, and garlic cloves on top.
2. Rinse the pheasant in cold water and pat it dry with paper towels. Place the pheasant in the roasting pan, breast side up, wings tucked under. Brush the olive oil over the pheasant and sprinkle it with the salt and pepper. Pour the water into the roasting pan.
3. Put the pan in the oven and roast for 45 minutes, or until the juices run clear.
4. Remove the pheasant from the oven and let it rest for 20 minutes before carving.

Serves 4

Chapter Four

Recipes from a Giant and an Elf

Hagrid is the bravest person Harry ever knew, and even if he's an awful cook, you have to admire his adventurous spirit in the kitchen. Foods that even experienced cooks leave to the professionals don't daunt him. He's not afraid to try his hand at treacle fudge (true, it will glue your teeth together) or even twice-raised Bath buns.

Hagrid, the Hogwarts gamekeeper, lives in a small one-room wooden hut near the outskirts of the Forbidden Forest. He is enormously proud of the two important tasks he's been entrusted with: delivering Harry to the Dursleys after his parents are killed and returning him to Hogwarts when he reaches school age. Hagrid takes a special interest in Harry, and a friendship springs up between them (see *Harry Potter and the Sorcerer's Stone*).

Harry and his friends often visit Hagrid for tea, where they learn that experience in cooking does not guarantee good results. They pretend to enjoy Hagrid's rock cakes, which break your teeth, or beef casserole with a talon mixed in. Have no fear: the recipes that follow, unlike Hagrid's, do yield excellent results, but if you have real Harry Potter spirit, follow the special instructions to make them turn out like Hagrid's.

Rock Cakes

This treat, if the word may be applied to something Hagrid made, is often found in his pantry, as it's mentioned no less than three times in the Harry Potter series in relation to Hagrid. Although Hagrid's rock cakes were nothing to write home about, you'll find these to be quite tasty (see *Harry Potter and the Sorcerer's Stone*, Chapter 8; *Harry Potter and the Goblet of Fire*, Chapter 3; *Harry Potter and the Half-Blood Prince*, Chapter 11).

Rock cakes, standard with tea, look like but don't taste like rocks, unless of course you leave them out for several days, which is probably what Hagrid did. Rock cakes have a short history and seem to have been invented by the Victorians.

2 cups all-purpose flour
½ cup granulated sugar
1 teaspoon baking powder
½ teaspoon cinnamon
¼ teaspoon salt

1 stick (8 tablespoons) cold butter,
*   cut into chunks*
1 large egg
⅓ cup whole milk
1 cup raisins

1. Preheat the oven to 350°F and grease and flour a large cookie sheet. Combine the flour, sugar, baking powder, cinnamon, and salt in a large mixing bowl. With your fingertips, rub the butter into the dry ingredients until the mixture reaches the consistency of wet sand.
2. Beat the egg together with the milk and pour it into the flour-butter mixture. Fold it together using a spatula to form a stiff dough. Fold in the raisins. Drop dough by rounded tablespoonfuls 2 inches apart on the prepared cookie sheet.
3. Bake for 25 minutes or until the bottoms are golden, rotating the pan midway through baking.

Makes 12

For rock-hard rock cakes like Hagrid's, just bake them for too long and eat them a week later at your own risk!

Harry's First Birthday Cake: Chocolate Layer Cake

It's hard to imagine a woman so heartless that she wouldn't ever, ever bake—or at least buy—a birthday cake for her motherless nephew. But such is indeed the case for Harry Potter, who meets his first birthday cake when he turns eleven, courtesy of Hagrid (see *Harry Potter and the Sorcerer's Stone*, Chapter 4).

Cocoa beans were so precious to the ancient Aztecs that they used them as money. The Spanish explorers brought the beans back to Spain in the 1500s, and from there it was only a matter of time for chocolate to catch on in the rest of Europe and for the final product to be perfected. We have the Dutch to thank for figuring out how to make chocolate and cocoa powder as we know it and the Swiss for thinking of adding milk.

Chocolate Cake

¾ cup boiling water
½ cup unsweetened cocoa powder
1 teaspoon instant coffee
1 cup all-purpose flour
1 teaspoon baking powder
¼ teaspoon salt
1 stick (8 tablespoons) butter, at room temperature
1 cup granulated sugar
½ cup packed dark brown sugar
3 large eggs, at room temperature
1 teaspoon pure vanilla extract

Chocolate Glaze

8 ounces chopped bittersweet chocolate
¾ cup heavy cream
¼ stick (2 tablespoons) butter
¼ cup corn syrup

Chocolate Frosting

1 stick (8 tablespoons) butter
1 cup confectioners' sugar
1 tablespoon heavy cream
1 teaspoon pure vanilla extract
½ of the above Chocolate Glaze recipe

Green Icing

1 cup confectioners' sugar
Water to form a paste
Green food coloring

Harry's First Birthday Cake: Chocolate Layer Cake

(continued)

1. To make the cake layers, preheat the oven to 350°F. Grease and flour two 8-inch round cake pans and line the bottoms with parchment paper.

2. Whisk together the boiling water, cocoa powder, and instant coffee in a measuring cup or small bowl until smooth; set aside. In a separate bowl, whisk together the flour, baking powder, and salt; set aside.

3. In the large bowl of an electric mixer, beat the butter, granulated sugar, and brown sugar until light and fluffy, scraping down the sides of the bowl as needed, about 5 minutes. Add the eggs one at a time, beating after each until incorporated and scraping down the sides as needed. Add the vanilla extract and beat until combined. Add the hot cocoa mixture and beat until combined, scraping down the sides as needed. Add the flour mixture and stir on the slowest speed until combined. Finish by scraping the bottom of the bowl with a spatula and folding it in. Divide the batter evenly between the prepared pans and bake for 20 minutes, until the cakes feel firm and a toothpick inserted in the center comes out with a few crumbs attached. Be careful, as this cake overbakes easily. Cool the layers in the pans for 10 minutes, then invert onto a wire rack and cool completely.

4. To prepare the glaze, place the chocolate, heavy cream, butter, and corn syrup in a bowl and microwave for 1 to 2 minutes. Whisk until smooth. Cool the glaze until it is thick but still pourable.

5. To prepare the frosting, place the butter, confectioners' sugar, heavy cream, and vanilla in a large mixing bowl and beat until light and fluffy, scraping down the sides as needed, about 7 minutes. Add half of the cooled glaze and beat until combined. If the frosting is too soft to spread, chill for 10 minutes and beat again. Chill another 10 minutes and beat again if necessary.

6. To make the icing, add 1 tablespoon of water at a time to the confectioners' sugar and mix to form a thick paste. Work in the food coloring to tint it to the desired shade of green.

7. To assemble the cake, place one layer top-side down on a cardboard round. Spread ¾ cup of the frosting over the cake and smooth it to the edges. Place the second layer top-side up over the first and spread the remaining frosting over the top and sides. Pour the remaining glaze over the cake and smooth it to the edges, allowing it to drip unevenly over the sides. (If the glaze is too stiff, warm briefly in the microwave and whisk to distribute the heat evenly. You may need to wait again for the glaze to cool.) If you have any frosting left, use it to pipe a decorative border around the bottom of the cake. Place the icing in a pastry bag fitted with a #3 round tip and write "Happy Birthday Harry" on top of the cake. The cake will look homemade. It's supposed to; Hagrid made it.

Serves 16

Instead of a pastry bag, you can use a sandwich bag. Snip off a small hole in one corner, fill it with the icing, and squeeze it through the hole.

Bath Buns

When Hagrid invites Harry and Ron to tea in *Harry Potter and the Prisoner of Azkaban* (Chapter 14), Ron thinks Hagrid wants to hear all about how he was almost attacked by Sirius Black. But Hagrid wants to talk to them about . . . Hermione. So they sit down, feeling guilty on two counts: they've forgotten about helping Hagrid with Buckbeak's trial and they haven't been good friends to Hermione. But their guilty feelings don't stop them from refusing Hagrid's Bath buns; they know only too well what to expect.

The city of Bath in the southwest of England is famous not only for its hot springs and Roman baths but also for a delightful pastry known as the Bath bun. The creation of this little cake is attributed, probably incorrectly, to eighteenth-century physician William Oliver. Historians question why a doctor who developed food (such as the Bath Oliver biscuit) to aid the digestion of his patients would prescribe such a rich pastry.

¼ cup warm water

2¼ teaspoons (1 packet) active dry yeast

1 tablespoon granulated sugar

½ cup whole milk

2 tablespoons (¼ stick) butter

2½ cups all-purpose flour

6 tablespoons granulated sugar

1 teaspoon salt

2 large eggs, at room temperature

Grated zest of 1 lemon

Grated zest of 1 orange

¾ cup dried currants or dried sweetened cranberries

1 teaspoon caraway seeds

1 egg beaten with 1 tablespoon water, for brushing over the buns

Turbinado sugar, for sprinkling (Introduction)

Bath Buns

(continued)

1. Grease and flour two cookie sheets or line with parchment paper and set aside. Spray a large bowl with cooking spray and set aside. Combine the water, yeast, and 1 tablespoon of sugar in a mixing bowl and set aside until the yeast is puffy, about 10 minutes. Heat the milk and butter in a saucepan until the butter is melted. Set aside but keep warm (not hot; if it's too hot it will kill the yeast).

2. Whisk together the flour, sugar, and salt. Whisk the eggs, lemon zest, and orange zest into the milk mixture. Add the yeast mixture, milk mixture, currants or cranberries, and caraway seeds to the flour mixture; mix to combine. Knead the dough in the bowl or on a lightly floured work surface 10 to 15 minutes until the dough is smooth and elastic. The dough will be sticky but will gradually become less sticky as you knead. If it remains sticky, add flour 1 tablespoon at a time, up to ½ cup. If you have a stand mixer you can knead the dough with the dough hook; the dough should clean the sides of the bowl.

3. Place the dough in the oiled bowl and turn the dough to coat (or spray the top with cooking spray). Cover the bowl with plastic wrap and set to rise in a warm, draft-free place until doubled in size, about 1 ½ hours.

4. Turn the dough out onto a clean work surface and divide in half. Divide in half again; then divide each quarter in half and then in half again to form 16 pieces of dough. Roll each piece into a ball. Put the dough balls onto the prepared baking sheets. Leave to rise until doubled in volume, about 2 hours.

5. Preheat the oven to 350°F. Brush the beaten egg over the buns and sprinkle with the turbinado sugar. Bake the buns for 15 minutes until the tops are golden brown, switching and rotating the pans midway through baking. Remove from the oven and transfer to a wire rack to cool completely.

Makes 8 to 16 buns

These buns do not keep well. They should be eaten within a few hours of baking.

Treacle Fudge

Hagrid's glue-your-teeth-together fudge turns out to be quite useful: after Hagrid's been taken to Azkaban, Harry feeds some to Fang to keep him quiet. Fang can't bark because his fangs are stuck together. Fudge is not foolproof, so it's no surprise Hagrid's didn't come out quite right (see *Harry Potter and the Chamber of Secrets*, Chapter 15).

Making fudge was the "in" thing to do at women's colleges in the 1880s. Can you imagine if that were the in thing to do at colleges today? Times have certainly changed. We don't know who invented fudge, though some speculate that a batch of caramels came out wrong—it was "fudged"—but it seems it was invented in the United States.

1 cup granulated sugar
1 cup packed dark brown sugar
1 stick (8 tablespoons) butter
½ cup heavy cream

2 tablespoons black treacle or dark molasses or blackstrap molasses
¼ teaspoon cream of tartar
1 teaspoon pure vanilla extract

1. Grease an 8-inch square pan and set aside. Combine the granulated sugar, brown sugar, butter, heavy cream, treacle, and cream of tartar in a medium saucepan. Cook over medium-high heat, stirring constantly, until the butter is melted and the ingredients are combined. Wash down the sides of the pot with a pastry brush dipped in hot water if sugar crystals form on the sides, to prevent recrystallization. Clip a candy thermometer to the side of the pot and continue to cook without stirring until the mixture reaches 240°F on the candy thermometer.

2. Remove the pan from the heat and stir in the vanilla. Allow the bubbles to subside and the mixture to cool slightly, about 5 minutes. Remove the thermometer and beat or stir vigorously with a wooden spoon until the mixture loses its gloss and is very thick, 15 to 20 minutes. Scrape the mixture into the prepared pan and smooth the top. You can use a piece of plastic wrap and the palm of your hand to do this.

3. Cool completely before cutting into 1-inch squares.

Makes 64 pieces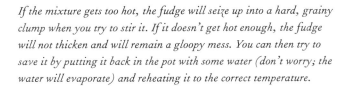

If the mixture gets too hot, the fudge will seize up into a hard, grainy clump when you try to stir it. If it doesn't get hot enough, the fudge will not thicken and will remain a gloopy mess. You can then try to save it by putting it back in the pot with some water (don't worry; the water will evaporate) and reheating it to the correct temperature.

Dundee Cake (Fruitcake) for Kids

Hagrid is about to offer fruitcake to Harry and Ron, but he is very nervous. He suspects that any moment he will be carted off to Azkaban for a crime he did not commit. When he hears the knock on the door, he is so agitated that he actually drops the cake on the floor (*Harry Potter and the Chamber of Secrets*, Chapter 14).

Once upon a time, in the faraway city of Dundee in Scotland, a factory produced marmalade. But it did not produce marmalade the whole year. So the rest of the year, the manufacturers came up with the idea to make a fruitcake with orange peel, also adding the almonds brought by the Spanish traders. Thus was born the Dundee cake.

Candied orange peel is next to impossible to find, so this recipe uses marmalade.

If you are an adult and you wish to make traditional Dundee cake, simply replace the apple juice with brandy.

2 cups all-purpose flour
½ cup finely ground almonds
1 teaspoon baking powder
½ teaspoon salt
1½ half sticks (12 tablespoons) butter
1½ cups granulated sugar
2 large eggs
¼ teaspoon almond extract
Juice and zest of 1 orange
¼ cup marmalade
¼ cup apple juice
½ cup dark raisins
½ cup golden raisins
½ cup currants or dried sweetened cranberries
¼ cup chopped candied cherries, optional
Whole raw almonds for covering the cake

1. Preheat the oven to 300°F. Grease and flour a 9-inch cake pan that is at least 2 inches deep and set aside. Whisk together the flour, ground almonds, baking powder, and salt.
2. In a separate bowl, beat the butter and sugar with an electric mixer until light and fluffy, scraping down the sides of the bowl as needed, about 5 minutes. Add the eggs one at a time, beating after each until incorporated. Add the almond extract and beat until combined. Add the orange zest and juice and the marmalade and beat until combined. Add the apple juice and beat until combined. Stir in the flour mixture at the lowest speed until combined, scraping down the sides. Stir in the dark raisins, golden raisins, currants or cranberries, and candied cherries, if using.
3. Scrape the batter into the prepared pan and smooth the top with a rubber spatula. Place the whole almonds in concentric circles on top of the cake. Bake for 1 hour; then reduce the temperature to 275°F and bake for another hour or until a toothpick inserted in the center comes out clean.
4. Remove from the oven and cool completely in the pan. When completely cool, invert the cake onto a cardboard round and immediately reinvert the cake onto a serving platter or another cardboard round.

Makes 16 thick slices or 32 thin slices

Almond-Ginger-Peach Treacle Tart

Harry is having a nasty turn. It's no fun seeing into Voldemort's mind. About to be really sick, he gets up from the table abruptly. Kreacher, out of newfound concern for his master, offers him treacle tart (see *Harry Potter and the Deathly Hallows*, Chapter 12).

Treacle is a byproduct of sugar refining, much like molasses. It's used mostly in England and has a delicious taste. If you can't find golden syrup (which is light treacle), you can use light molasses, dark corn syrup, or even pure maple syrup.

Tart Crust

1 cup all-purpose flour
½ cup finely ground almonds
¼ cup granulated sugar
¼ teaspoon salt
1 stick (8 tablespoons) cold butter or margarine, cut into pieces
1 large egg yolk
1 tablespoon heavy cream
1 teaspoon vanilla

Treacle Filling

1 large peach, thinly sliced
1 cup golden syrup or dark corn syrup
2 cups fresh bread crumbs (6 to 8 slices fresh bread processed to crumbs in a food processor)
½ cup chopped almonds
1 teaspoon ground ginger
1 egg beaten with 1 tablespoon water, for brushing the top

Almond-Ginger-Peach Treacle Tart

(continued)

1. Combine the flour, ground almonds, sugar, and salt in a large mixing bowl. Using a pastry cutter, two knives, or your fingertips, cut the butter into the flour until the flour is completely coated with fat; in other words, no white powdery flour remains and the mixture resembles coarse yellow meal. Or pulse in a food processor 15 to 20 times until the mixture resembles coarse yellow meal, and then transfer it to a large mixing bowl.

2. Beat the egg yolk with the cream and vanilla and pour it into the flour-butter mixture. Toss with a spatula until the dough clumps together, then knead briefly. Form ⅓ of the dough into one disk and the remaining ⅔ of the dough into another. Wrap in plastic wrap and refrigerate at least 2 hours or up to 3 days.

3. Preheat the oven to 350°F. Remove the larger disk from the refrigerator and sprinkle both sides generously with flour. On a heavily flour-dusted work surface, roll out the dough to an 11-inch circle. Fit the dough into a 9-inch tart pan and press in the bottom and sides. This dough is very, very hard to work with, but it's also very forgiving, especially if you use margarine in place of the butter (sacrificing some flavor, but oh, well). You can gather it up, knead it, and reroll several times without its becoming tough. If it gets too soft, put it back in the fridge to firm up.

4. Lay the thinly sliced peaches on the bottom of the tart. Warm the golden syrup in the microwave or a small saucepan just until it's runny. Combine the golden syrup, bread crumbs, chopped almonds, and ginger in a mixing bowl and mix well. Scrape the mixture into the tart shell and spread it evenly over the peach slices with a rubber spatula.

5. Remove the smaller disk from the refrigerator and sprinkle both sides generously with flour. On a heavily flour-dusted work surface, roll out the dough ⅛-inch thick. Cut the dough into strips with a sharp knife. Lay half the strips over the tart in one direction and lay the other half over the tart in the opposite direction to form a lattice. Don't try weaving the strips. Just laying them down will be hard enough, as the strips may break as you move them and you'll have to keep fixing and patching.

6. Brush the strips with the beaten egg and bake the tart for 45 minutes, until golden brown. Serve warm or at room temperature with or without a scoop of vanilla ice cream.

Serves 8

Sugar Biscuits

Harry's suffering from the shock of watching a schoolmate being murdered by Voldemort and barely escaping with his own life, and apart from Ron and Hermione, Hagrid is one of the few people he can confide in. Indeed, several days after this tragic episode, Harry finds himself in Hagrid's hut, having tea and Hagrid's "doughy" cookies (see *Harry Potter and the Goblet of Fire*, Chapter 27). If you wish to produce results like Hagrid's, you can try making the cookies twice as thick as specified or baking them for half the time.

"Biscuit" is the English word for "cookie." Biscuits are an old food, and the Romans, of course, made dry biscuits, which they fried and ate with honey and pepper. Once the Middle Ages were past, cooks learned to mix sugar with eggs, and to cream butter with sugar, so we have them to thank for the many varieties of "biscuits" that abound today.

3 cups all-purpose flour
½ teaspoon baking soda
¼ teaspoon salt
2 sticks (16 tablespoons) butter
1½ cups granulated sugar

2 large eggs
1½ teaspoons pure vanilla extract
Turbinado sugar or granulated sugar, for sprinkling (Introduction)

1. Whisk together the flour, baking soda, and salt.

2. In a separate bowl, beat the butter and sugar with an electric mixer until light and fluffy, scraping down the sides of the bowl as needed, about 5 minutes. Add the eggs one at a time, beating after each until incorporated. Add the vanilla and beat until combined. Stir in the flour mixture on the lowest speed until combined, scraping down the sides as needed. Divide the dough in half, form into disks, wrap in plastic wrap, and chill until firm, about 2 hours.

3. Preheat the oven to 350°F and line two cookie sheets with parchment paper. Remove the chilled disks from the refrigerator. Working with one disk at a time, roll out the dough ¼-inch thick. Using a 1½-inch or 3-inch cookie cutter, stamp out rounds of dough. Place the rounds on cookie sheets and sprinkle with turbinado sugar or granulated sugar.

4. Bake for 12 minutes, switching and rotating the pans midway through baking. Remove to a wire rack to cool. Repeat until all the dough is used up.

Makes 8 dozen 1½-inch or 4 dozen 3-inch cookies

For doughy cookies like Hagrid's, bake the cookies for half the time. But be aware that undercooked cookie dough may give you a foodborne illness or at the very least a stomachache!

Kreacher's French Onion Soup

Giving Kreacher Regulus's locket was a good move: Harry has never tasted better French onion soup (see *Harry Potter and the Deathly Hallows*, Chapter 12).

for at least 2,000 years, maybe more, onion soup has been a staple for the poor. But French onion soup is a staple for the not-so-poor, with its rich beef broth, croutons, and melted cheese.

To make French Onion Soup with Gruyère, preheat the oven to 325°F. Ladle the soup in heatproof cups. Sprinkle in 1 tablespoon of slivered Gruyère and ½ teaspoon grated raw onion per cup. Float a piece of buttered toast on top and sprinkle with a scant ¼ cup of grated Gruyère. Bake for 20 minutes or brown under the broiler.

4 medium onions
½ stick (4 tablespoons) butter, melted
1 baguette
½ cup grated Parmesan cheese
1 teaspoon salt
¼ teaspoon freshly ground black pepper

¼ teaspoon sugar
1 tablespoon all-purpose flour
6 cups beef or chicken stock (beef preferred)
Additional grated Parmesan, for serving

1. Preheat the oven to 350°F. Peel the onions, cut them in half from pole to pole, and slice as thinly as possible. In a heavy soup pot, heat the butter. Remove the pot from the heat.

2. Remove one end of the baguette and slice six 1-inch-thick slices for the croutons. Cover the cut end of the bread and save for the end. Dip a pastry brush into the hot butter that is in the pot and brush one side of each slice with the butter. Place the slices butter-side up on a baking sheet and sprinkle with the cheese. Toast the bread in the oven for about 10 minutes or until browned.

3. While the bread toasts, return the pot to the heat and add the onions. Season with salt and pepper. Stir in the sugar and continue to stir over medium-high heat until the onions have browned, about 15 minutes.

4. Blend in the flour. Gradually add the stock while stirring and bring the soup to a boil. Reduce the heat to a simmer and cook uncovered for 30 minutes.

5. Ladle the soup into warmed bowls and float a cheesy crouton in the center, then sprinkle cheese around the crouton.

Serves 6

Beef Stew with Herb Dumplings

Just when Harry is about to be sick from yet another excursion into Voldemort's mind, Kreacher tries to offer him some stew. Not a good thing to offer someone who's about to throw up, don't you agree? (See *Harry Potter and the Deathly Hallows*, Chapter 12.)

Not exactly haute cuisine, but you can't do better than this for a hearty and satisfying comfort food. The humble dumpling has been around for centuries. The Scots used to dump nettle leaves, hawthorn buds, and dandelion leaves into their dumplings—sounds more like a witch's brew than a food. Tastes have surely changed.

Herb Dumplings

1 cup flour

¼ teaspoon salt

1 teaspoon baking powder

¼ teaspoon freshly ground black pepper

¼ teaspoon ground sage

¼ teaspoon ground thyme

¼ teaspoon dried marjoram

2 tablespoons chopped fresh parsley

½ stick (4 tablespoons) butter or margarine, chilled and cut into small pieces

2 tablespoons milk

1 egg

Beef Stew

3 tablespoons vegetable oil

1½ pounds chuck steak, trimmed and cut into ½-inch cubes

1 onion, chopped

1 tablespoon flour

1 14-ounce can chicken broth

Salt and freshly ground black pepper to taste

2 carrots, cut into 1-inch pieces

2 celery ribs, cut into 1-inch pieces

4 red-skinned potatoes, unpeeled, scrubbed, and cut into 1-inch cubes

Beef Stew with Herb Dumplings

(continued)

1. To make the dumplings, whisk together the flour, salt, baking powder, black pepper, and herbs. Add the pieces of butter and rub with your fingertips until the mixture resembles coarse meal and no powdery bits remain.

2. Whisk the milk and egg together and add to the flour mixture. Toss with a rubber spatula until the mixture begins to clump together. Press plastic wrap down on top of the dough and refrigerate until needed.

3. To make the stew, heat 1 tablespoon of the oil in a Dutch oven or wide pot and add the meat in batches, searing on both sides over high heat 4 to 5 minutes until crusty brown, and transferring each batch to a dinner plate. Add the remaining 2 tablespoons oil to the skillet. Add the chopped onion and cook over medium-low heat until softened, scraping up the fond (browned bits) from the bottom of the pot with a wooden spoon.

4. Add the flour to the pot and stir until combined. Pour in the chicken broth and stir until well combined. Add the salt and pepper and the meat along with its accumulated juices to the pot and cook over medium-high heat, stirring occasionally, until thickened and bubbling. Reduce to a simmer and simmer the meat for 1½ hours.

5. Add the carrots, celery, and potatoes to the pot and simmer for 1 hour, stirring occasionally. Remove the dumpling dough from the refrigerator. Wet your hands and form the dumplings into 1-inch balls, dropping them onto the hot stew in the pot as you form them. Wet your hands as needed to prevent sticking. Cover the pot and simmer another 30 minutes until the dumplings have puffed up and feel set when pressed lightly with the fingertips, though they will be very soft.

Serves 6

Hot Rolls

Coffee and hot rolls for breakfast, yum . . . unfortunately, it's going to be the last meal Kreacher serves our favorite trio. After they escape the Ministry of Magic, they end up wandering from forest to forest, hungry and wishing for one of Kreacher's wonderful meals (see *Harry Potter and the Deathly Hallows*, Chapter 7).

Rolls became popular for breakfast because they rise and bake more quickly than whole loaves of bread, but you would still have to get up pretty early to make these for breakfast. If you like your sleep, prepare the rolls the day before and let them rise in the refrigerator overnight. Then all you have to do is pop them in the oven. Otherwise you are going to be very tired.

¼ cup warm water
1 tablespoon (1 packet) active dry yeast
1 tablespoon granulated sugar
½ stick (4 tablespoons) butter
½ cup whole milk
1 large egg
1 large egg yolk
2½ cups all-purpose flour
⅓ cup granulated sugar
½ teaspoon salt

1. Combine the water, yeast, and 1 tablespoon sugar in a mixing bowl and set aside until puffy. Place the butter and milk in a small saucepan and heat until the butter melts. Pour into a mixing bowl and whisk in the egg and egg yolk. In a separate bowl, whisk together the flour, sugar, and salt. Add the yeast mixture and milk mixture to the flour mixture and mix with a wooden spoon to combine. Knead in the bowl or on a lightly dusted work surface until smooth and elastic, 10 to 15 minutes. Place in an oiled bowl, turning the dough to coat it on all sides. Cover the bowl with plastic wrap and set it in a warm, draft-free place to rise until doubled in volume, about 2 hours.

2. Grease and flour a baking sheet. Turn the dough out onto a work surface. Cut the dough in half, then each half into half again to form quarters, and each quarter into halves again to form 8 pieces of dough. Roll each piece into a 4-inch rope and tie into a knot, tucking one end under. If you prefer, simply roll them into ball. Place the rolls on a baking sheet and set aside to rise until doubled in volume, 2 to 3 hours.

3. Preheat the oven to 350°F. Bake the rolls for 15 minutes, rotating once halfway through the baking time, until light golden brown. Remove to a wire rack to cool slightly. Serve while quite warm. The rolls become dense after a few hours and are best eaten fresh out of the oven, broken open and slathered with butter and jam.

Makes 8 rolls

Beef Casserole

Here's a nice, cozy scene: sitting around the table in Hagrid's hut, rain tapping against the windows, a fire crackling merrily in the hearth, while Harry, Ron, and Hermione rehash everything they know about the Triwizard Tournament. We have the ambiance, we have the sparkling conversation; the only thing missing is the good food. Our heroes and heroine have declined the beef casserole after finding a talon in one of their portions (see *Harry Potter and the Goblet of Fire*, Chapter 16).

Old-time Brits used to cook a huge roast for Sunday. Then they used the rest of the meat in other dishes with gravy or the like for the rest of week. Luckily, you can buy a small amount of beef and cook it fresh. Only a bit of work and well worth the effort, beef casserole is wonderful spooned over mashed potatoes, rice, or pasta (wide egg noodles look most elegant).

3 tablespoons vegetable oil
1½ pounds chuck steak, trimmed
   and cut into 1-inch pieces
1 onion, finely chopped
1 celery rib, finely chopped
3 tablespoons all-purpose flour
3 cups chicken broth
1 tablespoon tomato paste
10 ounces mushrooms, sliced
Salt and freshly ground black pepper

1. Preheat the oven to 350°F. Heat 1 tablespoon of the oil in a large oven-safe skillet over the stovetop. Add half the meat in a single layer and cook over high heat until crusty brown, about 5 minutes. Turn the meat over and brown the other side. Transfer the meat to a large plate. Wipe out the skillet and add the other tablespoon of oil. Repeat with the remaining meat.

2. Wipe out the skillet and add the remaining tablespoon of oil. Heat the oil and add the onion and celery. Cook over medium heat until the onion turns light brown, scraping up the fond (browned bits) from the bottom of the pan, 10 to 15 minutes.

3. Sprinkle the flour over the onion and celery and stir until it is dissolved. Add the broth while stirring. Add the tomato paste, mushrooms, salt, and pepper. Mix thoroughly and bring the casserole to a boil. Turn off the heat. Mix in reserved ground beef and any accumulated juices.

4. Cover the skillet and transfer it to the oven. Bake the casserole for 2 hours. Stir the casserole every 30 minutes to make sure the bottom doesn't burn, and add water as necessary. Serve over mashed potatoes, rice, or pasta.

Serves 4

A talon might not be easy to find to add to this casserole, but if you have a dragon for a pet and you've just clipped its claws, you can add the clippings.

Chapter Five

The Favorite Cook's Dishes

Mrs. Weasley is the mother of Harry's best friend, Ron. Plump, kind, and motherly, she can nevertheless be quite terrifying if her kids—and also her husband, Mr. Weasley—misbehave. Mrs. Weasley is almost like the mother Harry never had, and his favorite place to be after Hogwarts is the Burrow, the Weasleys' untidy house, which looks like it's about to fall down. There Harry gets to hang out with Ron and his brothers and his sister, Ginny, while eating home-cooked meals and being treated like a member of the family. The best cook Harry ever knew is Mrs. Weasley, and what a cook she is! She cooks everything from scratch, using fresh ingredients, and skillfully produces dishes that are beyond the ordinary home cook. Of course, a wand helps. But we'll have to do without one to replicate her wonderful food.

Homemade Fudge

Harry is astonished to find a pile of presents at his bedside on Christmas morning. Ron asks him if he expected turnips. But Harry hasn't ever seen a pile of gifts for him for any occasion—not for holidays, not for birthdays—and so he's delighted with the fudge and hand-knitted (or wand-knitted) sweater that Mrs. Weasley sent him for Christmas (see *Harry Potter and the Sorcerer's Stone*, Chapter 12).

Great fudge should have a slightly grainy but also smooth and creamy texture. It may take some practice to get right. Although we Americans associate fudge with the chocolate variety, in England it often means non-chocolate fudge, also called opera fudge. And it tastes absolutely amazing.

If the mixture gets too hot, the fudge will seize up into a hard, grainy clump when you try to stir it. If it doesn't get hot enough, the fudge will not thicken and will remain a gloopy mess. You can then try to save it by putting it back in the pot with some water (don't worry; the water will evaporate) and reheating it to the correct temperature.

2 cups granulated sugar
2 cups whole milk
2 tablespoons golden syrup or light or dark corn syrup
¼ stick (2 tablespoons) butter
¼ cup heavy cream
¼ teaspoon salt
¼ teaspoon cream of tartar
1 teaspoon pure vanilla extract

1. Grease an 8-inch square pan. Line it with parchment paper, allowing the paper to come up two of the sides. This will make it easy to remove the fudge and slice it.

2. Combine the sugar, milk, golden syrup or corn syrup, butter, heavy cream, salt, and cream of tartar in a large saucepan. (As you cook, the mixture will expand like crazy, so be sure the pot is large enough; it should be at least 4 quarts.) Cook over medium-high heat, stirring constantly, until the butter is melted and the ingredients are combined. Wash down the sides of the pan with a pastry brush dipped in hot water to get rid of sugar crystals. A few crystals on the sides can cause the fudge to recrystallize.

3. Clip a candy thermometer to the side of the pot and continue cooking, stirring frequently, until the mixture reaches 220°F. Continue cooking, stirring constantly, until the mixture reaches 238°F. This whole process may take more than 30 minutes, so be patient. Don't worry if the mixture looks curdled; it will smooth out as it thickens during the beating process.

4. Remove the pan from the heat and wait until the mixture cools to 115°F. Remove the thermometer, add the vanilla, and beat or stir vigorously with a wooden spoon until the mixture loses its gloss and is very thick, about 10 minutes. Scrape the mixture into the prepared pan and smooth the top. You can use a piece of plastic wrap and the palm of your hand to do this.

5. Cool completely before cutting into 1-inch squares.

Makes 64 pieces

Irish Soda Bread

Mrs. Weasley always seems prepared when it comes to food. Harry can burst in on her in the middle of the night and she'll still be able to serve him a nice meal. Fresh bread is part of it when Dumbledore brings Harry to the Burrow after taking him to Professor Slughorn's (see *Harry Potter and the Half-Blood Prince*, Chapter 5).

The Irish weren't very much into yeast breads (inadequate cooking utensils were the culprit), so they must have been very happy when baking soda arrived on the scene; they could quickly and easily make bread with it. And that's what they've been doing since the late 1800s. This is the bread to serve with soups and stews, and it makes awesome toast.

4 cups all-purpose flour, plus extra for dusting
1½ teaspoons baking soda
1½ teaspoons cream of tartar
1 teaspoon salt
3 tablespoons granulated sugar
½ stick (4 tablespoons) butter
1 large egg, beaten
1½ cups buttermilk

1. Preheat the oven to 425°F and grease and flour a 9-inch round baking dish.
2. In a large mixing bowl, whisk together the flour, baking soda, cream of tartar, salt, and sugar. Rub in the butter with your fingertips until it is completely rubbed in. The mixture will still be floury because of the much higher proportion of flour. With a wooden spoon stir or fold in the egg and buttermilk until a dough begins to form. Turn the dough onto a flour-dusted work surface and knead briefly just until the dough comes together. Form the dough into a round and dust the top with the extra flour. Place the dough into the prepared pan and score an X about ½-inch deep on the top of the dough.
3. Bake for 15 minutes; reduce heat to 350°F and bake another 40 minutes until the bottom is dark golden brown.
4. Cool completely on a wire rack before serving. Irish soda bread tastes best the day it is made but makes the best toast ever after the first day. Serve with soup or stew.

Makes 1 loaf

Treacle Pudding

Apparently, Harry loves anything treacle. He's always reaching for the treacle tart, and he seems to really like the treacle pudding Mrs. Weasley prepared for dessert the night before he left the Burrow for Hogwarts (see *Harry Potter and the Chamber of Secrets*, Chapter 5).

Treacle is like molasses and is made during sugar refining. Black treacle is like dark molasses, and light treacle is also called golden syrup, which can be found in some supermarkets and specialty food stores. The light variety is so good that if you buy it you might find yourself sneaking spoonfuls every now and then.

2½ cups all-purpose flour
1 teaspoon baking soda
1 teaspoon baking powder
¼ teaspoon salt
2 sticks butter, at room temperature
½ cup granulated sugar

⅓ cup golden syrup or light molasses
3 large eggs, at room temperature
Grated zest and juice of 1 lemon
⅔ cup milk, at room temperature
½ cup golden syrup or light molasses, plus more for serving

1. Fill a large pot with water and place a shallow bowl upside down inside the pot. Bring the water to a boil. Butter and flour a 2½-quart round baking dish or glass bowl and its lid; set aside.

2. Whisk the flour, baking soda, baking powder, and salt together in a mixing bowl and set aside. In a large mixing bowl, beat the butter, sugar, and the ⅓ cup golden syrup or molasses, scraping down the sides of the bowl as needed, until light and fluffy, about 5 minutes. Add the eggs one at a time, mixing at medium speed until incorporated, about 30 seconds after each. Add the lemon zest and juice and beat until incorporated. Scrape down the sides and add the flour mixture alternately with the milk, mixing on the lowest speed just until incorporated and beginning and ending with the flour. Use a rubber spatula to scrape the sides and bottom and fold the mixture together.

3. Pour the ½ cup golden syrup or molasses into the bottom of the baking dish or glass bowl. Scrape the batter into the dish and smooth the top with the rubber spatula. Cover tightly with the lid and place it in the pot on top of the overturned bowl, making sure the water comes halfway up the sides. Cover the pot and simmer for 2½ hours. Check every so often to see if more water needs to be added (don't let the pot boil dry).

4. Remove the pudding from the pot. Remove the lid and invert the pudding onto a serving dish. Serve with warmed golden syrup.

Serves 8

Hot Chocolate

After Harry's been spirited away in Mr. Weasley's Ford Anglia to the Burrow, he enjoys the rest of summer vacation with Ron. On the last night before start of term, he digs into a fabulous dinner prepared by fabulous cook Mrs. Weasley, finishing off with dessert and hot chocolate (see *Harry Potter and the Chamber of Secrets*, Chapter 5).

Before Coenraad van Houten was born, people enjoyed hot chocolate with pools of grease floating on top. But then along came the Dutch chemist, who figured out how to press out the cocoa butter from the cocoa beans in the early 1800s. Plus, he invented Dutch cocoa, which is leaps and bounds better than natural cocoa. We modern folk owe him a big debt of gratitude: every city should have a statue of this man, and every village and hamlet should have a Coenraad van Houten Street.

½ cup water
¼ cup granulated sugar
2 tablespoons unsweetened cocoa powder
2 teaspoons instant coffee
2 ounces chopped bittersweet chocolate

2 cups whole milk
½ teaspoon pure vanilla extract
Whipped cream, optional, for serving
Unsweetened cocoa powder, optional, for serving

1. Combine the water, sugar, cocoa powder, and coffee in a small saucepan and cook over medium-high heat, whisking constantly, until the mixture is hot and bubbling. Remove from the heat and whisk in the chopped chocolate until smooth. Return to the heat and add the milk, cooking and stirring until just heated through (do not boil). Remove from the heat and stir in the vanilla.
2. Pour the hot chocolate immediately into four teacups. You can top the hot chocolate with a dollop of whipped cream and a dusting of cocoa powder.

Serves 4

This hot chocolate is very rich. For a lighter version, put 1 heaping teaspoon cocoa powder, 3 to 4 heaping teaspoons granulated sugar, 1 teaspoon instant coffee, and a few drops of vanilla extract into a large mug. Pour in a little boiling water and stir until dissolved. Add more boiling water to come ¾ of the way up the mug. Stir well, then add milk or cream to fill the rest of the mug. Try adding a few mini-marshmallows to the cup before drinking. You can use a stick of cinnamon as a stirrer to add a bit of cinnamon flavor. For smooth creaminess, replace the dark chocolate with white chocolate.

Any-Nut Nut Brittle

In his third year at Hogwarts, Mrs. Weasley sends Harry lots of yummy treats, including nut brittle. But Harry barely notices these mouth watering items when he sees the Firebolt sent to him by a mysterious well-wisher (see *Harry Potter and the Prisoner of Azkaban,* Chapter II).

Nut brittle is one of the most delicious candies ever, and it's far too easy to crunch up a whole pound before you know it. It's been made for centuries, and with good reason. It's easy to make; you just need to watch the temperature carefully.

1 cup granulated sugar
½ cup golden syrup or light corn syrup
¼ cup water
¼ teaspoon salt
¼ stick (2 tablespoons) butter

1½ cups chopped raw nuts (almonds, pecans, peanuts, or any nut you like)
½ teaspoon pure vanilla extract
½ teaspoon baking soda

1. Grease a rimmed baking sheet and line it with parchment paper. Clip a candy thermometer to a saucepan that is at least 4 quarts. Place the sugar, golden syrup or corn syrup, water, and salt in the saucepan and cook over medium-high heat, stirring constantly, until the temperature reaches 280°F.

2. Add the butter and nuts and continue cooking, stirring constantly, until the mixture reaches 300°F. Remove the pan from the heat and stir in the vanilla and baking soda (the mixture will bubble and expand a lot).

3. Pour the mixture into the prepared pan and spread it with a wooden spoon as much as you can; it should be about ¼-inch thick. Cool completely before breaking into shards and eating.

Makes 1 pound

Nutty Chocolate-Covered Toffee

Mrs. Weasley's prowess in the kitchen is impressive. Most home cooks, even good ones, leave toffee to the professionals. Yet Mrs. Weasley sends Easter eggs filled with homemade toffee to Harry, Ron, and Hermione. To Hermione's dismay, Mrs. Weasley sends her a much smaller egg; she's "been reading Rita Skeeter" (see *Harry Potter and the Goblet of Fire*, Chapter 28).

1 cup granulated sugar
½ cup golden syrup or corn syrup
1½ sticks (12 tablespoons) butter
½ cup heavy cream
¼ teaspoon cream of tartar

¾ teaspoon salt
1 teaspoon soy lecithin* (optional)
1 teaspoon pure vanilla extract
1 pound bittersweet chocolate, chopped
2 cups chopped toasted pecans

A British-American dictionary is useful if you need to know, for instance, that "nappy" doesn't mean "napkin" or "a short nap," but "diaper." Less useful is the fact that "toffee" is British for "taffy" because in America, these two confections are very different. Toffee is made with lots of butter and can be either hard or soft, while taffy is very chewy and is likely to pull your teeth out. Toffee is very easy to mess up. You need to watch the temperature carefully and stir constantly to prevent scorching. Do not despair if you ruin your first few batches; it's worth it to learn how to make this delicious candy.

Soy lecithin is an emulsifier; that is, it keeps the fat in the candy from separating. You can find a bottle of liquid soy lecithin at a health food store. You can also make the toffee without it if you can't find it.

1. Grease a rimmed baking sheet and line it with parchment paper, allowing the parchment paper to climb up two opposite ends. This will make it easy to remove the toffee from the pan after it cools. Place the sugar, golden syrup or corn syrup, butter, heavy cream, cream of tartar, salt, and soy lecithin in a medium saucepan and cook over medium-high heat, stirring constantly, until combined. Reduce the heat to medium-low. Wash down the sides of the pan with a pastry brush dipped in hot water to get rid of sugar crystals. Just a few crystals on the sides can cause the toffee to recrystallize.

2. Clip a candy thermometer to the saucepan. Continue cooking, stirring constantly, until the temperature reaches 300°F.

3. Remove the pan from the heat and quickly stir in the vanilla. Quickly pour the mixture into the prepared pan and spread evenly to the edges with a wooden spoon. You need to move fast because the candy hardens quickly. Cool completely in the pan.

4. Melt the chocolate in a microwave. Spread half the chocolate over the toffee, then sprinkle half the pecans evenly over the chocolate, patting it down with your hands to make sure it sticks. Refrigerate for 10 minutes to allow the chocolate to set.

5. When the chocolate is hard, tug a corner of the parchment paper to loosen the toffee, then carefully flip it over and peel off the parchment paper. Spread the remaining chocolate over the toffee and sprinkle the remaining pecans over the chocolate, patting them down with your hands. When the chocolate is set, break the toffee into irregular pieces.

Makes about 2 pounds

Oversized Blueberry Muffins with Crunchy Tops

Harry is too nervous to eat on the morning of his fateful hearing, but Mrs. Weasley offers him muffins among several food choices for breakfast in Grimmauld Place. In the end, it doesn't matter what Harry chooses because he can barely get it down (see *Harry Potter and the Order of the Phoenix*, Chapter 7).

When chemical leaveners were discovered in America at the turn of the nineteenth century, muffins followed just as surely, with blueberry being one of the most popular. The Americans didn't keep the discovery to themselves, and so American muffins are enjoyed for breakfast in England as well.

2 cups all-purpose flour
2 teaspoons baking soda
¼ teaspoon salt
2 large eggs, at room temperature
1 cup granulated sugar
1 stick (8 tablespoons) butter, melted
Grated zest of 1 lemon

1 teaspoon pure vanilla extract
1 cup sour cream, at room temperature
1 pint blueberries, washed and well drained
Turbinado sugar for sprinkling (Introduction)

1. Preheat the oven to 350°F. Grease and flour a 12-cup muffin pan. In a mixing bowl, whisk together the flour, baking soda, and salt. Set aside.
2. In a large mixing bowl, whisk the eggs until smooth. Whisk in the sugar and continue whisking until light and fluffy. Drizzle in the melted butter while whisking vigorously. Whisk in the lemon zest and vanilla. Fold in the flour mixture and sour cream alternately, beginning and ending with the flour. The batter will be very stiff. Fold in the blueberries.
3. Divide the batter among the muffin cups (the batter should reach the rim of each cup). Sprinkle the tops generously with turbinado sugar. Bake the muffins for 25 minutes, rotating the pan halfway through the baking time, until the tops are golden brown.

Makes 12 muffins

To make apple-cinnamon muffins, add 2 teaspoons ground cinnamon to the flour in Step 1. Omit the vanilla and lemon zest in Step 2, and substitute 1 cup diced apples for the blueberries. Bake as directed.

Mince Pies

Mince pies are very Christmassy, and sure enough, Mrs. Weasley sends Harry some for Christmas along with other goodies (see *Harry Potter and the Prisoner of Azkaban*, Chapter 11).

If you eat a mince pie every day of the twelve days of Christmas, preferably in a different house each time, you will have a happy year, according to an old Yorkshire superstition. Mincemeat used to contain minced beef (hence the name) mixed with apples, dried fruit, suet, sugar, spices, and brandy. About 200 years ago beef gradually began to be left out, thank goodness. This recipe calls for butter rather than suet, as the latter is not readily available to the American consumer.

Pie Crust

2½ cups all-purpose flour

2 tablespoons granulated sugar

½ teaspoon salt

1 stick (8 tablespoons) cold butter, cut into pieces

½ cup (8 tablespoons) vegetable shortening, chilled and cut into pieces

½ to ¾ cup cold water

Mincemeat Filling

½ cup dark raisins

½ cup golden raisins

½ cup dried currants or dried sweetened cranberries

Juice and grated zest of 1 lemon

Juice and grated zest of 1 orange

1 cup apple cider

2 tart apples, such as Granny Smith, peeled, cored, and chopped

2 sweet apples, such as Braeburn or Gala, peeled, cored, and chopped

1 cup packed dark brown sugar

¼ teaspoon salt

1 teaspoon ground cinnamon

¼ teaspoon ground nutmeg

⅛ teaspoon ground allspice

⅛ teaspoon ground cloves

½ stick (4 tablespoons) butter

1 egg beaten with 1 tablespoon water, for brushing the tops

1 tablespoon ground cinnamon mixed with 3 tablespoons sugar, for sprinkling

Mince Pies

(continued)

1. Place the flour, sugar, and salt in the bowl of a food processor and pulse to combine. Scatter the pieces of butter and shortening over the flour mixture. Pulse until the mixture resembles coarse yellow meal without any white powdery bits remaining, about 15 pulses. Transfer the mixture to a large mixing bowl. Sprinkle ½ cup water over the mixture and toss with a rubber spatula until the dough sticks together. Add more water 1 tablespoon at a time if the dough is dry (better too wet than too dry). Divide the dough in half, form into disks, wrap in plastic wrap, and chill at least 1 hour or up to 3 days.

2. To make the filling, combine all the filling ingredients except the butter in a large saucepan. Cook over medium-high heat, stirring, until the mixture boils. Reduce heat to low and simmer for 1½ hours. Bring the mixture back to a boil and cook, stirring constantly, until the liquid has evaporated and the mixture is very thick, about 10 minutes. Remove the pan from the heat and stir in the butter. Cool to room temperature and then chill until cold.

3. Preheat the oven to 350°F. Remove one of the disks of dough from the refrigerator and roll it out on a floured surface ⅛-inch thick. Use a 4½-inch round cookie cutter to cut out ten circles of dough. Do not reroll the dough; if you have fewer than ten circles, that's okay (rerolling the dough will toughen it). Fit the circles of dough into a 12-cup muffin pan.

4. Fill each pie with a heaping tablespoon of the mincemeat filling (you will have a lot of leftover filling; see note for other uses). On a floured surface, roll out the second disk ⅛-inch thick. Use a 3½-inch round cookie cutter to cut out another ten circles of dough. Moisten the edges of the pies and attach the circles of dough to the edges by crimping with a fork (or your fingers).

5. Brush the tops of the pies with the beaten egg and sprinkle with the cinnamon sugar. Cut slits for vents. Fill the remaining empty cups halfway with water. Bake for 30 to 40 minutes until dark golden brown. Cool the pies completely in the pan. To remove them from the pan, slide a knife around the edges and lift them out.

Makes about 10 pies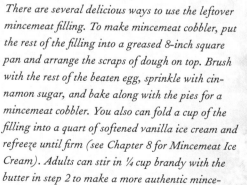

There are several delicious ways to use the leftover mincemeat filling. To make mincemeat cobbler, put the rest of the filling into a greased 8-inch square pan and arrange the scraps of dough on top. Brush with the rest of the beaten egg, sprinkle with cinnamon sugar, and bake along with the pies for a mincemeat cobbler. You also can fold a cup of the filling into a quart of softened vanilla ice cream and refreeze until firm (see Chapter 8 for Mincemeat Ice Cream). Adults can stir in ¼ cup brandy with the butter in step 2 to make a more authentic mincemeat. The filling will then keep well in the refrigerator for several months.

Rhubarb Crumble with Custard Sauce

Harry's first dinner at the headquarters of the Order of the Phoenix is a spectacular meal followed by a spectacular dessert cooked by Harry's favorite cook. The camaraderie that good food inspires disappears in a flash right after the rhubarb crumble and custard when Sirius invites Harry to ask whatever he wants about the Order of the Phoenix (see *Harry Potter and the Order of the Phoenix*, Chapter 5).

In the 1500s, you might have been offered stewed rhubarb when it was time to take your medicine. But that didn't work—it didn't get rid of bubonic plague. Three centuries later, rhubarb finally found its way into pies. It did take kind of a long time, but it's a good thing they figured it out. If you try this recipe, you will understand why Harry had three helpings.

Rhubarb Filling

1 pound frozen rhubarb

½ cup granulated sugar

1 teaspoon grated lemon zest

1 teaspoon baking soda

Crumble Topping

1 cup all-purpose flour

1 cup firmly packed dark brown sugar

½ cup pecans, chopped

½ teaspoon cinnamon

½ stick (4 tablespoons) cold butter, cut into chunks

Custard Sauce

¼ cup granulated sugar

Pinch salt

1 tablespoon cornstarch

1 cup whole milk and ½ cup heavy cream or 1½ cups milk

3 large egg yolks

1½ teaspoons pure vanilla extract

Rhubarb Crumble with Custard Sauce

(continued)

1. Preheat the oven to 350°F. Toss the rhubarb, sugar, lemon zest, and baking soda in a 9-inch pie pan. Bake for 10 minutes.

2. While the rhubarb is baking, make the Crumble Topping. Combine the flour, brown sugar, pecans, and cinnamon in a mixing bowl. Add the butter and rub it in with your fingertips until the mixture resembles wet sand.

3. Remove the rhubarb from the oven, toss the rhubarb mixture one more time, and pour the topping into the center, spreading it to the edges with your fingers. Return the pan to the oven and bake for 50 minutes, or until the rhubarb bubbles over the edges.

4. For the custard, combine the sugar, salt, and cornstarch in a small heavy-bottomed saucepan. Stir in the milk and cream and continue stirring until the cornstarch dissolves. Cook over medium-high heat, stirring constantly, until the mixture is hot but not bubbling. Reduce the heat to low and temper the egg yolks by slowly pouring ½ cup of the hot mixture into the yolks while whisking the yolks constantly. Pour the egg yolk mixture into the saucepan while stirring gently. Turn up the heat to medium and continue to cook, stirring constantly, until the mixture is thick and bubbling. Remove the saucepan from the heat and pour the custard through a sieve. Add the vanilla and stir to combine. Serve the rhubarb custard warm with the hot custard.

Serves 8

The addition of baking soda helps to neutralize some of the acid in the rhubarb, making it slightly more mellow and palatable. If you prefer an extremely tart dessert, omit the baking soda.

Creamy Onion Soup

Before the start of the school term, Dumbledore brings Harry to the Burrow in the middle of the night, where Mrs. Weasley serves the hungry boy a bowl of hot onion soup (see *Harry Potter and the Half-Blood Prince*, Chapter 5). This thick and creamy soup, warm and comforting, is the perfect dish to serve the weary traveler who bursts in on you at one in the morning. Serve with thick wedges of Irish Soda Bread (Chapter 5).

The Romans brought onions to Britain—although the Romans didn't mention them much in their own cookbooks. The one Roman cookbook we have today, called *Apicius*, barely mentions onions because the Romans didn't like that they make your breath smelly. But today we have breath mints, so bring on the onions!

¼ stick (2 tablespoons) butter
2 large onions, cut lengthwise and
    then sliced ⅛-inch thick
4 cups chicken broth or 4 cups water
    and 4 teaspoons chicken-flavored
    soup and seasoning mix

Freshly ground black pepper
Salt
2 cups whole milk, divided
⅓ cup flour

1. Heat the butter in a 4-quart pot. Add the onions to the pot, and cook over low heat until the onions are golden, about 30 minutes.
2. Add the chicken broth or the water and soup mix, and salt and pepper to taste. Bring to a boil, then reduce the heat and let it simmer until the onions are very soft, about 30 minutes.
3. Combine ⅓ cup of the milk with the flour in a bowl and mix well, beating out the lumps with a whisk. Add this mixture slowly to the soup while stirring constantly. Cook, stirring frequently, until the mixture thickens. Add the rest of the milk and just heat through; do not boil.

Serves 6

Molly's Meatballs with Onion Sauce

At the Ministry of Magic on the morning of Harry's hearing, Mr. Weasley bumps into Kingsley Shacklebolt. They pretend not to know each other, but Mr. Weasley manages to whisper to him that Mrs. Weasley is serving meatballs for dinner should he wish to stop by (see *Harry Potter and the Order of the Phoenix*, Chapter 7).

There's not much to say about meatballs. It doesn't take an awful lot of imagination to mince meat, mix it with other stuff, shape it, and cook it. In olden times, forcemeat, which is an old-fashioned word for the mixture of ground meat mixed with bread crumbs and seasonings, was used as a stuffing or by itself. You might still find recipes in British cookbooks that call it forcemeat balls. This recipe makes an interesting change from Italian meatballs and spaghetti.

Meatballs

1 pound extra-lean ground beef
½ cup fresh or dry bread crumbs
1 large egg
1 onion, finely chopped
2 tablespoons chopped fresh parsley
½ teaspoon salt
¼ teaspoon freshly ground black pepper
⅛ teaspoon ground nutmeg
2 tablespoons oil

Onion Sauce

2 tablespoons vegetable oil
1 onion, chopped
1 tablespoon all-purpose flour
1 14-ounce can chicken broth

1. For the meatballs, combine the beef, bread crumbs, egg, onion, parsley, salt, black pepper, and nutmeg in a large bowl and mix thoroughly.
2. Heat the oil in a skillet. Form the meat mixture into 1½-inch balls, and working in batches, fry the balls on each side until well browned, about 4 minutes per side. Transfer the meatballs to a dinner plate.
3. For the Onion Sauce, add 2 tablespoons oil to the skillet and heat. Add the chopped onion and cook over medium heat, stirring occasionally, until golden brown. Add the flour, and stir to combine. Pour in the chicken broth and cook, stirring constantly, until thickened and bubbling. Return the meatballs to the skillet and simmer for 15 minutes. Serve over rice, mashed potatoes, or wide egg noodles.

Serves 6

Brussels Sprouts with Chestnuts

While they prepare piles of sprouts to be used in a dish by Mrs. Weasley, Harry and Ron have a breathless discussion about Professor Snape and his sinister offer to help Draco Malfoy. To Ron's grumpy annoyance, he and Harry have to painstakingly prepare each sprout without using magic (see *Harry Potter and the Half-Blood Prince*, Chapter 16).

The Romans—no surprise there—brought the chestnut tree to Britain. Over the years and in many countries, chestnuts were ground up and mixed with flour, but these days we eat them roasted. They're also popular with Brussels sprouts at Christmas time.

1 pound frozen Brussels sprouts
1 cup water
½ teaspoon salt
¼ stick (2 tablespoons) butter
1 cup chopped canned chestnuts
2 tablespoons dark or light brown sugar
Pinch of nutmeg

1. Bring the sprouts, water, and salt to a boil in a medium saucepan. Reduce to a simmer and cook about 7 minutes, until sprouts are tender. Drain the sprouts and cut into quarters.
2. Heat the butter in a skillet until foaming. Add the sprouts, chestnuts, brown sugar, and nutmeg. Cook, stirring constantly, just until heated through. Serve immediately.

Serves 4 to 6

Double Strawberry Ice Cream

Do you sometimes wish you had a cook like Mrs. Weasley in your home? Imagine finishing off a weeknight supper with homemade strawberry ice cream. Harry enjoyed this sumptuous dessert, the finish to a sumptuous meal, the night before going to see the fateful international Quidditch match (see *Harry Potter and the Goblet of Fire*, Chapter 5).

> "Doubtless, God could have made a better berry, but doubtless, God never did," said Dr. William Butler, a sixteenth-century author. In those days, people ate strawberries with cream, still a favorite way to eat them—and what better way to improve upon it than to take these two simple ingredients and churn them into ice cream?

1 pound strawberries, chopped
¼ cup granulated sugar
1 cup strawberry jelly (not jam or preserves)
1½ cups milk
1½ cups heavy cream
3 egg yolks

1. Mix the strawberries and sugar together and let sit for 1 hour to allow the juices to be extracted. Drain well and reserve the juice. Set aside.

2. Combine the strawberry jelly, milk, and heavy cream in a medium saucepan and cook over high heat, whisking constantly, until the jelly has melted and the mixture is smooth—do not boil. Temper the egg yolks by whisking in 1 cup of the hot mixture; then return the yolk mixture to the saucepan while whisking constantly. Cook until the mixture thickens slightly; again, do not boil. Pour the mixture through a sieve.

3. Stir in the reserved juice. Lay a piece of plastic wrap directly on the surface to prevent a skin from forming and cool to room temperature. In separate containers, chill the custard mixture and chopped strawberries until completely cold, about 6 hours for the custard.

4. Freeze the custard mixture according to the manufacturer's instructions for your ice cream maker. Add the strawberries 2 minutes before the churning is over. Transfer to an airtight container and freeze until firm.

Makes about 6 cups

Apple Tart

No matter how annoyed he is, nothing interferes with Ron's appetite. While eating his apple tart, he fumes at his mother for making him clean up his room. Not bad, Ron (see *Harry Potter and the Half-Blood Prince*, Chapter 6).

An English cookbook from the 1300s called *The Forme of Curye*—yes, they really did have cookbooks in those days—mentions tarts. A tart is flatter than a pie and has no top crust. And that's pretty much all you need to know about tarts.

Tart Dough

1¼ cups all-purpose flour

½ cup granulated sugar

¼ teaspoon salt

1 stick (8 tablespoons) cold butter, cut into small pieces

1 large egg yolk

3 tablespoons heavy cream

1 teaspoon pure vanilla extract

Filling

5 tablespoons butter, divided

4 sweet apples, such as Fuji or Braeburn, peeled, cored, and sliced

½ cup granulated sugar, divided, plus more for sprinkling

½ teaspoon cinnamon

4 tart apples, such as Granny Smith, peeled, cored, and sliced

Apple Tart

(continued)

1. For the crust, place the flour, sugar, and salt in the bowl of a food processor and pulse to combine. Scatter the butter pieces over the flour and pulse until the mixture resembles coarse yellow meal, about 15 pulses. Transfer the mixture to a large mixing bowl. In a small bowl whisk together the yolk, cream, and vanilla. Pour it over the flour-butter mixture and fold it together using a rubber spatula until the dough clumps together. Gather the dough together and shape into a disk. Wrap it in plastic wrap and chill at least 2 hours or up to 3 days.

2. Preheat the oven to 400°F. Remove the dough from the refrigerator (if it is too stiff for rolling out, let it rest on the counter for 10 minutes) and roll it out on a floured surface to a 12-inch circle. Fold it into quarters, brushing off excess flour with a pastry brush after each fold, and then unfold it into a 9-inch tart pan with a removable bottom. Ease the sides gently into the pan and press the dough gently against the sides. Use the rolling pin to roll the overhang off the pan. Prick the bottom generously with a fork.

3. Line the pan with aluminum foil and fill with weights or beans. Bake until the dough is dry but still pale, about 20 minutes. Remove the shell from the oven and remove the foil and weights.

4. For the filling, melt 2 tablespoons of the butter in a large skillet. When it foams, add the sweet apples, ¼ cup of the sugar, and the cinnamon. Cook over medium-high heat, stirring frequently, until the apples soften. Continue cooking, mashing with the bottom of your largest-size heatproof measuring cup, until the apples are mostly mashed. Cook, stirring constantly, until the apples are golden brown and all the liquid is cooked out. The total cooking time should be about 20 minutes. Transfer the apples to a plate and cool to room temperature.

5. Wipe out the skillet with paper towels and heat 2 tablespoons of the remaining butter. When it foams, add the Granny Smith apples and the remaining ¼ cup sugar. Cook over medium-high heat, stirring frequently, until the apples begin to soften. Transfer to a plate and cool to room temperature.

6. Preheat the oven to 375°F. Spread the sweet apple mixture evenly over the bottom of the prepared tart shell. Arrange the tart apple slices in concentric circles over the top of the apple mixture. Melt the remaining tablespoon butter and brush it over the apple slices. Sprinkle generously with sugar and bake until the edges of the apples turn dark brown, about 25 minutes. Serve warm or at room temperature with a scoop of vanilla ice cream.

Serves 8

Herby Roast Chicken with Onion-Garlic Mashed Potatoes

Harry's appetite returns after the wizard court drops the charges against him, and he is glad to sit down to a Mrs. Weasley dinner of roast chicken and mashed potatoes. But then again, it's hard for him to eat as the thought of Dumbledore causes his scar to burn (see *Harry Potter and the Order of the Phoenix*, Chapter 9).

Herbs are very important to students at Hogwarts School of Witchcraft and Wizardry, and indeed to witches in many tales. Wiccans and other pagans (often called witches) use them in rituals, and naturopaths use herbs in remedies. The rest of us use them to flavor dishes, such as the following very delicious chicken.

Herby Chicken

1 medium onion, sliced

6 cloves garlic, peeled

1 3-pound chicken

2 tablespoons softened butter or margarine

¼ teaspoon ground thyme

¼ teaspoon ground sage

1 tablespoon chopped fresh parsley

Salt and freshly ground black pepper

½ cup water

Mashed Potatoes

2½ pounds (about 6) Yukon Gold potatoes, peeled and quartered

2 tablespoons vegetable oil

1 medium onion, chopped

2 cloves garlic, minced

½ cup vegetable oil

1 cup chicken broth

Salt and freshly ground black pepper to taste

Herby Roast Chicken with Onion-Garlic Mashed Potatoes

(continued)

1. Preheat the oven to 375°F and lay the onion slices and garlic cloves in a baking dish. Rinse the chicken and pat it dry.
2. Mix the butter or margarine with the thyme, sage, and parsley and spread it under the skin of the breasts and thighs; you will need to loosen the skin first by lifting up the flap of skin and sliding your fingers under it. Lay the chicken in the pan, breast-side up, on top of the onions and garlic and sprinkle with salt and pepper. Pour the water into the pan.
3. Bake for 50 minutes. Rotate the pan, raise the temperature to 450°F, and bake for another 30 minutes or until an instant-read thermometer inserted into the thigh reads 170°F.
4. While the chicken is roasting, prepare the mashed potatoes. Cover the potatoes with water in a large saucepan and bring to a boil. Reduce the heat and let it simmer until tender, about 25 minutes.
5. Heat the 2 tablespoons oil in a skillet and add the onions. Cook the onions over medium heat, stirring frequently, until nicely browned, about 10 minutes. Add the garlic and cook until fragrant, about 15 seconds. Remove from the heat.
6. Drain the potatoes. Add the onion-garlic mixture, ½ cup oil, chicken broth, and salt and pepper. Mash with a potato masher.

Serves 4

Four Delicious Pies

While Harry's friends, determined not to let him starve to death at the Dursleys', send him snacks and cakes, Mrs. Weasley sends heartier food. She sends him a variety of meat pies along with a fruitcake so he has better meals to eat than a quarter of a grapefruit (see *Harry Potter and the Goblet of Fire*, Chapter 3). The following four individual pie recipes are classic British recipes.

Small meat pies in England are popular snacks, so it's no surprise Mrs. Weasley sent a bunch to Harry.

Individual Beef Pies

Pie Crust

2½ cups all-purpose flour

1 teaspoon salt

1 stick (8 tablespoons) cold butter, cut into pieces

½ cup (8 tablespoons) vegetable shortening, chilled and cut into pieces

½ to ¾ cup cold water

Filling

3 tablespoons vegetable oil

8 ounces chuck steak, trimmed and cut into ¼-inch dice

1 medium onion, finely chopped

4–5 ounces mushrooms, chopped

1 tablespoon all-purpose flour

1 cup chicken broth

⅛ teaspoon ground thyme

1 tablespoon tomato paste

Salt and pepper

1 egg beaten with 1 tablespoon water

Four Delicious Pies

(continued)

1. Place the flour and salt in the bowl of a food processor and pulse to combine. Scatter the pieces of butter and shortening over the flour mixture. Pulse until the mixture resembles coarse yellow meal without any white powdery bits remaining, about 15 pulses. Transfer the mixture to a large mixing bowl. Sprinkle ½ cup water over the mixture and toss with a rubber spatula until the dough sticks together. Add more water 1 tablespoon at a time if the dough is dry (better too wet than too dry). Divide the dough in half, form into two disks, wrap in plastic wrap, and chill at least 2 hours or up to 3 days.

2. To make the filling, heat 1 tablespoon of the oil in a skillet and add the beef in two batches, searing over high heat on each side until crusty brown, about 4 minutes per side. Transfer each batch to a plate and set aside. Add the remaining oil to the skillet and heat it over medium heat. Add the onions and mushrooms and cook, stirring and scraping up the fond (browned bits), until the onions are well browned. Add the flour and mix until combined. Add the chicken broth and again mix until combined. Return the beef to the skillet; add the thyme, tomato paste, salt, and pepper. Simmer for 2 hours. Transfer to a bowl, cover with plastic wrap, and cool to room temperature.

3. Preheat the oven to 425°F. Remove the chilled dough from the refrigerator. On a generously floured surface, roll out one of the disks very thin. Use a 4½-inch cookie cutter to cut out circles. Fit the circles into a 6-cup muffin pan. Fill generously with the beef filling.

4. Roll out the second disk of dough. Use a 3½-inch cookie cutter to cut out six circles. You may have enough dough to cut out one more 4½-inch circle and one more 3½-inch circle to get one more pie. (If that's the case, use a 12-cup muffin pan and fill the empty cups halfway with water.) Brush the rims with water, lay the circles over the filling, and press with your fingers to seal. Brush the tops of the pies with the beaten egg and cut slits in the top of each pie to form vents. Bake for 10 minutes, then reduce the heat to 350°F and bake an additional 20 minutes, until the pies are golden brown.

Makes 6 or 7 pies

Four Delicious Pies

(continued)

Mutton, which is the meat from sheep, is not much used these days, so really you'll have to use lamb. Fortunately for us, the use of sugar, dried fruit, and sweet spices disappeared from mutton pies, and recipes for mutton pies have been savory since the 1700s. Like the following veal and pork pies, mutton pies are traditionally made with a hot-water crust, but this recipe uses pie dough to make a sort of pasty.

Individual Mutton Pies

1 pound mutton or lamb cubes for stew with bones attached

Mutton Stock

Bones from the mutton or lamb
1 bay leaf
½ carrot
½ celery rib
¼ onion
½ teaspoon salt
1 teaspoon dried rosemary leaves
Several sprigs parsley
Several sprigs dill

Mutton Filling

2 tablespoons vegetable oil (divided)
Mutton or lamb detached from the bones, trimmed, and cut into ¼-inch dice
1 small onion, chopped
1 tablespoon all-purpose flour
1 cup mutton or lamb stock
Freshly ground black pepper

Pasty Dough

2½ cups all-purpose flour
1 teaspoon salt
1 stick (8 tablespoons) cold butter, cut into pieces
½ cup (8 tablespoons) vegetable shortening, chilled and cut into pieces
½ to ¾ cup cold water
1 egg beaten with 1 tablespoon water, for brushing the tops of the pies

Four Delicious Pies

(continued)

1. To make the stock, cover the bones with water in a small pot, add the bay leaf, and bring to a boil. Reduce the heat to low and simmer for 1 hour. Add the carrot, celery, onion, salt, rosemary, parsley, and dill and simmer for another ½ hour. Strain the stock through a sieve and cool. Use a fat separator or chill the stock to remove the fat layer. Measure out 1 cup of stock and set aside.

2. To make the filling, heat 1 tablespoon oil in a large skillet and sear the mutton or lamb in batches over high heat 4 to 5 minutes on each side until crusty brown, transferring the batches to a large plate. Add the remaining tablespoon of oil to the skillet. Cook the onion over medium-low heat, scraping the fond (browned bits) from the bottom of the skillet, until the onions are softened. Add the flour and stir to combine. Add the reserved cup of stock to the skillet. Cook, stirring constantly, until thickened and bubbling. Add the meat back to the skillet along with any accumulated juices and the black pepper. Simmer for 1 hour, then cool to room temperature.

3. To make the pasty dough, place the flour and salt in the bowl of a food processor and pulse to combine. Scatter the pieces of butter and shortening over the flour mixture. Pulse until the mixture resembles coarse yellow meal without any white powdery bits remaining, about 15 pulses. Transfer the mixture to a large mixing bowl. Sprinkle ½ cup water over the mixture and toss with a rubber spatula until the dough sticks together. Add more water 1 tablespoon at a time if the dough is dry (better too wet than too dry). Divide the dough in half, form into disks, wrap in plastic wrap, and chill at least 1 hour.

4. To assemble the pies, preheat the oven to 450°F and line two baking sheets with parchment paper. Working with one disk at a time, roll out each disk ⅛-inch thick. Use a 4-inch cookie cutter to cut out circles of dough. Spoon 1 tablespoon of filling onto half the circles. Moisten the edges and cover with the rest of the circles. Use a fork dipped in flour to crimp the edges to seal them. Brush the tops with beaten egg and cut slits to make vents. Arrange the pies on the cookie sheets and bake for 15 minutes, rotating and switching the pans halfway through baking. Reduce the heat to 350°F and bake another 5 minutes until golden brown.

Makes 6 to 8 pies

To save the time and tedium of making a lamb stock from scratch, you can substitute 1 cup canned beef or chicken broth.

(continued)

It's interesting to find a food that people have been eating since medieval times. Veal pies belong to the family of "raised pies," which are pies made from a hot-water crust that can stand up on its own (you don't actually need a muffin pan, although it's easier if you use one). The typical veal pie usually contains ham or ham and eggs, but that would be a bit much for a small version, so only veal is used in this recipe.

Veal Pies

1 pound veal with bones attached

Veal Stock

Bones from the veal
1 bay leaf
½ carrot
½ celery rib
¼ onion
½ teaspoon salt
Several sprigs parsley
Several sprigs dill

Veal Filling

Veal, detached from the bones, trimmed, and finely chopped
1 teaspoon chopped fresh dill
½ teaspoon ground thyme
¼ onion, finely chopped
Freshly ground black pepper

Hot-Water Crust

2 cups all-purpose flour
1 teaspoon salt
½ cup water
½ cup (8 tablespoons) vegetable shortening
1 egg beaten with 1 tablespoon water, for brushing the tops of the pies

Aspic

1 cup veal stock
1 tablespoon (1 envelope) unflavored gelatin

Four Delicious Pies

(continued)

1. For the stock, put the bones in a small saucepan and cover with water. Add the bay leaf. Bring to a boil, then reduce the heat and simmer for 1 hour. Add the carrot, celery, onion, salt, parsley, and dill, and simmer another ½ hour. Cool to room temperature. Use a fat separator or chill the stock to remove the fat layer. Measure out 1 cup stock and set aside.

2. For the filling, combine the veal, dill, thyme, onion, and black pepper in a mixing bowl.

3. For the dough, whisk the flour and salt together in a large mixing bowl. Bring the water and vegetable shortening to a boil in a small saucepan. Make a well in the center of the flour and pour in the water-shortening mixture. Stir with a wooden spoon, then knead for a few seconds until a cohesive dough forms.

4. Preheat the oven to 350°F. To assemble the pies, roll out ¾ of the dough ⅛-inch thick. Use a 4-inch round cookie cutter to cut out ten circles of dough. (The dough can be briefly kneaded and rerolled to cut more circles.) Fit the dough circles into the cups of a muffin pan. Divide the filling among the pies. Roll out the remaining dough ¼-inch thick. Use a 3-inch round cookie cutter to cut out ten circles of dough. Use a 1-inch round cookie cutter to cut out holes in the centers. Brush the rims of the pies with water and attach the rings of dough to the tops of the pies, pressing with your fingers to seal. Brush the tops with the beaten egg. Fill any empty muffin cups halfway with water before putting the pan in the oven. Bake for 45 minutes to 1 hour, until pies are golden brown.

5. While the pies are baking, make the aspic. Boil the reserved cup of veal stock and whisk in the gelatin until dissolved. Reheat if necessary when the pies are finished baking. Using a funnel, slowly pour the stock into the holes in the pie crusts while the pies are still hot. You should use most of the stock. Cool the pies to room temperature and refrigerate until cold. Serve chilled.

Makes 10 pies

To save the time and tedium of making a veal stock from scratch, you can substitute 1 cup canned beef broth.

Four Delicious Pies

(continued)

Melton Mowbray Pork Pies

Another raised pie, this one hails from Melton Mowbray in Leicester (pronounced "lester") in central England. Pickled walnuts were standard in older recipes but are no longer used in modern recipes.

Pork Stock

3 pounds pork bones

3 cups water

1 teaspoon fresh sage

1 tablespoon fresh thyme

1 bay leaf

1 onion, quartered

Hot-Water Crust

2 cups all-purpose flour

2 pinches kosher salt

¼ cup (4 tablespoons) lard or vegetable shortening

¼ cup whole milk

¼ cup water

Flour for dusting

Pork Filling

2 pounds pork shoulder, ⅔ lean, ⅓ fat

6 slices bacon, diced

1 teaspoon fresh sage, or ½ teaspoon dried sage

1 anchovy fillet, minced, or 1 teaspoon oil from container of anchovy fillets

½ teaspoon ground allspice

Salt and pepper to taste

1 egg beaten with 1 tablespoon water, for brushing the tops of the pies

1 tablespoon (1 envelope) unflavored gelatin

English mustard, for serving

Four Delicious Pies

(continued)

1. To make the stock, combine all the stock ingredients in a heavy saucepan. Bring to a boil. Cover and reduce to a simmer for 1 hour. Strain the solids and return the liquid to the pan. Bring to a boil and reduce the total volume to 1¼ cups. Set aside to cool.

2. To make the pastry, combine the flour and salt in a large mixing bowl. Place the lard or vegetable shortening in a saucepan along with the milk and water; set the saucepan over high heat until the fat melts. Bring to a boil. Stir the fat and liquids together and pour into the bowl with the flour. Mix well. Turn the dough out onto a flour-dusted work surface. Form the dough into a ball and dust with flour. Knead for 5 minutes. Wrap in plastic wrap and let rest for 30 minutes.

3. For the filling, dice the pork into ¼-inch pieces or place chunks of pork into a food processor and pulse to coarsely chop. Place the pork in a large mixing bowl with the diced bacon, sage, minced anchovy or anchovy oil, and allspice. Add ¼ cup of the stock and mix well. Test the seasoning by heating a small amount of water in a sauté pan to a boil and cook a small amount of the pork mixture (1 teaspoon) in it. Taste the filling and adjust the salt and pepper as desired.

4. To assemble the pies, preheat the oven to 400°F, then decide on the size of finished pies desired. This recipe can be made in a muffin pan, popover pan, or 4-ounce ceramic ramekins. Cut off ¾ of the dough and place on a flour-dusted work surface. Roll it out ⅛-inch thick. To make the bottom crust, cut 4-inch circles for a muffin or popover pan and 4½-inch circles for the ramekins. Place the dough circles in the cups or ramekins and press the dough into the bottom and sides of each.

5. Fill the pastry-lined molds up to the rim. Fold any excess dough from the sides onto the top of the filling. Roll out the remaining dough and cut 3-inch circles to fit into the tops of the muffin or popover pan or ramekins. Place the tops onto the filling and press down lightly to seal. Cut a small hole in the center of each top. Reroll any excess dough. Using small pastry cutters, cut out shapes and decorate the tops. Brush the top of each pie with the beaten egg. Bake the pies for 20 minutes. Reduce the heat to 350°F and bake for 2 hours.

6. Remove the pies from the oven, brush with the beaten egg again, and bake for 10 minutes longer. Remove and let cool in the pan.

7. Bring the reduced stock back to a boil, remove from the heat, add the gelatin, and stir to dissolve. Using a funnel, spoon the stock mixture into the hole in the top of each pie, dividing the stock evenly among the pies. This is a slow process, and all of the liquid should be used. Chill overnight.

8. To serve, remove from the pan and serve with good English mustard.

Makes 8 pies

Beef and "Guinness" Stew for Kids

It doesn't exactly say that the Weasleys are Irish, but they are all redheaded, freckled, and fiery. Of course, we shouldn't stereotype, but . . . you know. So the night Harry arrives at Grimmauld Place, perhaps Mrs. Weasley would have served a classic Irish stew. There's a great moment when Mrs. Weasley displays her towering temper at Fred and George, who in trying to magic everything to the table, nearly spill the stew and stab Sirius (see *Harry Potter and the Order of the Phoenix*, Chapter 5).

Although it's been the favorite alcoholic drink of Ireland since the 1700s, when Arthur Guinness opened a brewery in Dublin, Guinness has another use. Its dark color and roasted barley flavor work really well in stews.

2 tablespoons vegetable oil, plus
    more as necessary
2 pounds chuck steak, trimmed and
    cut into ½-inch cubes
1 onion, chopped
2 tablespoons all-purpose flour
1 14-ounce can chicken broth
½ cup Coca-Cola
2 tablespoons tomato paste

¼ cup chopped prunes
1 teaspoon ground sage
Juice of 1 lemon
Salt and freshly ground black pepper
    to taste
6 Yukon Gold potatoes, peeled and
    cut into ½-inch cubes
2 carrots, peeled and chopped
¼ cup chopped fresh parsley

To make the stew for adults, replace the Coca-Cola with Guinness. Do not use Extra Stout. Add 2 tablespoons dark or light brown sugar along with the rest of the ingredients in Step 3.

1. Heat the oil in a Dutch oven or wide pot and add the meat in batches, searing on both sides over high heat 4 to 5 minutes until crusty brown and transferring each batch to a large plate. After the last batch of meat is cooked and removed from the pot, add another 2 tablespoons of oil if necessary and the onion. Cook the onion over medium-low heat until softened, scraping up the fond (browned bits) from the bottom of the pot with a wooden spoon.

2. Add the flour to the pot and stir until combined. Pour in the broth and Coca-Cola and cook over medium-high heat until thickened and bubbling. Add the meat back to the pot along with the accumulated juices and the tomato paste, chopped prunes, sage, lemon juice, salt, and pepper. Bring the mixture to a simmer, and simmer for 1½ hours.

3. Add the potatoes, carrots, and parsley and continue to simmer for another hour, stirring occasionally and adding more chicken broth or water as necessary to keep the stew from drying out and burning.

Serves 6 to 8

Mashed Parsnips

Percy got what he deserved when he barged in on the Weasleys during Christmas dinner and ended up with mashed parsnips all over his face. With all of the rest of the delicious food that is usually on the Christmas table, the Weasleys probably didn't miss the parsnips (see *Harry Potter and the Half-Blood Prince*, Chapters 16 and 17).

Run out of sugar while making plum pudding? No problem; just boil up some parsnips and add them to the batter. That's what was done in medieval times, when sugar was scarce. Parsnips have always been popular in Europe, but not very much so in America. This recipe just might make them a favorite here.

1½ pounds (about 10 medium-small) parsnips, peeled and chopped
1 14-ounce can chicken broth
2 tablespoons butter
¼ cup milk
Pinch of nutmeg
Salt and freshly ground black pepper to taste

In a medium saucepan, bring the parsnips and chicken broth to a boil. Reduce heat and simmer until tender, about 20 to 25 minutes. Drain the parsnips and add the butter, milk, nutmeg, salt, and pepper. Mash with a potato masher.

Serves 4 to 6

Canapés

Harry wryly observes that Voldemort won't get killed off while Harry's busy making canapés and vol-au-vents (although they might make good missiles in comedy shows). He's frustrated that Mrs. Weasley is keeping him so busy with preparations for Bill and Fleur's wedding that she leaves him no time for planning (see *Harry Potter and the Deathly Hallows,* Chapter 6).

Canapé is French for "couch." What's the connection? It takes a bit of imagination, but here goes: Just like you sit on a couch, the toppings for this elegant appetizer sit on a piece of fried or toasted bread.

You can cut the canapés into different shapes to represent different fillings. For example, you can cut the Sour Cream–Anchovy Canapés into squares, the Olive-Cheese into circles, and the Smoked Salmon into triangles. You can also come up with your own toppings. The ideas are endless.

Canapés

1 loaf good-quality sandwich bread
Butter, for greasing the skillet

The Toppings

Sour Cream–Anchovy Topping: sour cream, anchovy fillets packed in olive oil, grape tomatoes
Olive-Cheese Topping: mayonnaise, mozzarella cheese sliced into ¼-inch-thick slices, pitted green olives
Smoked Salmon Topping: cream cheese, smoked salmon, chopped scallions
Toothpicks for holding the fillings in place

1. To make the canapés, use a round 2-inch cookie cutter to cut circles out of the bread. Heat a skillet over medium heat. Take a cold stick of butter and rub the tip of it over the surface of the hot skillet. Add as many pieces of bread as fit into the skillet. Toast over medium heat on each side until golden brown, a few minutes per side. Repeat the buttering between batches. Make as many as desired.

2. For the Sour Cream–Anchovy Canapés, spread sour cream on the canapés. Dab the fillets with a paper towel, then cut in thirds and lay over the sour cream, 1 fillet per canapé. Push a toothpick through a grape tomato and press into place on top of the anchovy.

3. For the Olive-Cheese Topping, use the 2-inch cutter to cut out circles of cheese. Spread mayonnaise on the canapés. Lay the circles of cheese over the mayonnaise. Push a toothpick through an olive and press into place on top of the cheese.

4. For the Smoked Salmon Topping, spread cream cheese on the canapés. Lay a piece of smoked salmon on top, then sprinkle with the chopped scallions.

Makes as many as desired

Vol-au-Vents

Mrs. Weasley is really an amazing cook. To prepare all the food for her son's wedding, especially such elegant, classy savories as vol-au-vents, is just simply, well, impressive, to say the least (see *Harry Potter and the Deathly Hallows*, Chapter 6).

Marie Antoine Carême, known as the King of Chefs and the Chef of Kings, invented this beautiful and tasty appetizer around 1800. Its French name means "flying on the wind." You can fill the pastry cases with whatever you want; you are limited only by your imagination. The fillings here require no cooking, although traditionally a filling mixed with a velouté (a sauce thickened with a roux, which is a paste made of flour and butter) is used.

Puff Pastry

Puff pastry needs to be made at least a day in advance, as it takes so long to make. Forming the pastry cases is fussy work, so to save time you can use frozen puff pastry shells. Just prepare them according to the package directions.

Butter Block
3 sticks cold butter, cut into chunks
½ teaspoon lemon juice
½ cup flour

Dough
3 cups flour
1 teaspoon salt
½ stick cold butter, diced into ¼-inch pieces
1 cup plus 2 tablespoons cold water
1½ teaspoons lemon juice

Vol-au-Vents

(continued)

Sweet Cream—Blueberry Filling

8 ounces cream cheese

½ cup granulated sugar

1 teaspoon pure vanilla extract

1 cup heavy cream

1 pint blueberries, washed and drained

1 tablespoon currant jelly

Tomato-Feta Filling

5 ounces feta cheese, diced into ¼-inch pieces

1 cup grape tomatoes, sliced in half lengthwise

2 teaspoons olive oil

2 teaspoons balsamic vinegar

½ teaspoon dried basil

Pinch salt

Freshly ground black pepper to taste

Smoked Turkey-Olive Filling

1 cup diced smoked turkey breast (¼-inch pieces)

1 cup small green olives (if large, chop them)

1 tablespoon mayonnaise

Freshly ground black pepper

English mustard

1. For the butter block, combine the butter, lemon juice, and flour, and mix with your fingers. Knead briefly until combined. Form into a square and place between two sheets of parchment paper. Roll out the butter to a 7-inch square. Refrigerate until ready to use.

2. For the dough, whisk together the flour and salt. Add the ½ stick butter and rub it in with your fingers until the mixture becomes mealy. Add the water and lemon juice and stir to combine. Knead briefly until a rough dough forms. Shape the dough into a ball, flatten slightly, and cut a cross halfway through the dough almost to the edges with a sharp knife. Wrap in plastic wrap and refrigerate for 1 hour.

3. Remove the dough from the refrigerator and place on a flour-dusted surface. Pull the edges of the cross open from the center of the dough to create a rough square. Sprinkle flour on top and roll out the dough to an 11-inch square. Remove the butter block from the refrigerator and peel off the parchment paper. Place the block onto the square of dough so that the corners point to the center of the lines of the square (it should look like a diamond shape). Bring the dough up over the butter and pinch the edges together. Roll it out into a rectangle ½-inch thick. Fold the rectangle into thirds like a business letter. Wrap in plastic wrap and refrigerate for 1 hour. This is called the first turn.

Vol-au-Vents

(continued)

4. To make the second turn, remove the dough from the refrigerator and lay it horizontally on a flour-dusted work surface. Roll it into a rectangle ½-inch thick. Fold the rectangle into thirds like a business letter. Wrap in plastic wrap and refrigerate for 1 hour. Repeat the turns 3 more times, resting the dough in the refrigerator for 1 hour between each turn. This recipe makes about 2 pounds 10 ounces of puff pastry; you will not need all of it to make the vol-au-vents.

5. To make the pastry cases, line two baking sheets with parchment paper. Cut off ⅔ of the dough and roll it out ½-inch thick on a floured surface. Use a 3½-inch cutter to cut out twelve circles of dough. Use a 3-inch cutter to cut out centers, making thin rings. Set the rings aside on a sheet of parchment paper. Roll out the remaining centers one by one very thin (you will need to flour the work surface and the tops of the pastry circles again). Use the 3½-inch cutters to cut out new circles from the rolled-out centers. Prick holes in these circles with a fork and lay them on the prepared baking sheets, six circles to a sheet. Brush the edges with water and carefully attach the rings to the edges to form cases. Refrigerate the cases for 1 hour.

6. Preheat the oven to 400°F. Remove one baking sheet from the refrigerator and line each case with small pieces of aluminum foil. Fill the foil with beans or pie weights. Bake for 10 minutes.

Reduce the heat to 375°F and bake another 20 minutes until the dough is set. Remove the foil and weights and bake another 3 to 5 minutes until light golden brown. Raise the heat to 400°F and repeat with the second sheet. Cool completely on a wire rack before filling.

7. To make the Sweet Cream–Blueberry Filling, beat the cream cheese, sugar, and vanilla with an electric mixer until smooth and fluffy, about 4 minutes. In a separate bowl, beat the heavy cream until stiff peaks form. Fold the two mixtures together until smooth. Divide the mixture among the twelve vol-au-vents. Top with as many blueberries as fit. Melt the jelly in the microwave for about 20 seconds and brush the tops of the blueberries with the melted jelly, using a pastry brush. Refrigerate until ready to serve.

8. To make the Tomato-Feta Filling, combine all the filling ingredients and fill the cases.

9. To make the Smoked Turkey–Olive Filling, combine all the filling ingredients except for the mustard and fill the cups. After the cups are filled, drizzle the mustard on top.

Makes 12

Chapter Six

Breakfast Before Class

Breakfast is not just an important meal for Muggles; it's important for wizards too—but it's especially important at Hogwarts because that's when the owls arrive to deliver letters and packages from home. The flood of owls can be a bit much if you're receiving fan mail or hate mail, like Hermione after she was written up in a newspaper by reporter Rita Skeeter in *Harry Potter and the Goblet of Fire* (Chapter 28) or like Harry after he gave his fateful interview in *Harry Potter and the Order of the Phoenix* (Chapter 26).

How many different foods do *you* eat for breakfast every morning? One or two, maybe. A bowl of cereal. A muffin and hot chocolate if you have the time. Pancakes and sausages if someone loves you very much (or it's a holiday). If you don't completely skip this important meal, then how about a breakfast of bacon and eggs, sausages, fried bread, fried tomatoes, fried mushrooms, kippers, black pudding, baked beans, and toast and marmalade? Oh, and don't forget the porridge with cream and treacle.

What an enormous amount of food for breakfast. But that's the traditional English breakfast for you. In the 1700s the upper classes, and later also the Victorian middle class, were served all of that and more. This heavy-duty meal is also called the full English fry-up, but today our cousins across the ocean eat much the same things that we do: plain old cereal or a muffin and coffee in the morning. But not to worry—you die-hard Harry Potter fans can still find the traditional fry-up at some British hotels and bed-and-breakfasts if you ever travel to England.

In the Great Hall, we find a mix of the traditional and modern. Some mornings find Harry eating humdrum cereal, but other mornings he enjoys toast and marmalade, porridge with treacle, kippers, sausages, or fried tomatoes.

This chapter does not include a recipe for toast, although Victorian cookbooks devoted chapters to the art of making toast properly. Today, with toasters and toaster ovens, it's pretty simple if you just pay attention. If you don't want to make your own marmalade, you can find this favorite topping for toast next to the jams and jellies in your local supermarket. Treacle or golden syrup can be found at a specialty food store and some supermarkets, or you can substitute maple syrup, light molasses, or corn syrup.

Herbed and Spiced Fried Sausage Patties

Nothing says "Welcome home to Hogwarts" like sausage. You'll find sausages on the menu throughout the Potter books—most notably at the welcome feast that kicks off the new school year (see *Harry Potter and the Goblet of Fire*, Chapter 12). In that memorable scene, Dumbledore starts to announce the Triwizard Tournament—and is rudely interrupted by the bizarre-looking Professor Moody, who bursts into the Great Hall and without so much as a how-do-you-do helps himself to a sausage.

The Greeks didn't just run around naked throwing disks at each other, wearing laurel wreaths. They also ate sausages, as described in a comedy by Greek playwright Epicharmus brilliantly titled . . . *The Sausage.* Fifteen hundred years ago the Greeks figured out that you can use up and also preserve all the scraps of meats and unwanted parts of the animal by mixing it with a lot of salt and turning it into sausages. Sausages come in many shapes and forms, one of which is a fresh mixture of ground meat with a filler such as bread crumbs that is formed into patties or sausage shapes and fried.

½ pound ground veal
½ pound ground pork or beef
1 cup fresh bread crumbs
1 teaspoon grated lemon zest
1 teaspoon salt
¼ teaspoon ground nutmeg
1 teaspoon ground sage
⅛ teaspoon dried marjoram
⅛ teaspoon ground thyme
¼ teaspoon freshly ground black pepper
2 egg yolks
2 tablespoons butter or margarine

1. Combine all the ingredients except for the 2 tablespoons butter or margarine in a large mixing bowl and mix well.
2. Heat the butter or margarine in a skillet on a medium-high flame. Form the meat into sausage shapes and fry on each side, turning often, until the sausages are well browned.
3. Transfer the sausages to a paper-towel-lined plate. Repeat until all the mixture is used up.

Serves 6

Fried Tomatoes

The morning after a harrowing encounter with the dementor on the Hogwarts Express, Harry restores his peace and good humor with a little help from his friends—and sausages and fried tomatoes for breakfast (see *Harry Potter and the Prisoner of Azkaban*, Chapter 6).

Did you know that until the mid-1700s the British thought tomatoes were poisonous? They weren't far off the mark, though. Tomatoes are indeed related to the deadly nightshade, and the stems and leaves of the tomato plant do contain toxins. So when the tomato came to England in the late 1500s, it was cultivated as an unusual plant to look at. Thank goodness, someone finally figured out that we can eat them, and they began to appear in cookbooks in the 1700s.

3 tablespoons vegetable oil
2 medium-size red ripe tomatoes,
sliced into ¼-inch slices
Flour for dredging

Salt and freshly ground black pepper
to taste
Hot buttered toast, for serving

1. Heat the oil in a skillet on a medium-high flame.
2. Dredge the tomatoes in the flour and fry them on both sides until they are golden.
3. Transfer the tomatoes to a paper-towel-lined plate and sprinkle with the salt and pepper. Serve immediately with hot buttered toast.

Serves 4

English Farmhouse Scrambled Eggs and Bacon

Gilderoy Lockhart can't seem to stop embarrassing Harry, whether it's before the start of term or the first day of classes, when eggs and bacon are served for breakfast in the Great Hall (see *Harry Potter and the Chamber of Secrets*, Chapter 6). Poor Harry, the forced breakfast chef at the Dursleys', also serves bacon and eggs on Dudley's birthday after being warned he'd better not burn it (see *Harry Potter and the Sorcerer's Stone*, Chapter 2).

Who doesn't enjoy eggs with bacon on a weekend morning when there's actually time to make it and eat it? Feel like you're at home with Harry with this centuries-old breakfast classic. Throw in fried tomatoes with toast and a bowl of porridge to pretend you're eating the traditional English breakfast, which contains too much food for normal people to eat even occasionally.

2 slices bacon, diced
2 large eggs
1 tablespoon milk or heavy cream
Salt and pepper to taste
1 ounce English Cheddar cheese, shredded

1. Heat a skillet over medium-high heat. Add the diced bacon to the pan. Cook, stirring occasionally, until it reaches desired crispiness.
2. Break the eggs into a small bowl and beat with a fork until completely combined. Add the milk or cream and stir to combine. Add the salt and pepper and stir to combine. Pour the egg mixture over the cooked bacon in the pan, and as soon as they begin to set (become cooked), stir with a wooden spoon, moving them around and over until completely cooked.
3. Spoon the eggs onto a plate and top with the shredded Cheddar cheese.

Makes 1 serving

Sweet Orange Marmalade

Marmalade shows up often in the Harry Potter books; it's just that British. In one breakfast scene, Hermione determinedly avoids discussing her busy schedule and asks for the marmalade in response to Ron's questions (see *Harry Potter and the Prisoner of Azkaban*, Chapter 6).

How's this for a sweet little story? A Scottish merchant brought his wife a load of bitter Seville oranges, not very edible. Instead of saying, "What do you expect me to do with these?" as an ordinary housewife might have done, she marched into the kitchen to experiment, and thus orange marmalade was born.

3 oranges
2 cups sugar
2 cups water

1. Place the oranges in a medium saucepan and cover with water. Bring to a boil, then reduce to a simmer and cook for 1½ hours. Remove the oranges from the pot to a cutting board. Discard the cooking water and rinse the pot.

2. Peel the oranges and scrape off the pith (the white underside of the peel), using a metal spoon. Discard the pith, as it's bitter. Mince the orange peel and add to the clean pot. Chop the peeled oranges, discard the pits, and process in a blender or food processor until smooth. Pour through a sieve, pressing down with a rubber spatula to extract as much juice as possible. Discard the pulp and add the juice to the pot, along with the sugar and water. (As the mixture boils, it will expand like crazy, so make sure your pot is large enough to handle at least double what you're putting in.)

3. Cook the mixture over medium-high heat, stirring constantly, until the sugar is dissolved and it begins to bubble. Clip a candy thermometer to the side of the pot, and continue cooking, stirring constantly, until the mixture registers 220°F on the candy thermometer. Remove from the heat.

Makes enough to fill one 14-ounce jar

If you don't have a candy thermometer, you can do the wrinkle test: Put a small amount of marmalade on a saucer and cool it in the fridge. In the meantime, turn off the flame. When it's cool, push the edge in with your finger; if it wrinkles, it's done. Otherwise, reheat the marmalade, cook it for a few more minutes, and try again.

Thick Porridge with Cream and Treacle

What's more filling than a bowl of thick, sticky porridge? Harry loads up on this wholesome brain food while asking Ron about his schedule. Ron worries about Potions with the Slytherins: will Professor Snape favor the Slytherins as rumored? Little does he know! (See *Harry Potter and the Sorcerer's Stone*, Chapter 8.) Even the evil and toad-like Professor Umbridge has some porridge—while glaring at the teachers who dare to discuss in her presence the mass outbreak from Azkaban (see *Harry Potter and the Order of the Phoenix*, Chapter 25).

Often when we hear the word "porridge," we think of "Goldilocks and the Three Bears," but it's actually a real food that real people in the United Kingdom eat, especially the Scots, who've been eating porridge since before the arrival of the Anglo-Saxons in the fifth and sixth centuries.

4 cups water
1 cup steel-cut oats
Milk or cream, for serving
Golden syrup, for serving

1. Bring the water to a boil in a medium-size saucepan. Slowly pour in the oats while stirring constantly. Simmer on a low flame, stirring occasionally, for about 30 minutes, until all the water is absorbed.
2. Serve with the milk or cream and generous amounts of golden syrup. Don't mix the golden syrup in or you will lose its unique caramel-like flavor.

Serves 4

Crispy Fried Bacon

Harry is too worried that the dragon in his first Triwizard task will fry his bacon to be tempted by the crispy fried bacon served the morning before the tournament. He's too nervous and, frankly, terrified to eat at all, but he takes comfort in knowing he would rather face a dragon than go back to the Dursleys' (see *Harry Potter and the Goblet of Fire*, Chapter 20).

The British were much luckier than their contemporaries in other countries. In bad times, they had more food to eat than did the rest of Europe. Bacon was available even when a depression hit the country some 700 years ago. By the 1800s the lower classes were eating bacon almost every day for breakfast.

8 slices of bacon

1. Heat a large skillet. Add the bacon and fry on both sides until it is crisp.
2. Remove the bacon to a paper-towel-lined plate. Repeat until all the bacon is used up.

Serves 4

Cheesy, Chivy Scrambled Eggs

On the morning of a Quidditch match, Captain Oliver Wood excitedly dishes out scrambled eggs to his team members. The weather is excellent; what could possibly go wrong? He doesn't know yet that the match will be canceled due to a couple more mysterious attacks (see *Harry Potter and the Chamber of Secrets*, Chapter 14).

Eggs are a truly miraculous food. They have many uses, from simply being cooked and eaten (for which there are a million methods) to enriching breads and cakes, acting as a leavener or emulsifier, thickening sauces and custards . . . the list goes on and on. And that's without even mentioning what you can do with the whites and yolks separately. But for our purposes here, it's enough that scrambled eggs make a delicious and healthful breakfast.

1 tablespoon butter

6 eggs

¼ cup heavy cream

½ teaspoon salt

Freshly ground black pepper

1 tablespoon chopped fresh chives

½ cup shredded mozzarella cheese

Buttered toast, for serving

Tomatoes, for serving

1. Heat the butter in a large skillet. Whisk together the eggs, heavy cream, salt, pepper, and chives. Whisk in the shredded cheese. Pour the mixture into the skillet and cook over medium-low heat, stirring constantly and gently with a wooden spoon until set.
2. To serve, sprinkle more chopped chives on top. Serve with buttered toast and tomatoes.

Serves 3 to 4

Cinnamon Pull-Apart Breakfast Rolls

To deflect questions about what Ginny was about to tell Harry, Percy (man, he has a guilty conscience!) asks for the breakfast rolls. But Ginny was about to tell Harry something much, much more important . . . good thing Percy interrupted, or she would've spoiled the plot (see *Harry Potter and the Chamber of Secrets*, Chapter 16).

Cinnamon rolls, or buns, are a classic breakfast treat. Most people don't know this, but the cinnamon you buy is more likely powdered cassia bark, which tastes like cinnamon and is more plentiful and therefore cheaper. Real cinnamon is said to be superior, but who would know?

Dough

¼ cup warm water

1 tablespoon (1 packet) active dry yeast

1 tablespoon granulated sugar

⅔ cup whole milk

½ stick (4 tablespoons) butter

3 cups all-purpose flour

½ teaspoon salt

2 large eggs

⅓ cup granulated sugar

Cinnamon Filling

1 tablespoon butter, melted

¼ cup packed dark brown sugar

1 tablespoon cinnamon

Icing

1 cup confectioners' sugar, sifted

4 ounces cream cheese, softened

1 tablespoon heavy cream

½ teaspoon pure vanilla extract

Cinnamon Pull-Apart Breakfast Rolls

(continued)

1. Combine the water, yeast, and 1 tablespoon sugar in a mixing bowl and set aside until puffy. Heat the milk and butter in a small saucepan or the microwave until the butter is melted. Set aside. Whisk together the flour and salt; set aside. In a separate bowl, whisk together the eggs and sugar, then whisk in the milk-butter mixture. Add the yeast mixture and egg mixture to the flour mixture and stir to combine. (If making this dough by hand, first whisk ½ cup of the flour mixture into the egg mixture until smooth, then add the egg mixture to the rest of the flour mixture.) Knead the dough in the mixing bowl of an electric mixer fitted with a dough hook or by hand either in the bowl or on a lightly floured surface until the dough is smooth and elastic, about 10 minutes. Place in an oiled bowl, turning to coat, and cover with plastic wrap. Set aside in a warm place until doubled in size, 1½ to 2 hours.

2. Grease and flour a 9" × 13" pan. Turn the dough out onto a lightly floured surface and roll into a 16" × 12" rectangle. Brush the tablespoon of melted butter over the dough. Combine the brown sugar and cinnamon and spread it over the dough until within ½ inch of the borders. Roll up the long side. Slice off the messy ends.

3. The best way to cut the roll is using dental floss. Sounds crazy, but a knife exerts too much pressure and squashes the roll. First, slide a length of floss under the roll until you reach the center. Bring the two ends over the roll and cross them, pulling until a neat cut has been made. In this manner, cut the two halves in half again, then each quarter into 3 slices to make 12 rolls in all. Lay the rolls in the prepared pan and leave to rise until the rolls are touching each other and reach the rim, 1½ to 2 hours.

4. Adjust the oven rack to the middle position and preheat the oven to 350°F. Bake the rolls for 20 minutes until golden brown, rotating the pan halfway through baking. Remove from the oven. Cool for 10 minutes in the pan, then invert the pan and reinvert the rolls onto a serving platter.

5. To make the icing, beat the icing ingredients together with a wooden spoon until smooth. Be sure to sift the confectioners' sugar or you will have lumps. Spread the icing over the rolls while they are still warm, or pipe the frosting using a #3 round tip. Eat immediately. The rolls do not keep well and should be eaten within a few hours of being made.

Makes 12 rolls

If you want the rolls for breakfast, prepare the rolls the day before through Step 3, but instead of setting them to rise, cover the rolls with plastic wrap and allow them to rise in the refrigerator overnight, then pop them in the oven in the morning. You can also prepare the icing ahead of time and keep it in the refrigerator; just allow it to come to room temperature before using.

Kippers

Ron gets really mad at Hermione for stirring up the house-elves in the Hogwarts kitchens. She just doesn't get it: House-elves like being slaves. Now he's sure the food they'll send up from the kitchens will be horrible, but the next morning he's relieved to see that the kippers are fine (see *Harry Potter and the Goblet of Fire*, Chapter 28).

To "kipper" a fish means to split it, clean it, and then cold-smoke it. Kippers are often eaten for breakfast with eggs and toast. Whole, cold-smoked kippers are hard to find in the United States. In this country they are sold as kipper snacks, small chunks or fillets of smoked, salted herring that can be eaten straight out of the container. If you don't mind spending a lot on food, you can order this delicacy online from companies based in the United Kingdom.

4 kippers
Butter, for serving
Salt and pepper to taste

1. Broil or grill the kippers for 5 minutes. Remove them from the oven or grill and brush butter over the kippers. Sprinkle with the salt and pepper.
2. Serve with toast.

Serves 4

Chapter Seven

Lunch and Dinner in the Dining Hall

The Great Hall is magnificent. Look up at the ceiling—wait a minute, where *is* the ceiling? It's there, but it's charmed to look like the outdoor heavens, reflecting the weather and time of day. You take your seat at one of the four long tables, one for each House, and if you glance up at the podium, you will see another smaller table, reserved for the staff. Fantastic food magically appears on platters in front of you, and you dish it out onto your golden plate. Where does all this bounty come from? In the kitchens directly below the Great Hall, four long tables correspond to the tables above. The house-elves send up the food by magic (see *Harry Potter and the Goblet of Fire*, Chapter 21).

The kitchens provide hearty lunches and dinners with such mouthwatering specials as steak and kidney pie and shepherd's pie. Great desserts—such as Harry's favorite, treacle tart—accompany each meal.

Harry probably did not know this, but in the nineteenth century, men were generally too busy to eat lunch; they ate a big breakfast and a big dinner and nothing or a small snack in between. You weren't a real man if you ate lunch—that was only for women and children. Men everywhere should be grateful that this has changed . . . and today, as everyone knows, lunch is the light meal eaten between breakfast and dinner. In some countries, dinner is eaten in the afternoon and then a light supper is eaten in the evening, but it seems that at Hogwarts both lunch and dinner were heavy-duty meals. All that wand-waving and magic-making must really stimulate the appetite.

The Roast Beef of Old England

Ron has just discovered that leprechaun gold is fake, and he rants about it as he serves himself roast beef and Yorkshire pudding. As always, nothing spoils his appetite, and even as he complains about being poor, he continues to scarf down potatoes (see *Harry Potter and the Goblet of Fire*, Chapter 28).

The English developed a reputation for excellence in roasting beef. Roast beef is so important to the Britons that they even have a song about it called "The Roast Beef of Old England," which in turn inspired a famous painting of someone holding a humongous chunk of raw beef. Interestingly, the U.S. military plays this song when roast beef is served at formal dinners.

1 4- to 5-pound rib roast (or shoulder roast if you want a leaner meat)

3 tablespoons kosher salt
1 tablespoon fresh coarsely ground black pepper

1. Preheat the oven to 375°F. Grease a roasting rack and place it in a roasting pan.
2. Rinse the roast and pat it dry with paper towels. Generously sprinkle the roast with the salt and black pepper. Place the roasting pan in the oven and cook until the thermometer registers 120°F for rare, about 1 hour and 20 minutes; 125°F for medium rare, about 1 hour and 30 minutes; 132°F for medium, about 1 hour and 35 minutes; or 145°F for well done, about 1 hour and 45 minutes.
3. Remove the roast from the oven and tent a piece of aluminum foil over the roast. Let the roast rest 15 to 20 minutes before carving and serving. The resting time is important, as the roast will continue cooking for a few minutes due to residual heat; the resting time also allows the juices to redistribute themselves throughout the roast.

Serves 8

To prevent food-borne illness, it is recommended to cook roast beef to an internal temperature of at least 145°F.

Yorkshire Pudding

Roast beef and Yorkshire pudding go together like peas and carrots. They are almost always served together, and lunch after a niffler lesson with Hagrid is no exception (see *Harry Potter and the Goblet of Fire*, Chapter 28).

There was only so much meat to go around, so how to serve less of it but still leave the dinner table satisfied? Thrifty housewives always served the Yorkshire pudding before the roast beef at the traditional Sunday dinner to take the edge off the appetite. In the old days, when they cooked the roast on a spit over an open fire, they used to put a pan under the roast to catch the drippings, and the batter was poured into the hot drippings. As it baked, it soaked up the juices that continued to drip down from the meat.

1 cup all-purpose flour
½ teaspoon salt
2 large eggs

3 tablespoons butter, melted
1 cup whole milk
2 tablespoons vegetable oil

1. Whisk together the flour and salt in a large mixing bowl. In a separate bowl, whisk the eggs until smooth, then whisk in the butter, then the milk. Pour the egg mixture into the flour mixture and whisk until smooth. Refrigerate for 30 minutes.
2. Preheat the oven to 450°F. Pour the vegetable oil into an 8-inch pan or baking dish and put it in the oven while it's preheating. The oil needs to be hot before you pour in the batter.
3. Remove the batter from the refrigerator. It may need to be whisked again for a few seconds. Carefully pour the batter into the hot baking dish. Bake for 10 minutes. Reduce the heat to 350°F and continue baking for another 10 minutes, until it puffs up around the edges and the edges are golden. Serve hot or warm.

Serves 6

Breaded Pork Chops

At the Yule ball, the feast in the Great Hall is a bit different from usual. Instead of food magically appearing on the table, a menu has been placed next to each setting. Dumbledore demonstrates how this works by saying out loud the item he wants to eat, which in his case is pork chops (see *Harry Potter and the Goblet of Fire*, Chapter 23).

If you were just a common man living in the old days, you may have chosen pigs to raise as livestock. Almost every poor family owned a pig. Pigs don't cost anything to feed, since they eat garbage and can forage for themselves. They also produce a lot of meat, and everything but "the eyes and the squeak," as they say, can be used. (Try not to think too hard about that.)

4 6-ounce pork chops
Salt and freshly ground black pepper
*   to taste*
1 cup all-purpose flour
2 large eggs, whisked
2 cups seasoned bread crumbs
Vegetable oil as needed

1. Remove the pork chops from the package and pat dry with paper towels. Sprinkle with salt and pepper.
2. The breading process has three steps. The coating (breading) is a series of layers. Be sure to coat the food completely at each step of the process. You will need a bowl or large plastic bag for the flour; a bowl for the eggs; and a bowl for the bread crumbs.
3. Place the pork chops in the bowl of flour and turn them to coat evenly (or place the pork chops into the bag of flour and toss to coat evenly). Remove the chops from the flour and place in the bowl of beaten eggs; turn to coat completely. Lift out and let the excess eggs drain back into the bowl. Place the egg-coated chops in the third bowl of bread crumbs and turn to coat completely.
4. Fill a heavy skillet with enough oil to reach a depth of ¼ inch and heat to 350°F. If you don't have a thermometer to check the temperature, watch for the oil to begin moving (dancing) in the pan. Once that happens, sprinkle a pinch of bread crumbs into the oil. If they sizzle, the oil is ready. If the oil is smoking, it is too hot. If that happens, remove the pan from the heat and let it cool until the smoking stops. Then return the pan to the heat.
5. Carefully add the breaded chops to the oil and fry the chops about 4 minutes per side until they are browned and the internal temperature reaches 145°F. Use a pair of tongs to turn the chops. Do not use a fork. If the chops are pierced too many times, they will become dry.
6. Remove the chops to a paper-towel-lined plate to drain.

Serves 4

Braised Lamb Chops

Harry gloomily eats his lamb chops and potatoes. He's just been yelled at by the captain of the Quidditch team for getting detention from Professor Umbridge—like it was his fault—and he knows she'll never let him off for Quidditch tryouts. Not to mention the huge pile of homework waiting for him when he finishes his detention with her. Well, he'd be a whole lot gloomier if he knew what horrors Umbridge has in store for him (see *Harry Potter and the Order of the Phoenix*, Chapter 13).

"Lamb" refers to a baby sheep up to a year old. Once it's celebrated a birthday, it becomes tough and gamy and is called mutton. Because lamb is very fatty, it's usually cooked with an acid such as wine (which contains tannic acid) to cut the fattiness.

3 tablespoons vegetable oil
4 shoulder lamb chops
Salt
Freshly ground black pepper
1 medium onion, chopped

1 tablespoon all-purpose flour
1 cup white wine for adults or 1 cup
    canned chicken broth for children
1 teaspoon dried rosemary leaves
½ teaspoon ground sage

1. Heat 1 tablespoon of the oil in a large skillet.
2. Rinse the lamb chops and pat them dry. Sprinkle them on both sides with the salt and pepper. Sear the lamb chops on both sides over high heat, about 3 minutes per side, and transfer them to a large plate.
3. Wipe the fat gently off the skillet so as to leave the browned bits on the bottom of the pan. Heat the remaining 2 tablespoons of oil in the skillet. Add the onion and sauté until it is browned. Sprinkle the flour over the onion, then stir until well blended. Pour in the wine or broth while stirring. Stir in the rosemary and sage. Cook and stir, scraping up the fond (the browned bits), until the mixture is thickened and bubbling.
4. Return the lamb chops to the skillet. Cover the skillet and simmer for 15 to 20 minutes, until the meat is tender. Serve with the pan sauce, passing extra sauce at the table.

Serves 4

Classic Roast Chicken

At the Dursleys', Harry has never been allowed to eat as much as he wanted. So at his first-ever Hogwarts feast his eyes must have been popping out of his head with amazement at the huge variety of dishes that suddenly appeared on the table in front of him, including roast chicken (see *Harry Potter and the Sorcerer's Stone*, Chapter 7).

Chicken is the most popular poultry in the world. This may be because compared to cows, sheep, and goats, it costs much less and is easier to raise, it can be prepared in a staggering number of different ways, and very little of it goes to waste.

1 medium onion, sliced into ¼-inch-thick slices
2 celery ribs, cut into 2-inch chunks
2 carrots, cut into 2-inch chunks
4 garlic cloves, peeled
1 3-pound roasting chicken
Olive oil for brushing on the chicken
Salt and freshly ground black pepper
1 cup water

1. Preheat the oven to 375°F. Lay the onion slices in a roasting pan and scatter the celery, carrots, and garlic cloves on top.
2. Pat the chicken dry. Place the chicken in the roasting pan, breast side up, wings tucked under. There is no need to truss the chicken. Brush the olive oil over the chicken and sprinkle it with the salt and pepper. Pour the water into the roasting pan.
3. Put the pan in the oven and roast for 50 minutes. Raise the temperature to 450°F. Rotate the pan and continue roasting for 30 to 40 minutes, until an instant-read thermometer inserted into the thigh registers 170°F. Remove the chicken from the oven and let it rest for 20 minutes before carving.

Serves 4

Boiled Potatoes with Herb Vinaigrette

One of the astounding variety of dishes that magically appear before an astonished Harry at his first Hogwarts feast is boiled potatoes (see *Harry Potter and the Sorcerer's Stone*, Chapter 7).

When you think "history of the potato" (if you think "history" at all), you probably think "Ireland and the potato famine." But actually the Irish weren't so keen on the potato at first. The Spanish brought the potato back from South America in the 1500s and it took a very long time before the English and Irish started eating it. They thought it was poisonous, because, like the tomato, it belongs to the nightshade family.

3 pounds small new potatoes
¼ cup olive oil
2 tablespoons tarragon vinegar (you can substitute a different vinegar, such as balsamic)

Salt to taste
Freshly ground black pepper to taste
2 tablespoons chopped fresh dill

1. Scrub the potatoes and place in a pot. Fill the pot with water to cover the potatoes. Bring to a boil, then reduce the heat and simmer until the potatoes can be pierced easily with a fork, about 25 minutes.
2. Drain the potatoes and transfer to a large mixing bowl.
3. Add the oil, vinegar, salt, pepper, and dill, and toss to combine. Serve warm.

Serves 6

A traditional vinaigrette is made by whisking the ingredients to form a temporary emulsion (a process that suspends the oil in the vinegar), but in this recipe we take the easy way out and just toss all the ingredients together.

Roast Potatoes with Garlic and Rosemary

Ron stuffs his mouth with so many roast potatoes that no one can understand a word he's saying. What can he do? He's hungry, after all. It took a while for the feast that kicks off the school year to get started because of the extra-long sorting, when the hat sang an extra-long song warning everyone to stick together in the troubled times ahead (see *Harry Potter and the Order of the Phoenix*, Chapter **11**).

If you've been reading this book in order, you know that it took a long time (two centuries, in fact) from the introduction of the potato into England to its being eaten. Some people knew potatoes were safe to eat, but no one believed them. So they resorted to tricks. One Benjamin Thompson realized that the government could save lots of money feeding potatoes to poorhouse residents. He boiled the potatoes behind closed doors until they fell apart and no one could tell what food it was. Otherwise, no one would have eaten it. Sneaky, sneaky . . . but this way, the residents were well-fed, the government saved loads of money, and everyone was happy.

6 red potatoes (about 2 pounds), scrubbed and chopped into ½-inch cubes

¼ cup olive oil

1 teaspoon salt

1 teaspoon dried rosemary leaves

2 cloves garlic, minced

Freshly ground black pepper

1. Preheat the oven to 400°F. Combine the potatoes with the oil, salt, rosemary, garlic, and black pepper, taking care to coat the potatoes thoroughly and evenly.
2. Spread the potatoes in a large, shallow roasting pan or rimmed baking sheet. Roast the potatoes for about 45 minutes, until the potatoes are slightly crisp around the edges and soft in the middle. Halfway through baking, remove the pan briefly to toss the potatoes again, then replace it in the oven and continue baking.

Serves 4

Fluffy Mashed Potatoes

Ron is starving—as usual—at the start-of-term feast, where the Triwizard Tournament will be announced. He loads up on mashed potatoes, observed by a wistful Nearly Headless Nick (see *Harry Potter and the Goblet of Fire*, Chapter 12).

There are a zillion and one ways to prepare potatoes, and it seems as though at least half of them are mentioned in the Harry Potter books. But this is one of the best ways to eat them. For mashing, use starchy potatoes, such as russet. Waxy potatoes like the red-skin variety don't lose their shape after a long cooking time and are best reserved for roasting and stewing. They don't make good mashed potatoes.

6 Idaho or russet potatoes (about 2½ pounds), peeled and quartered
1 stick (8 tablespoons) butter
1 cup whole milk
2 teaspoons salt
Freshly ground black pepper to taste

1. Place the potatoes in a pot and cover with water. Bring to a boil, then reduce the heat and simmer about 25 minutes or until the potatoes break apart when pierced with a fork.
2. Drain the potatoes. Add the butter, milk, salt, and black pepper. Mash with a potato masher until the potatoes are light and fluffy.

Serves 4

You can have a lot of fun with mashed potatoes. Boil 2 peeled cloves of garlic along with the potatoes and mash them together with the potatoes, along with a dash of garlic powder, for garlicky mashed potatoes. Add a sautéed onion and 1 tablespoon onion powder for onion mashed potatoes. Sprinkle shredded cheese on top for cheesy mashed potatoes. Or mash in your favorite herbs, minced. And serve with lots of gravy.

Potatoes Baked in Their Jackets

Harry is about to have his very first Halloween feast at Hogwarts, complete with live bats (for show, not for eating), when Professor Quirrell bursts into the Great Hall to warn everyone about a troll, throwing the Hall into chaos. Harry doesn't get to finish the baked potato he had been about to help himself to, but he has adventures far more exciting than eating potatoes (see *Harry Potter and the Sorcerer's Stone*, Chapter 10).

Another interesting fact about potatoes: They used to be called "earth apple" in English and German (*Erdapfel*). They are still called "earth apple" in French (*pommes de terre*), Hebrew (*tapuchei adama*), Dutch (*aardappel*), and other languages.

6 Idaho or russet potatoes, scrubbed
Salt and freshly ground black pepper
Butter, sour cream, or plain yogurt, for serving

1. Preheat the oven to 400°F. Slice the potatoes in half lengthwise and spread them, cut-side up, on a baking sheet.
2. Bake the potatoes for 1 to 1½ hours, until the tops are crusty and golden and the potatoes can be easily pierced with a fork. Season with salt and pepper to taste and serve with lots of butter or with sour cream or plain yogurt.

Serves 6

For a hearty meal on its own, bake the potatoes whole, then split them in half and scoop out the insides. Mash with tuna and mayonnaise—using the proportions of tuna and mayo to potato that you like—and return the mixture to the shells. If desired, pop them into the oven for a few minutes to reheat just until hot throughout.

French Fries

Fried potatoes, one of the three ways potatoes are served at Harry's first Hogwarts feast, appear magically on the table in front of Harry, who tastes all the foods except the humbugs (see *Harry Potter and the Sorcerer's Stone*, Chapter 7).

To get the French to start eating potatoes—like other people, they too were reluctant—scientist Antoine-Augustin Parmentier got creative. He gave Queen Marie Antoinette potato blossoms to wear and he planted a potato field and had it heavily guarded. He figured, rightly, that the locals would be curious about the valuable crop. Indeed, they snuck in at night and stole potatoes, which they then planted and ate, finding that they were quite good after all. Such shtick! But it worked. So grateful are the French to Monsieur Parmentier that today any dish with the word *parmentier* in it means the main ingredient is potatoes.

6 large Idaho potatoes, peeled
Peanut oil, for frying (see note)
Salt to taste

1. Cut a thin slice off the ends and all four sides of the potatoes, which will turn the potatoes into rectangles. Slice the potatoes into ¼-inch slices along the length. Turn the first set of slices onto their broad side, and then cut lengthwise to form ¼-inch sticks. Rinse the potatoes in cold water until the water runs clear, then dry with a towel. Keep the potatoes wrapped in a towel until ready to fry. (You can reserve the leftover slices to make mashed potatoes.)

2. Fill a medium saucepan with enough oil to come 2 inches up the sides. Clip a candy thermometer to the pot and heat the oil to 350°F. Add the potatoes in batches, bringing the temperature back up to 350°F in between batches. Cook each batch until darker yellow, about 5 minutes. Transfer the potatoes to paper towels to drain. Reserve the pot of oil for the next step.

3. Before serving, reheat the pot of oil to 350°F. Fry the potatoes again in batches until crisp and golden, about 2 minutes, bringing the temperature back up to 350°F in between batches. Transfer to paper towels, sprinkle with salt, and serve.

Serves 4 to 6

Peanut oil is one of the best oils for deep-frying, as it has a high smoking point and delivers beautiful crispiness. But it is horribly expensive, so you can substitute canola or vegetable oil for the peanut oil.

Buttered Peas

The most food ever mentioned in one place in the Harry Potter books is at Harry's first Hogwarts feast. About twenty-five dishes are named, including peas. Who can eat that much food in one meal (see *Harry Potter and the Sorcerer's Stone*, Chapter 7)?

The Romans introduced peas to Great Britain, and a good thing too, because peas became an important staple in the diet of medieval peasants, who ate it in the form of a pottage (a very thick soup). If there is ever a vegetable you want to steal, peas should be the one. The tall, flowering plants could so easily conceal a thief that medieval laws were enacted to protect them (the peas, not the thieves).

1 pound frozen peas
1 cup water
½ teaspoon salt
¼ teaspoon pepper
2 tablespoons butter
1 tablespoon granulated sugar

1. Combine the peas and water in a small pot and bring them to a boil. Reduce the heat and simmer for about 5 minutes, until the peas are tender. Drain the peas and return them to the pot.
2. Add the salt, pepper, butter, and sugar. Toss until the butter melts and is well combined.

Serves 6

Frozen peas, hard as it is to believe, have an advantage over fresh. Unlike most produce, peas begin to get starchy and lose flavor within a few hours of being picked, so by the time you buy them in the supermarket, they're not that great. Because frozen peas are picked and frozen at the peak of their freshness, they are better for this recipe.

Glazed Carrots

Carrots are yet another of the myriad dishes served at the feast in the Great Hall following Harry's sorting ceremony into Gryffindor House (see *Harry Potter and the Sorcerer's Stone*, Chapter 7).

British fighter pilots, in an effort to keep radar technology from the Germans, claimed that their super night vision came from eating a lot of carrots. The Germans actually bought the story, hard though that may be to believe. Carrots really do improve your night vision, but you can't use them instead of radar. And you will still have to wear your glasses.

6 medium carrots, peeled and sliced into ¼-inch-thick slices on the bias

½ cup water

2 tablespoons golden syrup or maple syrup or corn syrup

¼ teaspoon salt

1 teaspoon ground cinnamon

1. Combine the carrots, water, golden syrup or maple or corn syrup, salt, and cinnamon in a skillet and bring to a boil, stirring occasionally with a wooden spoon. Reduce the heat and simmer the carrots, uncovered, for about 5 minutes, until the carrots are somewhat softened but not yet tender.

2. Raise the heat and boil until all the liquid evaporates. As the liquid starts to reduce, begin stirring more frequently. Keep cooking until the glaze starts to turn brown, stirring and scraping the bottom of the pan. Turn off the heat and serve immediately.

Serves 4

Classic Gravy

Gravy is not really a food; it's something you put on your food. It's served at Harry's first Hogwarts feast and first Hogwarts Christmas dinner, probably to pour over all the many potato dishes (see *Harry Potter and the Sorcerer's Stone*, Chapters 7 and 12).

It's amazing how sophisticated British cooks were in the 1200s and 1300s. They made gravy from a purée of ground almonds, broth, ginger, and sugar, to be poured over rabbit, chicken, eel, or oysters. The expression "fit for a king" certainly had great significance in those days. The peasants didn't get to dine on this kind of fare, to be sure!

3 tablespoons vegetable oil
3 tablespoons all-purpose flour
2 cups chicken, turkey, or beef stock
½ cup chicken, turkey, or beef drippings, after fat has been skimmed off the top (see note)
Salt to taste

1. Heat the oil in a small saucepan. Add the flour and stir until the flour turns brown and foams. Slowly pour in the stock, stirring constantly. Add the drippings.
2. Cook, stirring occasionally, until the gravy is thickened and bubbling.
3. Taste, and adjust salt accordingly.

Makes about 2½ cups

This gravy is not truly classic. Technically, gravy contains no thickeners, so the following recipe is really a sauce. This type of thick sauce, however, is associated with classic gravy by many.

If drippings are not available, you can use all stock.

English Tomato Ketchup

If ketchup is worth mentioning at Harry's very first Hogwarts banquet, then it can't be a typical bottled variety. The house-elves no doubt make their own signature ketchup, which they send up to the Great Hall along with the rest of the meal (see *Harry Potter and the Sorcerer's Stone*, Chapter 7).

Originally ketchup in England was made with pickled mushrooms and no tomatoes, and although tomato ketchup is pretty much the only kind that is made these days, ketchup really refers to any condiment that is concentrated and that contains a lot of sugar and vinegar. It's easy to make homemade ketchup and it tastes great—but ironically it costs a lot more to make it from scratch than to buy a bottle.

2 pounds (about 4 large) ripe tomatoes, cut into quarters
1 medium onion, cut into chunks
2 cloves garlic, cut into small chunks
¼ cup packed brown sugar
½ cup white wine vinegar or distilled white vinegar
1 teaspoon salt
1 cup water
1 stick cinnamon
5 whole cloves
5 whole allspice
5 peppercorns

1. Place all the ingredients in a large pot. Bring to a boil, then reduce heat to a simmer and cook until the tomatoes are very soft, about 30 minutes.
2. Remove the pot from the heat. Pour the contents into a large sieve set over a large bowl and push it through with a rubber spatula until all the juice is extracted. Discard the remaining pulp, skin, seeds, and spices.
3. Return the cooked tomato mixture to the pot and boil, uncovered, stirring occasionally until it is reduced and very thick, about 30 minutes.

Makes ¾ cup

Steak and Kidney Pudding

Malfoy has just been attacked by Buckbeak the hippogriff—Malfoy's fault entirely, as he wasn't paying attention to Hagrid's warning not to insult these sensitive animals. But it's Hagrid's first lesson as a teacher, and Hermione is so worried he might get into trouble that she can't eat her steak and kidney pudding (see *Harry Potter and the Prisoner of Azkaban*, Chapter 6).

This national British dish first appeared in the mid-1800s. To feel authentic, bring it to the table in the bowl it was cooked in, wrapped in a clean white napkin or cloth. Suet puddings are uniquely British, but butter or margarine, easier to find, yields acceptable results. Serve this dish with boiled new potatoes and Brussels sprouts or with mashed potatoes and steamed peas and carrots for a very traditional British meal.

"Suet" Crust

2 cups all-purpose flour

½ teaspoon salt

¼ teaspoon black pepper

1½ sticks (12 tablespoons) butter or margarine, cut into small chunks

½ cup ice water

Filling

1 pound chuck steak, chopped into ¼-inch pieces

3 tablespoons vegetable oil

1 medium onion, finely chopped

1 clove garlic, minced

3 tablespoons all-purpose flour

1 cup chicken broth

3 tablespoons tomato paste

½ teaspoon salt

¼ teaspoon freshly ground black pepper

1 pound lamb or ox kidneys, cut into ¼-inch pieces

Steak and Kidney Pudding

(continued)

1. For the crust, whisk together the flour, salt, and pepper in a large mixing bowl. Scatter the chunks of butter or margarine over the flour and rub it in using a pastry cutter or your fingertips. Sprinkle the ice water over the flour and fold it in with a spatula until the dough sticks together. If it's too dry, add ice water one tablespoon at a time. Remove ⅓ of the dough for the lid and reserve the rest for the base. Form both pieces of dough into disks, wrap them in plastic wrap, and refrigerate them while you prepare the filling, at least 30 minutes.

2. For the filling, sear the meat in batches over high heat in a large skillet on both sides until deeply browned. Do not overcrowd the skillet or the meat will exude too much liquid and will not brown well. Set the meat aside and wipe out the skillet.

3. Add the oil to the skillet and heat it. Add the onions and sauté over medium heat until the onions are golden brown. Add the garlic and sauté for just a few seconds until it's fragrant.

4. Stir in the meat. Sprinkle the flour over the meat and mix well. Slowly stir in the broth, then the tomato paste. The mixture will be very thick. Add the salt, pepper, and kidneys and cook, covered for 10 minutes. Uncover, raise the heat, and boil until the mixture is even thicker, about 5 minutes. Pour the filling onto a rimmed baking sheet and spread it around to cool it quickly. Cool the filling to room temperature.

5. To assemble the pudding, place a shallow bowl upside-down in a large pot and fill the pot ⅓ of the way with water. Bring to a boil. Grease and flour a 2-quart bowl with a tight-fitting lid. On a generously floured surface, roll out the larger disk of dough to a 14-inch circle. Fold the dough in quarters and unfold it in the prepared bowl, carefully easing the dough into the bowl and letting the edges hang over the rim. Roll out the second disk to an 8-inch circle.

6. Scrape the filling into the pastry-lined bowl. Cover the filling with the second round of dough. Press the edges together and fold them over (not under). You should have a rim of at least ½ inch to allow room for the dough to expand. Snap the lid tightly onto the bowl and carefully place it in the pot. The water should come halfway up the sides. Simmer for 2½ hours, checking the water level occasionally and adding more water as necessary.

7. Use oven mitts to carefully lift out the bowl. To serve, simply scoop out servings with a large spoon.

Serves 6

If you can't find kidneys or prefer not to use them, use a pound of sliced mushrooms instead.

Steak and Kidney Pie

Ron, the man with the indestructible appetite, actually forgets to eat his steak and kidney pie in his amazement that Harry, instead of being punished for flying on a broomstick, is placed on the Quidditch team as the youngest Seeker in a century (see *Harry Potter and the Sorcerer's Stone*, Chapter 9).

Steak and kidney pie is the same as the pudding, just baked in a pie crust, which is a whole lot easier.

Pie Crust

2¼ cups all-purpose flour

1 teaspoon salt

9 tablespoons chilled vegetable shortening, cut into chunks

8 tablespoons (1 stick) cold butter, cut into chunks

½ to ¾ cup ice water

Filling

Use the same ingredients as the filling for Steak and Kidney Pudding

1 egg, beaten with 1 tablespoon water, for brushing over the crust

Steak and Kidney Pie

(continued)

1. To make the crust, place the flour and salt in a standing mixer or food processor and stir or pulse to combine. Scatter the shortening and butter over the flour mixture and stir or pulse until the mixture resembles coarse meal.

2. Transfer the mixture to a bowl. Sprinkle ½ cup of the ice water over the mixture and fold it in with a spatula until the dough holds together. Add the rest of the water 1 tablespoon at a time if the dough is too dry (better too much water than too little).

3. Divide the dough in half, form the two halves into disks, wrap them in plastic wrap, and refrigerate for at least 2 hours or up to 3 days before using.

4. To make the filling, follow the instructions for cooking the filling in the Steak and Kidney Pudding recipe.

5. To assemble the pie, preheat the oven to 425°F. Place a baking sheet on the lowest rack to catch any drips. Remove one disk of dough from the refrigerator and roll it out on a generously floured surface to a 12-inch circle. Fold the circle into quarters and unfold it in a 9-inch pie pan, easing it in gently.

6. Scrape the filling into the pastry-lined pan and smooth it to the edges. Roll out the second disk of dough to a 12-inch circle. Fold the dough in quarters and unfold it over the filling. Trim the overhang about ¾ inch over the rim of the pan. Fold the overhang under and crimp the edges together with a fork or your fingers. Brush the egg over the top of the pie and then cut four slits in the top for the vents. You can use dough scraps to create leaves or other shapes to decorate the pie. Attach the decorations with a bit of water to create a "glue."

7. Carefully place the pie on the baking sheet and bake for 25 minutes, then reduce the heat to 350°F and bake until golden brown, another 30 minutes. If the edges start to burn, cover them with strips of aluminum foil. At the end of the baking time, remove the pie from the oven and let it set for 20 minutes before cutting it to give the filling a chance to firm up.

Serves 8

Shepherd's Pie

The day Harry is to spend time in detention with Professor Lockhart (helping him to answer his fan mail), Harry eats his shepherd's pie without much appetite, dreading his upcoming detention. If he could foretell the future, he'd have a lot more on his mind, because during his detention he will hear a terrifying, murderous voice in the walls that no one else can hear (see *Harry Potter and the Chamber of Secrets,* Chapter 7).

There's nothing like a mincing machine to grind up meat for you. Victorian housewives were delighted with the invention of the mincing machine because it helped them mince leftover roast lamb from Sunday to be used during the week in dishes such as shepherd's pie.

1½ pounds ground lamb or beef
2 tablespoons vegetable oil
1 medium onion, finely chopped
1 clove garlic, minced
1 tablespoon all-purpose flour
1 cup chicken stock
2 tablespoons tomato paste
1 carrot, peeled and chopped
½ teaspoon salt
Freshly ground black pepper
3 large Idaho potatoes, peeled and cut into quarters
½ stick (4 tablespoons) butter
½ cup half-and-half or whole milk
1½ teaspoons salt

Shepherd's Pie

(continued)

1. Place a baking sheet on the lowest oven rack to catch drips. Preheat the oven to 350°F.

2. In a large skillet or wide saucepan, brown the meat, breaking up the clumps with a wooden spoon, until it is completely browned and crumbly. Drain the fat off the meat and transfer to a plate. Wipe out the skillet with a paper towel. Add the oil. Heat the oil and add the onions. Sauté the onions over medium heat until they turn golden brown. Add the garlic and sauté a few seconds until fragrant. Return the meat to the skillet; stir to combine.

3. Sprinkle the flour over the meat mixture and stir it in. Slowly pour in the chicken stock while stirring. Add the tomato paste, chopped carrots, salt, and pepper; raise the heat and bring to a simmer. Cook until the filling is thick and bubbling and the carrots have softened, about 15 minutes.

4. Cover the potatoes with water in a saucepan and bring to a boil. Reduce the heat and simmer until the potatoes break apart when pierced with a fork, about 25 minutes. Drain the potatoes and return them to the pot. Add the butter, half-and-half or milk, and salt, and mash everything together with a potato masher.

5. Pour the meat mixture into a deep 9-inch baking dish. Spoon the mashed potatoes on top. You can make peaks and swirls with the back of a spoon or a crosshatch pattern with a fork. For a festive look, you can pipe out the mashed potatoes through a pastry bag fitted with a ¾-inch star tip. Bake the pie until it is bubbling around the edges and the potato crust turns a deeper yellow, about 45 minutes.

Serves 8

Technically, shepherd's pie is made from lamb, and cottage pie from beef, but often the term "shepherd's pie" is used for both. Whatever you call it, you can't fail to please with this ultimate comfort food.

Bangers and Mash

On the evening that Dumbldore's Army (the D.A.) is to meet for the first time, Harry eats bangers and mash for dinner, referred to as sausages and mash in the American version of *Harry Potter and the Order of the Phoenix* (Chapter 18).

During wartime rationing, sausages were so waterlogged that they made exploding noises while they fried, earning the British nickname "bangers." This dish is delicious smothered in onion gravy. You can use good-quality sausages instead of homemade sausage patties.

Bangers

½ pound ground veal

½ pound ground pork or beef

1 cup fresh bread crumbs

1 teaspoon grated lemon zest

1 teaspoon salt

¼ teaspoon ground nutmeg

1 teaspoon ground sage

⅛ teaspoon dried marjoram

⅛ teaspoon ground thyme

¼ teaspoon freshly ground black pepper

2 egg yolks

2 tablespoons butter or margarine

Mashed Potatoes

6 potatoes, peeled and quartered

2 teaspoons salt

4 tablespoons (½ stick) butter

1 cup whole milk or half-and-half

Freshly ground black pepper to taste

Onion Gravy

3 tablespoons vegetable oil

1 medium onion, finely chopped

3 tablespoons all-purpose flour

2 cups chicken broth

Salt to taste (this will need to be adjusted according to the saltiness
   of the broth)

Bangers and Mash

(continued)

1. For the bangers, combine all the ingredients except for the 2 tablespoons butter or margarine in a large mixing bowl and mix well. Heat the butter or margarine in a skillet. Form the meat into sausage shapes and fry on each side over medium-high heat, turning often, until the sausages are well browned. Transfer the sausages to a paper-towel-lined plate. Repeat until all the mixture is used up.

2. For the mashed potatoes, place the potatoes in a pot and cover with water. Bring to a boil, then reduce the heat and simmer about 25 minutes or until the potatoes break apart when pierced with a fork.

3. Drain the potatoes. Add the salt, butter, milk or half-and-half, and black pepper. Mash with a potato masher until the potatoes are light and fluffy.

4. For the onion gravy, heat the oil in a medium saucepan. Add the onions and cook over low heat, stirring occasionally, until the onions are golden, about 30 minutes. Add the flour and stir until smooth. Add the chicken broth. Cook over medium heat, stirring constantly, until thick and bubbling. Taste the gravy and add salt, if necessary.

5. To serve, place 2 or 3 sausages on a plate. Mound the mashed potatoes on the side, and spoon generous amounts of onion gravy over the whole lot.

Serves 6

Chiddingly Hotpot

Hermione and Ron are in a fight . . . so what else is new? Ron made fun of Hermione in a lesson with Professor McGonagall, and now she's sitting alone at the Gryffindor table, not really eating her stew. She's mad, and it doesn't help that he's dating Lavender and not her (see *Harry Potter and the Half-Blood Prince*, Chapter 15).

This stew hails from Chiddingly in East Sussex, an important Roman mining town. There's practically no information of how this dish evolved and how olives came to be a part of it. But it tastes good, and that's all that matters.

3 tablespoons vegetable oil

1 pound chuck steak or eye roast, trimmed and cut into 1-inch cubes

Flour for dredging

1 onion, chopped

1 celery rib, chopped

½ cup chopped green olives

2 tablespoons tarragon vinegar

2 tablespoons malt vinegar

¼ teaspoon ground cloves

Salt

Freshly ground black pepper

3 large red-skinned potatoes, thinly sliced

About 1 cup chicken broth

1. Preheat the oven to 350°F. Heat 1 tablespoon of the oil in a large skillet. Dredge the meat pieces in the flour and cook in batches over medium-high heat, tossing the meat as it cooks, until well-browned. Transfer to a large plate.

2. Heat the remaining 2 tablespoons oil and add the onion and celery. Cook over medium heat, scraping up the fond (the browned bits on the bottom), until vegetables are softened, about 5 minutes.

3. In a medium-size deep round baking dish, layer half the celery-onion mixture, then half the olives. Sprinkle with 1 tablespoon of each of the vinegars, ⅛ teaspoon of the cloves, salt, and pepper. Then layer over that half the meat. Arrange half the potato slices on top. Repeat this layering once. Pour in chicken broth to come halfway up the sides of the dish. Sprinkle the top layer of potatoes with more salt and pepper. Cover tightly and cook for 2½ hours.

4. Remove the cover and check that the stew is not too dry; if it is, add some more chicken broth. Bake uncovered another 30 minutes until browned on top.

Serves 4

Scotch Collops
(Pan-Seared Steak with Onions and Mushrooms)

What a way for Hermione to find out about the house-elves at Hogwarts—at the start-of-term feast, when everyone is starving. Harry has just finished swallowing his steak when Nearly Headless Nick talks about the trouble Peeves caused in the kitchen with the house-elves. Hermione is hungry, but she feels it's wrong to eat any more. Harry and Ron are unaffected, of course (see *Harry Potter and the Goblet of Fire*, Chapter 12).

"Collops" is a quaint word that means "slices," specifically slices of meat. The Victorians had very strong feelings about how their collops should be prepared. The cookbook *Great British Cooking* by Jane Garmey repeats a story related by the famous Victorian cookbook author Isabella Beeton: a woman was asking around about a cook she was thinking to hire. When told about the cook's high moral character, she said, "Oh, d'n [sic] her decency; can she make good collops?"

2 tablespoons vegetable oil
1½ pounds strip steak, cut against the grain into ⅛-inch-thick slices
1 onion, sliced
1 10-ounce package mushrooms, sliced
Salt and freshly ground black pepper to taste

1. Heat the oil in a skillet and brown the meat over high heat, about 1 to 2 minutes per side, in batches, taking care not to overcrowd the pan. Remove each batch of meat to a plate. Add the onions and mushrooms to the pan and reduce the heat to medium-high. Cook, stirring often and scraping the bottom of the pan to loosen the flavorful fond (browned bits), until the onions are brown and the mushrooms are soft.
2. Remove the skillet from the heat and add back the meat, tossing to combine. Serve alongside buttered egg noodles.

Serves 6

Brussels Sprouts with Béchamel Sauce

Hermione knows she can't help the house-elves by starving herself to death, but she can go to the library. That's her mantra: when in doubt, go to the library. She stuffs her mouth as fast as she can with lamb chops, potatoes, and sprouts so she can use the remaining lunch period to read up on elf rights (see *Harry Potter and the Goblet of Fire*, Chapter 13).

Brussels sprouts have a bad rap as being one of the least desirable veggies out there. A good reason many don't like this veggie is simply that they've only had it overcooked. To get scientific about it, overcooking releases sulfuric compounds that taste just, well, gross. So be very careful not to braise the sprouts for longer than 7 minutes.

1 pound frozen Brussels sprouts
  (use frozen sprouts for easier
  preparation)
1 cup water
1 tablespoon butter

1 tablespoon all-purpose flour
1 cup whole milk
¼ teaspoon salt
⅛ teaspoon ground nutmeg
Freshly ground black pepper, to taste

1. Bring the sprouts and water to a boil in a medium saucepan. Reduce heat to a simmer and cook sprouts about 7 minutes, until tender. Drain the sprouts and transfer to a serving dish.
2. Heat the butter in a skillet until foaming. Add the flour and stir to combine. Pour in the milk while stirring. Add the salt, nutmeg, and pepper, and continue to cook, stirring constantly, until thick and bubbling.
3. Pour the sauce over the sprouts. Serve warm.

Serves 6

The sprouts can be stored with the sauce in the refrigerator up to 1 week but should be reheated gently over a low flame or in the microwave.

Bouillabaisse

To make the foreign students feel at home, the dishes of their native cuisines appear along with the usual Hogwarts fare on the Great Hall tables at the feast welcoming Durmstrang and Beauxbatons (see *Harry Potter and the Goblet of Fire*, Chapter 16).

If you've been wondering how in the world to pronounce it, your search is over. Ready? Here goes: bool-yuh-BAYSS. Any dish with a French name sounds fancy, but this stew originated with simple fishermen. A very logical story: the fisherman comes home with the catch he hasn't been able to sell, an assortment of fish and shellfish. The wife dumps it all in a pot with veggies and herbs, wine and olive oil if available, and boils it up to serve with bread. Simple enough—although the variety of ingredients in this recipe is anything but.

½ cup olive oil
1 cup chopped onion
3 ribs celery, chopped
2 cloves garlic, minced
2 cups clam juice
¼ cup fresh flat-leaf parsley, minced
1½ cups chopped tomatoes
2 teaspoons salt
1 teaspoon chopped fresh thyme
1 tablespoon paprika
½ cup dry white wine
Pinch of saffron

¼ teaspoon crushed red pepper flakes
3 pounds firm white fish like halibut, sea bass, or snapper, cut into bite-size pieces
1 pound lobster meat, cut into bite-size pieces
1 pound crabmeat
1 pound shrimp, shelled and deveined
2 dozen clams
1 baguette per serving
Butter, for serving

1. In a large soup pot, heat the oil over medium heat. Add the onions and celery and cook, stirring, until tender, about 3 minutes. Add the minced garlic, clam juice, parsley, tomatoes, salt, thyme, paprika, wine, saffron, and red pepper flakes. Bring to a boil, reduce the heat to medium-low, and cover the pot. Simmer for 30 minutes.
2. Bring the soup to a boil over high heat. Add all the seafood, cover again, and reduce the heat to a simmer for 45 minutes.
3. Divide the soup among 6 bowls. Serve with the fresh bread and butter.

Serves 6

Nine Recipes from the Goblet

The following nine recipes are based on a quote from *Harry Potter and the Goblet of Fire*: "The pale blue Beauxbatons carriage looked like a large, chilly, frosted pumpkin . . . while the Durmstrang ship's portholes were glazed with ice, the rigging white with frost. The house-elves down in the kitchen were outdoing themselves with a series of rich, warming stews and savory puddings" (Chapter 23).

Toad in the Hole

1 cup all-purpose flour
½ teaspoon salt
2 large eggs
3 tablespoons butter, melted

1 cup whole milk
2 tablespoons vegetable oil
1 pound of your favorite sausages

The Oxford Companion to Food tantalizingly asks about Toad in the Hole, "How did it get its name?" but doesn't answer the question! Wikipedia explains that maybe it's because the sausages poking out of the batter look like toads poking their heads out of their holes. They don't, but oh, well. Someone had too much imagination.

1. To make the batter, whisk together the flour and salt. In a separate bowl, whisk the eggs until smooth, then whisk in the butter, then the milk. Pour the egg mixture into the flour mixture and whisk until smooth. Refrigerate for 30 minutes.

2. Preheat the oven to 450°F. Pour the oil into a medium-size rectangular baking dish and put into the oven to heat. In the meantime, brown the sausages in a skillet on both sides. When the oil in the baking dish is hot, carefully remove the pan from the oven. Lay the sausages in the pan. Remove the batter from the refrigerator, give it one final whisk, and pour it over the sausages. Return the pan to the oven and bake for 10 minutes. Reduce the temperature to 350°F and bake another 10 minutes, until the pudding is puffed up around the edges and the edges are brown.

Serves 4

Nine Recipes from the Goblet

(continued)

The point of this pudding is similar to Yorkshire pudding: to round out the meal so less meat could be served. The trademarks of the Derby (pronounced "darby") pudding are lots of sage and onions.

Derby Savory Pudding

2 cups bread crumbs

1 cup rolled oats (old-fashioned, not quick-cooking or instant)

2½ cups whole milk

3 large eggs

2 teaspoons salt

¼ teaspoon freshly ground black pepper

2 teaspoons ground sage

2 onions, finely chopped

½ stick (4 tablespoons) butter, melted

1. Preheat the oven to 350°F and grease an 8-inch square pan. Combine the bread crumbs and oats in a large mixing bowl. Pour the milk over it and let it stand 15 minutes until absorbed, stirring occasionally (it will be hard to stir, as it will be very stiff).

2. Whisk together the eggs, salt, pepper, and sage. Add the egg mixture to the oats mixture and stir to combine. Add the onions and mix well. Add the melted butter and mix until thoroughly combined. Scrape the batter into the prepared pan and bake for 1 hour until the top is dry and the pudding feels firm. Cool in the pan for 15 minutes, then cut into 2-inch squares. Serve hot or cold.

Makes 16 (2-inch) squares

Nine Recipes from the Goblet

(continued)

> "Pease porridge hot, pease porridge cold, pease porridge in the pot nine days old." This famous nursery rhyme was inspired by pease pudding (which used to be called pease pottage in the Middle Ages) or pease porridge. This is a very, very old dish, but it's still eaten today, often with bacon or sausages, and it's surprisingly good.

Pease Pudding

2 tablespoons vegetable oil
1 medium onion, finely chopped
3 cloves garlic, minced
3 14-ounce cans chicken broth
1 pound yellow or green split peas, rinsed and drained
1 teaspoon salt
Freshly ground black pepper

1. Heat the oil in a large skillet or pot. Add the onion and cook over medium heat until browned, stirring occasionally, 10 to 15 minutes. Add the garlic and cook until fragrant, about 15 seconds. Add the chicken broth, peas, salt, and pepper and simmer over low heat, covered, until very thick, about 1½ hours. Once the pudding begins to thicken, stir every 10 minutes to avoid scorching. Taste and adjust seasonings accordingly.
2. Serve hot or cold as an accompaniment to bacon or sausages, or if you prefer, roast beef or chicken.

Serves 6

Nine Recipes from the Goblet

(continued)

Irish Stew

2 tablespoons vegetable oil

3 pounds lamb chops, trimmed of fat and gristle and cut into 1-inch pieces

1 medium onion, chopped

6 potatoes, about 2 pounds (Yukon Gold preferred), peeled and cut into 1-inch pieces

2 cups chicken broth

Salt and freshly ground black pepper to taste

½ teaspoon ground thyme, optional

> *Traditional Irish stew is easy: layer onions, chunks of lamb, and chunks of potato in a pot, add water and seasonings, and off you go. It's also very bland. For a deeper, richer flavor, we modern cooks prefer to sear the meat first, brown the onions, and simmer the stew in chicken broth instead of water. The results are worth the bit of extra bother.*

1. In a Dutch oven or wide pot, heat a teaspoon of the oil. Working in two or three batches, sear the cubes of meat in a single layer over medium-high heat until well browned, about 4 minutes per side. Transfer the meat to a large plate and repeat, wiping out the pot and adding a teaspoon of oil between each batch.

2. Wipe out the pot and heat the remaining tablespoon of oil. Sauté the onion over medium-low heat until light brown, scraping up the fond (browned bits) on the bottom of the pot with a wooden spoon, 10 to 15 minutes.

3. Add the meat and accumulated juices to the pot, along with the potatoes and broth. Add salt and pepper to taste and the thyme, if using. Bring the stew to a boil, then reduce the heat and simmer for 2 to 2½ hours.

Serves 4 to 6

Nine Recipes from the Goblet

(continued)

We use the word "hodgepodge" to mean a mix of odds and ends, so it kind of makes sense to call a stew a hodgepodge, as they did in the Middle Ages. That term survives today as "hotpot," a stew covered by a lid of thinly sliced potatoes. Lancashire, where the townsfolk often join for community suppers featuring the hotpot, is most famous for this dish.

Lancashire Hotpot

2 tablespoons vegetable oil
3 pounds neck of lamb chops, trimmed, rinsed, and patted dry
2 onions, thinly sliced and separated into rings
6 red-skinned potatoes, peeled and thinly sliced
¼ teaspoon ground thyme
Salt and freshly ground black pepper
1 cup chicken stock

1. Preheat the oven to 400°F. Heat the oil in a Dutch oven or wide pot. Sear the lamb chops on each side over high heat in batches until well browned, about 3 minutes per side. Remove from the pot and set aside.
2. Add the onions and stir constantly over high heat, until they are limp and pale brown. Set aside.
3. Spread half the onions over the bottom of the Dutch oven or a very deep casserole dish. Layer half the meat over the onions. Layer half the potato slices over the meat. Sprinkle the potatoes with the thyme, salt, and pepper.
4. Repeat the layering process. Sprinkle the last layer of potatoes with more salt and pepper. Pour in the chicken stock. Cover the pot or casserole dish. Bake the hotpot for 1½ hours. Remove the lid and bake for another 30 to 45 minutes, until the potatoes turn golden brown.

Serves 6

If you're not partial to lamb, you can use beef instead. Cut 3 pounds of chuck steak into six pieces and proceed with the recipe as directed.

Brown Windsor Soup

Brown Windsor Soup has a bad reputation, which it deserves. The traditional method calls for puréeing the soup, meat and vegetables and all, and then adding a bunch of herbs, including too much thyme, and a ridiculous amount of wine. It's hardly fit for human consumption, and it's hard to imagine why this soup was popular with Queen Victoria. However, three simple but important changes result in a satisfying, delicious soup you can serve as a complete supper, since it has everything in one pot. First, add the meat back to the soup *after* puréeing the rest of the soup. Second, omit the thyme; it gives the soup a very unpleasant flavor. And finally, reduce the wine to a very small amount, which is all that is needed to give a bit of complexity. In fact, the soup is fine without it as well.

3 tablespoons vegetable oil
2 pounds chuck steak, trimmed and cut into ¼-inch dice
1 large onion, finely chopped
¼ cup all-purpose flour
4 14-ounce cans chicken broth
Salt to taste
½ teaspoon dried marjoram
½ teaspoon ground sage
½ teaspoon dried tarragon
2 russet potatoes, peeled and diced into ¼-inch pieces
4 carrots, peeled and diced into ¼-inch pieces
3 celery ribs, cut into ¼-inch dice
Freshly ground black pepper

1. Heat 1 tablespoon of the oil in a Dutch oven or wide pot and add the meat in batches, searing on both sides over high heat 4 to 5 minutes until crusty brown and transferring each batch to a large plate. Add the remaining 2 tablespoons oil to the skillet. Add the chopped onion and cook over medium-low heat until softened, scraping up the fond (the browned bits) from the bottom of the pot with a wooden spoon.

2. Add the flour to the pot and stir until combined. Pour in 2 cans of the chicken broth and stir until well combined. Add the rest of the chicken broth, the salt, and the meat, along with its accumulated juices. Cook over medium-high heat, stirring occasionally, until thickened and bubbling. Reduce the heat and simmer the meat for 1½ hours.

3. Remove the meat from the pot with a slotted spoon and cover to keep it from drying out. Skim the fat off the top of the soup. Add the herbs, potatoes, carrots, celery, and black pepper. Simmer for 1 hour until the vegetables are very soft. Process most of the soup, leaving some chunks. You can do this in a food processor or blender in batches, or you can use an immersion blender and process the soup directly in the pot. Return the meat to the pot. Reheat if necessary.

Serves 6–8

Scotch Broth

This is arguably one of the most delicious soups ever created, but don't follow the original recipe from the 1700s. It called for boiling a chicken with celery and marigolds. Even though the marigold would probably give it a nice color, it wouldn't suit the modern palate.

3 tablespoons vegetable oil

1 pound chuck eye roast, chuck steak, or lamb, cut into ½-inch cubes

1 large onion, finely chopped

4 14-ounce cans chicken broth

½ cup pearl barley

1 tablespoon salt, or more to taste

4 carrots, chopped into ¼-inch dice

1 large turnip, chopped into ¼-inch dice

1 leek, chopped

3 celery ribs, chopped into ¼-inch dice

4 cloves garlic, minced

Freshly ground black pepper

1 cup shredded green cabbage

2 tablespoons chopped fresh parsley

1. Heat 1 tablespoon of the oil in a Dutch oven or wide pot and add the meat in batches, searing on both sides over high heat 4 to 5 minutes until crusty brown and transferring each batch to a large plate. Add the remaining 2 tablespoons oil to the skillet. Add the chopped onion and cook over medium-low heat until softened, scraping up the fond (the browned bits) from the bottom of the pot with a wooden spoon.

2. Add the broth, barley, meat with its accumulated juices, and salt to the pot and stir to combine. The barley will absorb a lot of the salt, so it's a good idea to taste the soup again later and adjust the salt. Simmer for 1½ hours.

3. Add the carrots, turnip, leek, celery, garlic, and black pepper and simmer another hour. Then add the cabbage and parsley and simmer another 30 minutes.

Serves 8

Nine Recipes from the Goblet

(continued)

Cock fighting is a cruel and abhorrent sport, but like it or not, it did take place in days of old (unfortunately also today in some parts of the world). After a fight, the Scots took the dead cock (another word for rooster) and served it up to the sports lovers in a soup made with leeks, barley, and most unusual, prunes. This version includes rice but leaves out the prunes to create a full meal in one dish. If you want a more authentic dish, leave out the rice and add 2 cups pitted prunes to the soup a ½ hour before it finishes cooking.

Cock-a-Leekie

2 teaspoons plus 1 tablespoon
    vegetable oil
6 chicken thighs, rinsed and patted
    dry
1 medium onion, chopped

1 pound leeks, washed and cut into
    ½-inch pieces
6 cups water
½ cup long-grain white rice
Salt and freshly ground black pepper

1. Heat 1 teaspoon oil in a wide pot. Add 3 of the chicken thighs, skin-side down, and cook on both sides until they are golden brown, about 5 minutes per side. Transfer to a large plate. Pour out the fat, wipe out the pot, and add another teaspoon of oil. Repeat for the remaining 3 pieces of chicken.

2. Pour out the rest of the fat, wipe out the pot, and heat the remaining tablespoon oil. Add the onions and cook until they are translucent, scraping up the fond (browned bits) from the bottom of the pot, about 5 minutes. Add the leeks and cook, stirring frequently, for another 5 minutes.

3. Add the water, rice, and chicken. Bring the soup to a boil, then reduce the heat and simmer for about 1 hour, until the chicken is tender. The rice will be completely soft and almost melted into the soup.

4. Remove the chicken from the soup. Using a wide spoon such as a serving spoon, skim the fat off the top of the soup. Remove the chicken meat from the skin and bones and chop into bite-size pieces; then return it to the soup. Season the soup with the salt and pepper.

Serves 8

Nine Recipes from the Goblet

(continued)

Queen Victoria's Soup

1 cup water
¼ cup pearl barley
6 cups chicken stock

1 cup heavy cream
Salt and white pepper to taste

The name says it all. This soup was one of Queen Victoria's favorites, and this recipe is derived from one used by Charles Elmé Francatelli, chief chef to Queen Victoria from 1841 to 1842.

1. Bring the water to a boil in a heavy 2-quart saucepan or soup pot. Add the barley and cook for 5 minutes. Drain the barley and rinse with cold water.
2. Wipe out the pan. Add the chicken stock and the drained barley and bring to a boil. Reduce the heat to a simmer and cook for 1 hour and 15 minutes.
3. Transfer ⅔ of the soup to a large bowl, leaving ⅓ of the soup in the pot. In batches, purée the soup removed to the bowl until very smooth, and then return it to the pot. Add the heavy cream, stir to combine, and season with salt and white pepper to taste.

Serves 6

Lightly Seasoned Broiled Chicken Drumsticks

Harry is happy to bring Sirius chicken legs to eat—poor Sirius has been subsisting on rats while hiding out—but he's not happy to see Sirius. He's worried Sirius will get caught by the Ministry, which believes Sirius is a vicious murderer (see *Harry Potter and the Goblet of Fire*, Chapter 27).

Drumsticks are a popular take-along food because they're good cold and are easy to eat with your fingers. This is about the easiest way to prepare flavorful drumsticks.

1 pound drumsticks
¼ cup olive oil
½ teaspoon salt
¼ teaspoon freshly ground black pepper

1 teaspoon dried rosemary
2 cloves garlic, minced

1. Wash the drumsticks and pat them dry.
2. Whisk together the oil, salt, pepper, rosemary, and garlic.
3. Coat the drumsticks with the mixture and lay them in a 9-inch pan.
4. Broil for 10 minutes on each side, until crisp and golden.

Serves 3

Cornish Pasties

Not quailing under his mother's stern look as he explains how he bluffed his way through his History of Magic exam, Ron reaches for a Cornish pasty on the day Harry is to perform the final task in the Triwizard Tournament (see *Harry Potter and the Goblet of Fire*, Chapter 31).

Also called "tiddy oggies," these pasties were taken by the Cornwall tin miners to work. The mines were a scary place, full of evil, hungry spirits called "knockers." To appease these terrifying beings, the miners threw their crusts (now full of arsenic from their fingers anyway) down the mine shafts. The pasties were a meal in one. Literally. Some women put vegetables in one end, meat in the middle, and fruit in the other end. They also stamped their husband's initials in the corner so each miner could find his pasty on the big oven where the pasties were kept warm until lunchtime.

Pasty Dough

2½ cups all-purpose flour

1 teaspoon salt

2½ sticks cold butter or margarine, cut into chunks

½ to ¾ cup ice water

Filling

8 ounces chuck steak, finely chopped (not ground)

1 potato, finely diced

1 carrot, finely diced

1 small onion, finely chopped

Salt to taste

Freshly ground black pepper to taste

1. Place the flour and salt in the bowl of a food processor and pulse to combine. Scatter the pieces of butter or margarine over the flour mixture. Pulse until the mixture resembles coarse yellow meal without any white powdery bits remaining, about 20 pulses. Transfer the mixture to a large mixing bowl. Sprinkle ½ cup of the water over the mixture and toss with a rubber spatula until the dough sticks together. Add more water 1 tablespoon at a time if the dough is dry (better too wet than too dry). Divide the dough in half, form into disks, wrap in plastic wrap, and chill at least 2 hours or up to 3 days.

2. Just before you are ready to roll out the dough, combine the steak, potatoes, carrots, onion, salt, and pepper in a mixing bowl.

3. Preheat the oven to 425°F. On a floured surface, roll out each circle of dough ⅛ inch thick. Use a saucer to cut out 6-inch circles. Place about ⅓ cup filling in the center of each circle. Moisten the edges of the circles with water. Fold the dough over and crimp the edges with a fork to seal them. Cut slits in the top to make vents.

4. Move the pasties to an ungreased cookie sheet and bake for 10 minutes. Lower the heat to 375°F and bake for 1 hour until golden brown.

Makes 8 pasties

Haggis

Naturally Ron is the one to discover that food is served at the ghostly death day party of Nearly Headless Nick. But the three friends quickly realize that this food is not fit for humans. Among the "delicacies" laid out for the ghosts to view is a rotten haggis covered with crawling maggots (see *Harry Potter and the Chamber of Secrets*, Chapter 8).

Haggis is the national dish of Scotland. Most Americans are not used to the concept of eating the offal (the parts that "fall off" or "off fall" the animal during butchering), which haggis is made of, so you may find this recipe a bit, well, repulsive. The following recipe has not been tested, so proceed at your peril (if you can even find all the ingredients).

1 sheep's heart
1 sheep's lung
1 sheep's liver
2 cups chopped suet
1 cup oatmeal

1 cup chicken broth
1 onion, finely chopped
1 teaspoon salt
½ teaspoon black pepper
Artificial casings

1. Bring a large pot of water to a boil. Finely chop the heart, lung, and liver.
2. Combine the chopped offal with the suet, oatmeal, broth, onion, salt, and pepper, and mix well. Stuff the casings with the mixture, leaving room for the mixture to expand. Tie the casings well with a bit of kitchen twine so water can't get in.
3. Add the haggis to the pot and reduce to a simmer. Simmer for 3 hours, but keep an eye on the haggis. If they look like they're going to burst, prick them with a needle.

Serves 6

Sausage Rolls

The Gryffindors are celebrating. Harry has just successfully completed the first task in the Triwizard Tournament, and Fred and George have snuck food into the common room from the kitchens for what promises to be a great party. But when Harry opens the golden egg at the urging of his curious friends, Neville drops his sausage rolls in fright. He is sure the unearthly wailing coming from the egg is the sound of someone being tortured (see *Harry Potter and the Goblet of Fire*, Chapter 21).

There's not much to be said about the sausage roll, a modern innovation. You might find it at parties or fast-food places, but it greatly resembles the French *rissole*, which is a ground meat mixture baked in puff pastry.

Approximately 1 pound store-bought pre-rolled puff pastry sheets, thawed

Spicy brown mustard, optional

1 pound of your favorite sausages or frankfurters

1 egg beaten with 1 tablespoon water

1. Preheat the oven to 425°F. Grease and flour a cookie sheet or line it with parchment paper.
2. Unroll the puff pastry sheets and cut out eight to ten 4½-inch squares (depending on how many sausages you have). Spread the mustard on each square, if using. Place a sausage at the edge of each square and roll the pastry around each sausage. If the sausages are longer than the squares, the ends will poke out; this rather adds to the appeal.
3. Lay the rolls on the cookie sheet seam-side down and brush with the beaten egg. Cut three slits on top of each sausage roll. Bake for 10 minutes, rotate the pan, then reduce the heat to 375°F and bake another 15 minutes until puffed and golden.

Makes 8–10 rolls

For the filling, you can use the ground beef mixture from the Herbed and Spiced Fried Sausage Patties (Chapter 6) instead of using store-bought sausages.

Black Pudding

Fleur Delacour takes Ron's breath away when she asks for the bouillabaisse. He tells her it's very good, but has to ask Hermione what that "bless-you" stuff is. No thanks, he'll stick to black pudding (see *Harry Potter and the Goblet of Fire*, Chapter 16).

Black pudding, also called blood sausage, is made of blood mixed with animal fat such as suet as well as oats, onion, salt, and seasonings. The mixture is stuffed into casings and boiled in water. You can't make your own, because you can't legally purchase animal blood in the United States, but a recipe for black pudding follows. Since you are more likely to buy a premade pudding, be sure to slice the sausage thickly and reheat it gently, as it's crumbly.

3½ cups blood (pig's or sheep's)
1½ cups shredded suet
1 cup whole milk
⅔ cup oatmeal
3 onions, finely chopped

1 tablespoon salt
½ teaspoon cayenne pepper
1 teaspoon basil
¼ teaspoon nutmeg
Sausage casings

1. Bring a large pot of water to a boil. Mix all the ingredients together in a large mixing bowl. Stuff the casings with the mixture and drop them into the pot. Bring it back to a boil, then reduce the heat and simmer gently for 3 hours.
2. Remove the sausages from the pot and cool. To use, slice thickly and fry on both sides.

Serves 6

The following recipe is based on Black Pudding from TheFoody.com. This recipe has not been tested, so proceed at your own risk! Assuming you can get hold of the blood, of course.

Chicken and Ham Pie

Professor Umbridge is so evil, she must be defied. Right under her nose, Harry secretly trains a group of friends in Defense Against the Dark Arts, but he rebels openly by giving an interview that will be read by the whole school. Seamus Finnigan gobbles up a delicious chicken and ham pie while listening to Harry talk about his interview with Rita Skeeter, and he will finally be convinced Harry's not a "nutter" when he reads the interview in *The Quibbler* (see *Harry Potter and the Order of the Phoenix*, Chapter 26).

There are so many wonderful things you can do with chicken, not least of which is to bake it into a pie. This recipe is easy to prepare and tastes delicious.

Chicken and Ham Pie, Version I, Easy

1 3-pound store-bought rotisserie chicken

2 pounds ham, in one piece or steaks

3 cups prepared or store-bought chicken gravy

1 large onion, chopped

1 teaspoon dried thyme

1 cup frozen peas

1 box refrigerated pie crust, 2 circles in a box

1. Remove the meat from the chicken and discard the skin and bones. Cut the ham into ½-inch strips.
2. Place the chicken gravy in a saucepan and add the chopped onion and thyme. Bring to a simmer and cook for 10 minutes.
3. Adjust the oven rack to the middle position and preheat the oven to 375°F. Place the peas in a bowl. Using a slotted spoon, remove the cooked onions from the chicken gravy and add them to the peas.
4. Place one of the dough circles into an 8- or 9-inch deep-dish pie plate and press it into the bottom and the sides. Place the chicken in the pie pan and top with the peas and cooked onions. Add the ham. Pour the gravy evenly over the filling. Place the other dough circle on top and crimp the edges to seal. Cut two or three 1-inch slits in the top crust to form vents. Place the pie on a baking sheet and place in the oven. Bake for 35 to 45 minutes until brown and bubbly.

Serves 6

Chicken and Ham Pie

(continued)

Chicken and Ham Pie, Version II

1 3-pound chicken, cut into quarters or eighths

2 pounds ham, in one piece or steaks

1 large onion, chopped

2 bay leaves

1 teaspoon dried thyme

3 tablespoons cornstarch

½ cup cold water

1 cup frozen peas

1 box refrigerated pie crust, 2 circles in a box

1. Place the chicken in a heavy pot with the ham, onion, bay leaves, and thyme. Cover with water, bring to a boil, cover, and reduce to a simmer. Simmer for 1½ hours.

2. Remove the chicken and ham from the pot. Remove the bay leaves and discard. Strain the liquid and reserve. Transfer the cooked onions to a small bowl.

3. When the chicken is cool enough to handle, remove the meat from the bones and cut into bite-size pieces. Slice the ham into ½-inch-thick strips.

4. You will need 3 cups of the chicken broth. If you have too much liquid, return it to the pot and boil to reduce the volume to 3 cups. Bring the 3 cups of chicken broth to a boil and reduce to a simmer. Dissolve the cornstarch in the cold water and whisk into the hot chicken broth until thickened.

5. Adjust the oven rack to the middle position and preheat the oven to 375°F. Place one of the dough circles into an 8- or 9-inch deep-dish pie plate and press into the bottom and sides. Place the chicken in the pie plate and top with the peas and cooked onions. Add the ham. Pour the gravy (the thickened chicken broth) evenly over the filling. Place the other dough circle on top and crimp the edges to seal. Cut two or three 1-inch slits in the top crust to form vents. Place the pie on the baking sheet and place in the oven. Bake for 35 to 45 minutes until brown and bubbly.

Serves 6

Chapter Eight

Desserts and Snacks at School

The British are a nation of sugar fiends. (So are the Americans, but that's another story.) So much so that in early times, without dental care like we have today, their teeth rotted and fell out. You really would not have wanted to see them smile. The peasants, ironically, had healthier teeth because sugar was too expensive for them.

"Pudding" is the English word for dessert, and the Pudding King was George I. ("Georgey-Porgey pudding and pie" refers to him.) He insisted he be served Christmas pudding although Oliver Cromwell had banned it because one, it was too sinfully rich (true, especially if you're trying to lose weight) and two, it echoed pagan Celtic customs (also true, the flaming pudding represented the fires the druids and Celts lit at the winter solstice to strengthen the sun).

Here are some of the quaintly named sweets they ate:

- Frumenty, a pudding of wheat kernels cooked in milk and sweetened (it was served at King Henry IV's wedding feast—not the Henry with the six wives; that's Henry VIII).
- Flummery, an oatmeal dish that evolved into a blancmange-type of jelly made with cream or ground almonds.
- Junket, a sweetened curd cheese.

None of these dishes appear in the Harry Potter books; it's just an interesting bit of info.

Desserts and Snacks at School *cont'd*

Of course, the British have also been eating apple pies and custards for eons. So it's no surprise that the desserts at Hogwarts follow the fine English tradition of being sweet, yummy, and unwholesome. The lucky students get fancy desserts on golden platters with each meal. These recipes are fun to make, even more fun to eat, and are okay to have as long as you save them for special occasions.

Lemon Drops

With Harry, it's often a case of being in the wrong place at the wrong time, but when another student is attacked and Harry is yet again found at the scene of the crime, Professor McGonagall decides enough is enough: this is something for Professor Dumbledore to handle. The password to his quarters is "lemon drop"; no surprise there, as he confessed to Professor McGonagall that he was fond of this Muggle sweet (see *Harry Potter and the Chamber of Secrets*, Chapter 11).

¼ cup water
1 cup granulated sugar
½ cup light corn syrup

¼ teaspoon cream of tartar
1 teaspoon lemon extract

*L*emon drops, as you might expect, are lemon-flavored candies. They are basically the same as acid drops, a more sour candy, just prepared with lemon extract instead of citric acid. In England there's a popular sweet called a sherbet lemon, which is a lemon-flavored sucking candy with sherbet powder in the center, but specialized equipment is needed to produce it.

1. Line two baking sheets with parchment paper and set aside. Combine the water, sugar, corn syrup, and cream of tartar in a small saucepan. Cook over medium heat, stirring constantly, until the sugar is dissolved and the mixture begins to bubble. Wash down the sides of the pan with a pastry brush dipped in hot water if sugar crystals have formed on the sides. Clip a candy thermometer to the pan and continue cooking over medium heat, stirring occasionally, until the mixture reaches 300°F.

2. Remove the pan from the heat. Stir in the lemon extract. When the bubbling has subsided, use an oiled teaspoon to drop teaspoonfuls of the sugar syrup onto the prepared sheets.

3. To store the candies, wrap them in sheets of parchment paper, making sure the candies don't touch, as they will stick to each other.

Makes about 40 candies

Peppermint Humbugs

Harry doesn't understand why peppermint humbugs are served along with the roasts and chops and potatoes at his first Hogwarts feast. But it makes sense if you think about it. Maybe the candies were supposed to be like after-dinner mints to freshen your breath (see *Harry Potter and the Sorcerer's Stone*, Chapter 7).

Scrooge's famous "Bah, humbug!" exclamation and peppermint humbugs are unrelated, though some people in England give out humbugs on Christmas as a joke. The only other thing you need to know about a humbug is that it's a type of pulled candy, literally pulled, as you will see in the instructions. Traditional humbugs are striped white and black, but it's easier for home cooks to tint the candy one color. If you make the candy with a friend, double the recipe, divide the hot candy, and tint it two different colors. When the candy is stiff enough, you can twist and pull the two colors together.

⅓ cup water
1 cup granulated sugar
¼ teaspoon cream of tartar
¼ teaspoon peppermint extract
Few drops green food coloring or other desired color

Peppermint Humbugs

(continued)

1. Spray an 8-inch pan with cooking spray and set aside. In a medium saucepan, combine the water, sugar, and cream of tartar and cook over medium-high heat, stirring constantly, until the sugar is dissolved and the mixture begins to boil. If sugar crystals form on the sides of the pan, wash down the sides with a pastry brush dipped in hot water.

2. Clip a candy thermometer to the side of the pot. Reduce the heat to medium and continue cooking, stirring occasionally, until the temperature reaches 260°F. Remove the pan from the heat. Add the peppermint extract and food coloring and mix well.

3. Pour the syrup into the prepared pan. Let the syrup cool for a few minutes. Put on a pair of clean heavy rubber gloves and spray the gloves with cooking spray. Rub your hands together to evenly distribute the oil. If you can tolerate the heat, you can skip the gloves and just oil your hands.

4. Pick up the hot candy and begin pulling it, twisting along the rope as you pull. This will be difficult at first, as the candy will be a mushy glob and will seem to just gloop and droop. Gradually it will stiffen and be easier to pull. Fold the rope in half and then half again and twist and pull again. Repeat and repeat and repeat. As you pull and twist, the candy will begin to look more opaque and will take on a pearlescent sheen, very pretty to behold. When the candy is too stiff to pull, snip the rope at ¾-inch intervals onto a sheet of parchment paper. The candies will look like teeny-weeny pillows. Do not let the humbugs touch each other; instead wrap each piece individually in parchment paper or plastic wrap to prevent sticking. Store in an airtight container. The humbugs will begin to recrystallize after two or three days.

Makes about 20 ¾-inch pieces

Eat these candies with caution. They can really cement your teeth together!

Classic and Unique Ice Cream Flavors

The dessert course at Harry's first Hogwarts feast is a kid's fantasy (or an adult's, if the adult has a sweet tooth). Pies, cakes, tarts—and ice cream in every imaginable flavor—it doesn't get better than that. A separate cookbook would be needed to cover that many ice cream flavors, so this book includes just a small sample of unique or popular British flavors (see *Harry Potter and the Sorcerer's Stone*, Chapter 7).

The Europeans used vanilla to flavor chocolate and tobacco at first, but as everyone knows, it's used today to flavor lots of other things. The most basic ice cream is vanilla, and it can be used as a base for other flavors. See the note for great variations, or use your imagination and come up with your own flavors.

Classic Vanilla Ice Cream

2 cups heavy cream

2 cups whole milk

1 cup granulated sugar

5 large egg yolks

1 tablespoon pure vanilla extract

1. Combine the cream, milk, and sugar in a medium saucepan and cook over medium heat, stirring constantly, until hot but not bubbling. Temper the egg yolks by slowly pouring 1 cup of the hot mixture into the egg yolks while whisking constantly. Pour the egg yolk mixture into the pot while stirring and cook until slightly thickened and steaming, but not bubbling. Remove from the heat.

2. Pour the mixture through a sieve and stir in the vanilla extract. Cover the surface directly with plastic wrap to prevent a skin from forming, and cool to room temperature. Chill until very cold, about 6 hours or overnight. Freeze in an ice cream maker according to the manufacturer's instructions.

Makes about 5 cups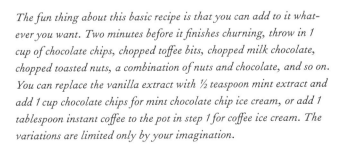

The fun thing about this basic recipe is that you can add to it whatever you want. Two minutes before it finishes churning, throw in 1 cup of chocolate chips, chopped toffee bits, chopped milk chocolate, chopped toasted nuts, a combination of nuts and chocolate, and so on. You can replace the vanilla extract with ½ teaspoon mint extract and add 1 cup chocolate chips for mint chocolate chip ice cream, or add 1 tablespoon instant coffee to the pot in step 1 for coffee ice cream. The variations are limited only by your imagination.

Classic and Unique Ice Cream Flavors

(continued)

Tea Ice Cream

People often think of tea ice cream as using green tea and hailing from Asia, but the truth is that traditional British cookbooks with an ice cream section invariably include a tea flavor.

2 cups whole milk

10 bags black tea

2 tablespoons pure instant tea, unsweetened

2 cups heavy cream

1 cup granulated sugar

5 large egg yolks

1. Heat the milk in a medium saucepan over medium heat until it's hot but not bubbling. Remove from the heat, add the tea bags and instant tea, and steep for 10 minutes. Remove the tea bags and discard. Add the cream and sugar and return to the heat.

2. Cook over medium heat, stirring constantly, until hot but not bubbling. Temper the egg yolks by slowly pouring 1 cup of the hot mixture into the egg yolks while whisking constantly. Pour the egg yolk mixture into the pot while stirring and cook until slightly thickened and steaming, but not bubbling. Remove from the heat.

3. Pour the mixture through a sieve. Cover the surface directly with plastic wrap to prevent a skin from forming, and cool to room temperature. Chill until very cold, about 6 hours or overnight. Freeze in an ice cream maker according to the manufacturer's instructions.

Makes about 5 cups

Classic and Unique Ice Cream Flavors

(continued)

Brown Bread Ice Cream

About 4 slices cinnamon bread
2 cups heavy cream
2 cups whole milk

1 cup packed dark brown sugar
5 large egg yolks
¾ teaspoon rum extract

1. Process the bread in a food processor until it turns into crumbs. Measure out ½ cup, spread it on a baking sheet, and toast until dark brown but not burned. Cool to room temperature.
2. Combine the cream, milk, and brown sugar in a medium saucepan and cook over medium heat, stirring constantly, until hot but not bubbling. Temper the egg yolks by slowly pouring 1 cup of the hot mixture into the egg yolks while whisking constantly. Pour the egg yolk mixture into the pot while stirring and cook until slightly thickened and steaming, but not bubbling. Remove from the heat.
3. Pour the mixture through a sieve and stir in the rum extract. Cover the surface with plastic wrap to prevent a skin from forming, and cool to room temperature. Chill until very cold, about 6 hours or overnight. Freeze in an ice cream maker according to the manufacturer's instructions. Add the bread crumbs and churn another 2 minutes before transferring to an airtight container and placing in the freezer.

Makes about 5½ cups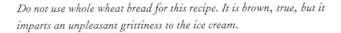

Do not use whole wheat bread for this recipe. It is brown, true, but it imparts an unpleasant grittiness to the ice cream.

Can't think what to do with the bread that's going stale on the counter? Don't throw it out—use it in your next batch of ice cream instead. It sounds like a strange combination, but British cookbooks have been giving recipes for it since the first recipe appeared in a cookbook in 1772.

Classic and Unique Ice Cream Flavors

(continued)

Apple Crumble is a popular dessert, and if you serve it with ice cream anyway, why not just combine the two? This is one of the best ice creams you'll ever eat.

Apple Crumble Ice Cream

Apple "Filling"

¼ stick (2 tablespoons) butter

1 tart apple, such as Granny Smith, peeled, cored, and chopped into ¼-inch pieces

1 sweet apple, such as Gala, peeled, cored, and chopped into ¼-inch pieces

2 tablespoons dark brown sugar

¼ teaspoon cinnamon

Crumble "Topping"

½ cup all-purpose flour

2 tablespoons dark brown sugar

2 tablespoons granulated sugar

½ teaspoon cinnamon

⅛ teaspoon ground nutmeg

½ stick (4 tablespoons) butter, chilled and cut into small pieces

Ice Cream

1½ cups heavy cream

1½ cups whole milk

⅔ cup granulated sugar

3 large egg yolks

2 teaspoons pure vanilla extract

Classic and Unique Ice Cream Flavors

(continued)

1. For the apples, heat the butter in a skillet and add the apples, brown sugar, and cinnamon. Cook over medium-high heat, stirring and scraping constantly, until the apples are softened and caramelized, about 10 minutes. Remove from the heat, cool to room temperature, and chill until cold.

2. For the crumble, preheat the oven to 350°F. Whisk together the flour, sugars, cinnamon, and nutmeg. Rub in the butter with your fingertips until the mixture resembles wet sand. Spread the mixture on a baking sheet and bake 15 to 20 minutes until crisp and golden. Cool to room temperature, then chill until cold, uncovered to keep it from getting soft.

3. For the ice cream, combine the cream, milk, and sugar in a medium saucepan and cook over medium heat, stirring constantly, until hot but not bubbling. Temper the egg yolks by slowly pouring ½ cup of the hot mixture into the egg yolks while whisking constantly. Pour the egg yolk mixture into the pot while stirring and cook until slightly thickened and steaming, but not bubbling. Remove from the heat.

4. Pour the mixture through a sieve and stir in the vanilla extract. Cover the surface with plastic wrap to prevent a skin from forming, and cool to room temperature. Chill until very cold, about 6 hours or overnight. Freeze in an ice cream maker according to the manufacturer's instructions. Add the apples and crumble and churn another 2 minutes before transferring to an airtight container and placing in the freezer.

Makes about 6 cups

Classic and Unique Ice Cream Flavors

(continued)

Mincemeat Ice Cream

This is a great way to use up your mincemeat filling if you're making mince pies—and if you don't want the bother of making the ice cream itself, just soften a quart of store-bought vanilla ice cream, fold in the mincemeat filling, and refreeze the ice cream until firm.

1½ cups heavy cream
1½ cups whole milk
⅔ cup granulated sugar
3 large egg yolks

2 teaspoons pure vanilla extract
1 cup mincemeat filling from Mince Pies (Chapter 5)

1. Combine the cream, milk, and sugar in a medium saucepan and cook over medium heat, stirring constantly, until hot but not bubbling. Temper the egg yolks by slowly pouring ½ cup of the hot mixture into the egg yolks while whisking constantly. Pour the egg yolk mixture into the pot while stirring and cook until slightly thickened and steaming, but not bubbling. Remove from the heat.

2. Pour the mixture through a sieve and stir in the vanilla extract. Cover the surface with plastic wrap to prevent a skin from forming, and cool to room temperature. Chill until very cold, about 6 hours or overnight. Freeze in an ice cream maker according to the manufacturer's instructions. Fold in the mincemeat filling with a rubber spatula before transferring ice cream to an airtight container and placing in the freezer.

Makes about 5 cups

This is a surprisingly good recipe. Rather than folding in a cup of crumbled Christmas pudding, as some recipes suggest, this recipe imitates the flavors of the famous pudding by incorporating some of the ingredients that go into making it.

Christmas Pudding Ice Cream

1½ cups heavy cream

1½ cups whole milk

¾ cup packed dark brown sugar

2 cinnamon sticks

About 10 whole cloves

About 10 whole allspice

3 large egg yolks

¾ teaspoon rum extract

¼ cup dark raisins

¼ cup golden raisins

¼ cup dried currants or dried
    sweetened cranberries

½ cup chopped toasted almonds

1. Combine the cream, milk, brown sugar, cinnamon sticks, cloves, and allspice in a medium saucepan and cook over medium heat, stirring constantly, until hot but not bubbling. Temper the egg yolks by slowly pouring ½ cup of the hot mixture into the egg yolks while whisking constantly. Pour the egg yolk mixture into the pot while stirring and cook until slightly thickened and steaming, but not bubbling. Remove from the heat and stir in the rum extract.

2. Pour the mixture through a sieve. Cover the surface with plastic wrap to prevent a skin from forming, and cool to room temperature. Chill until very cold, about 6 hours or overnight.

3. Freeze in an ice cream maker according to the manufacturer's instructions. Add the dried fruits and the almonds and churn another 2 minutes before transferring to an airtight container and placing in the freezer.

Makes about 5½ cups

Chocolate Custard Trifle with Toffee Crunch

Whenever Hagrid pats someone, the result is usually dramatic, meaning the recipient gets knocked down. So when Hagrid shows his appreciation to Harry and Ron for getting him out of Azkaban, he pushes them into their plates of trifle (see *Harry Potter and the Chamber of Secrets*, Chapter 18).

Although the classic trifle should be some kind of cake or biscuit placed in the bottom of a dish, wetted with wine, and then layered over with custard or fruit and whipped cream, trifle appears so many times in the Harry Potter books that a chocolate variation is called for. Any chocoholic will agree!

1 recipe Chocolate Cake from Harry's First Birthday Cake, baked and cooled (Chapter 4)
1 recipe Chocolate Glaze from Chocolate Éclairs, prepared with 1 teaspoon instant coffee

1 recipe Chocolate Pastry Cream from Chocolate Éclairs, prepared and chilled
1 cup heavy cream
¼ cup confectioners' sugar
1 teaspoon pure vanilla extract
1 cup toffee bits

1. Place 1 cake layer in the bottom of a round 9-inch serving dish, preferably clear glass, about 3 inches deep. Eat the other cake layer as you work.
2. Pour the glaze over the cake layer and spread to the edges of the dish. Allow it to harden (you can refrigerate it for a few minutes to speed it up), then pour the pastry cream on top of the glaze and spread it to the edges. Cover the surface with plastic wrap and refrigerate until cold, or up to 2 days.
3. Before serving, combine the heavy cream, sugar, and vanilla extract in a large mixing bowl and beat until stiff peaks form. Remove the plastic wrap and spread or pipe the whipped cream over the chocolate pastry cream. Sprinkle the toffee bits on top and serve.

Serves 8 to 10

You can simplify this recipe by using chocolate cake mix and instant chocolate pudding. It won't be as good, but it will look impressive. And if you're still a kid, or a kid at heart, you'll enjoy it anyway.

Jam Doughnuts

The whole ordeal is over. The monster behind the mysterious attacks has been destroyed—by Harry Potter, of course—and Harry's good name, as well as Hagrid's, is restored. The feast following Harry's recuperation is one of the best he's ever seen, and life just gets better when Professor Dumbledore announces, while Ron eats a jam doughnut, that Lockhart is leaving for good (see *Harry Potter and the Chamber of Secrets*, Chapter 18).

Do oily cakes sound appetizing? Well, that's what the Dutch settlers called them (*oeliekoeken*) when they introduced these little fried cakes in America. In England, when most people celebrate Pancake Day, the residents of the town of Baldock (about 30 miles north of London) celebrate their own version, called Doughnut Day. In England the most popular type of doughnut has no hole and is filled with jam.

½ cup warm water

4½ teaspoons (2 packets) dry yeast

1 tablespoon granulated sugar

1 stick (8 tablespoons) butter

1 cup whole milk

2 large eggs

5 cups all-purpose flour

⅔ cup granulated sugar

1½ teaspoons salt

4 cups peanut oil (see note)

Raspberry jam, for filling (pastry bag with metal tip required)

Confectioner's sugar, for dusting

Jam Doughnuts

(continued)

1. Combine the water, yeast, and 1 tablespoon sugar in a mixing bowl and let it stand until the yeast is dissolved and the mixture is puffy. Heat the butter and milk in the microwave or in a small saucepan over low heat until the butter is melted. Whisk the eggs into the milk mixture.

2. In the bowl of an electric mixer, combine the flour, sugar, and salt. Whisk together the milk and yeast mixtures and pour it into the flour mixture. Attach the dough hook and knead the dough on the slowest speed for about 10 minutes; after the first few minutes the dough should clean the sides of the bowl. If the dough is very sticky, add more flour ¼ cup at a time. Remove the dough from the mixer and knead it for 30 seconds on a lightly dusted surface. You can also knead this dough by hand, either in the bowl or on a floured surface. Transfer the dough to an oiled bowl, turning to coat the dough on all sides. Cover the dough with plastic wrap and leave it to rise in a warm, draft-free place, about 1½ to 2 hours, until doubled in size.

3. Remove the dough from the bowl and roll it out ½-inch thick on a floured surface. Cut circles of dough with a 3-inch cutter. Cut the remaining scraps into 3-inch pieces. Place the dough circles and scraps on a piece of floured parchment paper and leave them to rise for 1½ to 2 hours until doubled in size.

4. Line two or three baking sheets with four layers of paper towels. Clip a candy thermometer onto a 4-quart pot and pour in the peanut oil. Heat the oil over a medium flame until the thermometer registers 350°F (or a piece of bread dropped in the oil bubbles instantly but doesn't turn dark brown right away).

5. Carefully place three or four doughnuts into the oil. Fry until golden, about 1 to 1½ minutes per side. Bring the temperature back up to 350°F between batches. Transfer the doughnuts with a metal slotted spatula to the paper-towel-lined baking sheets. Repeat until all the doughnuts and scraps are fried.

6. Sift the confectioners' sugar generously over the warm doughnuts. When the doughnuts are cool, fill a pastry bag fitted with a plain metal tip with the jam. Plunge the tip into the bottom of each doughnut and squirt in a small amount of jam.

Makes about 1½ dozen doughnuts

If you plan to make these doughnuts often, it is worthwhile to invest $5 in a flavor injector, the kind with a sharp needlelike squirter. If you use one of these, plunge the needle tip through the side; it will leave a barely detectable hole.

Apple Pie

Harry is furious. He just lost his temper with Professor Umbridge, and when he enters the Great Hall for dinner everyone's talking about it. Unable to eat, he angrily asks why no one believes Dumbledore anymore. An equally angry but sympathetic Hermione forcefully suggests they leave the Great Hall, and a hungry Ron sadly leaves his apple pie behind (see *Harry Potter and the Order of the Phoenix*, Chapter 13).

Apple pie's always been a favorite dessert, so much so that Elizabethan playwright Robert Greene complimented the ladies by comparing their breath to apple pies. Don't try it on your girlfriend, though. If you tell her, "Thy breath is like the steame of apple pyes," she will run very fast in the other direction.

Pie Crust

2½ cups all-purpose flour

3 tablespoons granulated sugar

½ teaspoon salt

1¼ sticks (10 tablespoons) cold butter, cut into chunks

10 tablespoons vegetable shortening, chilled and cut into chunks

½ cup ice water

Filling

8 Granny Smith apples, peeled, cored, and chopped

Juice and grated zest of 1 lemon

¾ cup granulated sugar

1 teaspoon ground cinnamon

¼ teaspoon ground nutmeg

1 egg, lightly beaten, to brush over the crust

Sugar, for sprinkling the crust

Apple Pie

(continued)

1. For the crust, place the flour, sugar, and salt in the bowl of a food processor and pulse to combine. Scatter the pieces of butter and shortening over the flour mixture. Pulse until the mixture resembles coarse yellow meal without any white powdery bits remaining, about 20 pulses. Transfer the mixture to a large mixing bowl. Sprinkle ½ cup water over the mixture and toss with a rubber spatula until the dough sticks together. Add more water 1 tablespoon at a time if the dough is dry (better too wet than too dry). Divide the dough in half, form into disks, wrap in plastic wrap, and chill at least 2 hours or up to 3 days.

2. To assemble and bake the pie, adjust the oven rack to the lowest position and place a baking sheet on the rack. Preheat the oven to 350°F.

3. Remove one of the disks of dough from the refrigerator and roll it out on a floured surface to an 11-inch circle. Fold the dough into quarters, brushing off the excess flour with a pastry brush after each fold. Unfold the dough inside a 9-inch pie pan. Trim the overhang to 1 inch. Put the pan in the refrigerator while preparing the filling.

4. Combine the filling ingredients and pour them into the prepared crust, mounding the apples in the center.

5. Remove the second disk of dough from the refrigerator and roll it out on a floured surface to a 10-inch circle. Fold the dough into quarters and then unfold it onto the pie. Trim the dough even with the edges of the pan. Fold the overhang over the edges of the top crust and crimp it to seal the edges, either by pressing down with the tines of a fork or by pinching with your fingers. If desired, cut out shapes of leaves from the scraps of dough and attach them with a little water.

6. Brush the beaten egg over the crust with a pastry brush. Cut slits in the top crust to form air vents. Sprinkle the crust generously with sugar. Place the pie in the oven in the middle of the baking sheet (the baking sheet will catch drips and prevent smoking). Bake the pie for 1½ to 2 hours, or until the crust is golden and the juices are bubbling out.

Serves 8

A helpful hint to prevent a soggy crust and soupy filling: put the filling ingredients into a pot and bring to a simmer. Simmer for about 20 minutes until the apples are softened and release their juices. Drain the filling thoroughly and cool to room temperature before using. You may need to reduce the baking time by ½ hour.

Treacle Tart

Ron and Hermione are quarreling. Again. Hermione is furious because Ron can't apologize for insulting Nearly Headless Nick—his mouth is stuffed too full of food. Harry's not getting involved. He'd rather enjoy his dinner, finishing off with his favorite dessert of treacle tart (see *Harry Potter and the Order of the Phoenix*, Chapter 11).

Treacle tart is a favorite dessert in England—and is also Harry Potter's. If you're a fan of pecan pie, chances are you'll love the similar chewy texture and over-the-top sweetness of treacle tart. For a truly decadent dessert, serve it warm with a scoop of vanilla ice cream on top. It's also delicious with warm custard.

Tart Crust

2½ cups all-purpose flour

1 cup confectioners' sugar

½ teaspoon salt

2 sticks cold butter, cut into chunks

2 cold large egg yolks

⅓ cup cold heavy cream

1 teaspoon pure vanilla extract

Filling

1 cup golden syrup or light molasses or corn syrup

2¼ cups fresh bread crumbs

Grated zest and juice of 1 lemon

1 egg, beaten with 1 tablespoon water, for brushing over the crust

Treacle Tart

(continued)

1. For the crust, place the flour, confectioners' sugar, and salt in the bowl of a food processor and pulse to combine. Scatter the pieces of butter over the flour mixture. Pulse until the mixture resembles coarse yellow meal without any white powdery bits remaining, about 20 pulses. Transfer the mixture to a large mixing bowl. Beat the egg yolks with the cream and vanilla and pour them into the flour-butter mixture. Toss with a spatula until the dough clumps together. If the dough is dry, add 1 more tablespoon heavy cream (better too wet than too dry). Divide the dough in half, form into disks, wrap in plastic wrap, and chill at least 2 hours or up to 3 days.

2. Just before you are ready to roll out the dough, prepare the filling. Warm the golden syrup in a saucepan until it is runny, or microwave it for 1 minute. Combine the golden syrup, bread crumbs, lemon zest, and lemon juice in a mixing bowl and mix well.

3. Preheat the oven to 400°F. Remove the dough from the refrigerator. On a floured surface, roll out the larger disk to an 11-inch circle. Fold it into quarters, brush off the excess flour with a pastry brush after each fold, then unfold it into a 9-inch tart pan, easing the sides gently into the pan and pressing the dough into the fluted edges. Trim the dough even with the rim. Roll out the second disk ⅛-inch thick. Cut the dough in long strips for the lattice topping.

4. Scrape the filling into the prepared crust and smooth the top with a rubber spatula. Lay half the strips of dough over the filling in one direction and the other half in the opposite direction to form a lattice. Trim the overhang. Gently brush the beaten egg over the lattice.

5. Bake for 10 minutes, then reduce the temperature to 375°F and bake another 25 minutes until the crust is browned and the filling puffs up in the center. Serve warm with custard or whipped cream.

Serves 8

Tart dough is hard to roll out because it is sticky and tears easily. Make sure the surface you work on is generously floured. If the dough sticks, simply scrape it off, clump it back together, and reroll it. If the dough breaks or tears, don't worry. You can easily patch it in the pan with extra pieces of dough and a bit of water.

Chocolate Éclairs

To show his gratitude to Dobby for the gillyweed that saved him in the second task, Harry descends to the Hogwarts kitchens, where Dobby works, to give him a pair of socks (Dobby's favorite gift). In the kitchen, Hermione is disgusted by Ron's greed. Why he's asking for éclairs when he's just had breakfast is beyond her. But the house-elves are delighted to present him with a huge platter-full (see *Harry Potter and the Goblet of Fire*, Chapter 28).

Éclair comes from the French word for "lightning," but how it's related to this yummy dessert is anybody's guess. Perhaps it's because it disappears as quickly as lightning.

Choux Pastry

1 cup water
½ stick (4 tablespoons) butter
¼ teaspoon salt
1 tablespoon granulated sugar
1 cup all-purpose flour
4 large eggs
Pastry bag for forming éclairs

Chocolate Pastry Cream

1 cup whole milk
½ cup heavy cream or whole milk
1 tablespoon cornstarch
1 tablespoon unsweetened cocoa powder
½ cup granulated sugar
Pinch salt
3 large egg yolks
1 teaspoon pure vanilla extract
2 ounces bittersweet chocolate, chopped
2 tablespoons butter ONLY if using all milk

Chocolate Glaze

½ cup heavy cream
6 ounces bittersweet chocolate, chopped

Chocolate Éclairs

(continued)

1. For the choux pastry, combine the water, butter, salt, and sugar in a small saucepan and bring to a boil. Reduce the heat and add the flour all at once, mixing quickly with a wooden spoon until the mixture pulls away from the sides of the pot and forms a ball around the spoon. Transfer the dough to the bowl of a stand mixer and allow it to cool slightly.

2. Add the eggs one at a time, beating after each until combined, and scraping down the sides of the bowl.

3. Preheat the oven to 425°F and grease and flour a baking sheet. Cut a 1½-inch slit at the edge of a disposable pastry bag and fill it with the choux paste. Pipe 3-inch logs onto the baking sheet in two rows of six or seven each. Bake for 15 minutes, rotating the baking sheet halfway through the baking time. Reduce the heat to 375°F and bake another 20 minutes, again rotating halfway through the baking time, until the éclairs are puffed and golden. It's better to overbake than to underbake, as the éclairs will collapse and be impossible to fill if they are underbaked. Remove from the oven and cool to room temperature. After they are cooled, the shells can be sealed in an airtight container or zipper bag and frozen for 2 months. They should not be unwrapped until they are completely defrosted, or they will turn soggy from the condensation.

4. To make the pastry cream, combine the milk, heavy cream if using, cornstarch, cocoa powder, sugar, and salt in a medium saucepan and cook over medium-high heat, stirring constantly, until hot but not bubbling. Reduce the heat. Slowly pour ½ cup of the hot mixture into the egg yolks while whisking constantly, then pour the egg yolk mixture into the saucepan while stirring constantly. Return the heat to medium-high and cook, stirring constantly, until the mixture is thick and bubbling. Remove from the heat.

5. Add the vanilla and chocolate (and butter, if using all milk). Stir to combine. Pour the mixture through a sieve, using a rubber spatula to push it through. Cover the surface directly with plastic wrap to prevent a skin from forming, and cool to room temperature. Refrigerate until cold, or up to 2 days.

6. To make the glaze, combine the cream and chocolate in a microwave-safe bowl. Microwave on high for 2 minutes, stopping the microwave and stirring every 30 seconds; then stir until smooth. Cool until it is thick enough to spread.

7. To assemble the éclairs, split them in half with a knife. Fill the bottom halves with about 2 tablespoons of the pastry cream. Replace the top halves and spread with about 2 teaspoons of the glaze. Allow the glaze to set. Éclairs are best eaten right after the glaze has set. They can be refrigerated for a few days, but they will be a bit soggy.

Makes 12 to 14

Choux pastry, or pâte à choux (pronounced pott-ah-SHOO), is a sticky dough used to make cream puffs and éclairs, among other baked or fried goods, such as beignets. "Choux" comes from the French word for "cabbage" and is so named because it was used in France to make little cakes that looked like cabbages.

Banana Fritters with Caramel Sauce

As far as we know, no one actually eats banana fritters in the Harry Potter books; it's just the password to get through the portrait of the Fat Lady to the Gryffindor common room. Maybe the Fat Lady liked 'em (see *Harry Potter and the Goblet of Fire*, Chapter 25).

The Romans used to make a type of fritter similar to funnel cakes; it's amazing how in some ways the food we eat has changed so little. Even this medieval recipe for fritters (spelled *frytours*) sounds familiar (except for the parsnips): "Take skyrwater [whatever that is] and pasternakes [parsnips] and apples and parboil them, make a batter of flour and eggs, cast thereto ale and saffron and salt, wet them in the batter and fry them in oil or in grease, do thereto almond milk and serve it forth."

Caramel Sauce

½ cup granulated sugar

2 tablespoons water

½ cup heavy cream

1 tablespoon butter

½ teaspoon pure vanilla extract

Banana Fritters

½ cup all-purpose flour

1 teaspoon baking powder

Pinch salt

2 large eggs

2 tablespoons granulated sugar

2 tablespoons butter, melted and cooled

2 tablespoons whole milk

Oil for frying

3 ripe but firm bananas, sliced at an angle into ¼-inch slices

Banana Fritters with Caramel Sauce

(continued)

1. For the caramel sauce, in a small saucepan, cook the sugar and water over medium heat, stirring constantly, until the sugar dissolves and the mixture begins to bubble. Continue cooking over medium-high heat, stirring occasionally, until the mixture turns a deep amber color.

2. Remove the pan from the heat and add the cream and butter; the mixture will bubble up violently. Stir until it turns back to liquid; if hard lumps of the caramelized sugar remain, stir over low heat until they liquefy. Add the vanilla and stir to combine. Keep warm until ready to serve.

3. Whisk together the flour, baking powder, and salt in a large mixing bowl. In a separate bowl, whisk the eggs with the sugar until combined. Add the melted butter to the egg mixture and whisk until combined. Add the egg mixture to the flour mixture and whisk until smooth. Add the milk and whisk until smooth.

4. Fill a large skillet with enough oil to come ¼-inch up the sides. Heat the oil until it begins to shimmer. Using a fork, coat the banana slices in the batter, lift the slices out, and place them in the hot oil. Fry on both sides until golden brown, about 1 minute per side. Remove from the pan to a paper-towel-lined plate to drain. Repeat until all the banana slices are used up.

5. To serve, place 4 to 6 fritters on a dessert plate and drizzle with the warm caramel sauce. Serve immediately, as the fritters don't keep well and turn soggy quickly. Also, the bananas will turn black and be inedible.

Serves 6

You can skip the sauce or serve the fritters with a chocolate sauce instead: Heat ½ cup heavy cream and pour it over 4 ounces chopped bittersweet chocolate. Let it stand a few minutes and then stir until smooth. The sauce will stiffen as it cools; you can reheat it gently over a low flame or in a microwave.

Rice Pudding

The list of desserts served at Harry's first Hogwarts feast makes your mouth water. Among the many foods that suddenly appear on the table is rice pudding (see *Harry Potter and the Sorcerer's Stone*, Chapter 7).

Rice pudding has traveled around, beginning as a dessert for the very rich in medieval times and ending up as the plain-Jane of desserts today. Rice pudding is good, but really isn't anything to make a fuss about. It's a nice ending to an ordinary weeknight dinner, but is not recommended as dessert for a formal affair.

½ cup white rice (short grain preferred, but long-grain also works)
4 cups whole milk
½ cup granulated sugar
¼ teaspoon salt
2 tablespoons butter
2 teaspoons pure vanilla extract
¼ teaspoon ground nutmeg

1. Preheat the oven to 300°F and grease a 2-quart baking dish. Combine the rice, milk, sugar, and salt in a large saucepan and bring to a boil. Reduce the heat and simmer for 15 minutes, stirring occasionally.

2. Remove the pan from the heat and add the butter, vanilla, and nutmeg. Stir to combine. Pour the mixture into the baking dish and bake for 1 hour, stirring every 20 minutes or so. Bake another 30 to 45 minutes until spotty golden brown. Serve warm or at room temperature with whipped cream or vanilla ice cream or jam.

Serves 4 to 6

Spotted Dick

Hermione refuses to eat after discovering that enslaved house-elves cooked her food. Ron has no such qualms and naughtily tries to tempt her with spotted dick (see *Harry Potter and the Goblet of Fire*, Chapter 12).

This is one dish that makes a lot of Harry Potter fans wonder what in the world is that? It's an old-fashioned Victorian-era suet pudding (suet being the hard fat that encases beef kidneys). The story of its name is not very exciting: It's called "spotted" because it's spotted with raisins and "dick" because that's a Victorian word that means "pudding." Don't worry about where to find suet: This recipe uses butter, which makes a fine substitute.

2 cups all-purpose flour
2 cups fresh bread crumbs (see note)
1 cup granulated sugar
2 teaspoons baking powder
1 teaspoon salt
2 teaspoons ground cinnamon
½ teaspoon ground nutmeg
¼ teaspoon ground cloves
2 sticks cold butter, cut into pieces
½ cup dark raisins
½ cup golden raisins
1 cup dried currants or cranberries
¾ cup whole milk

1. Fill a large pot with water and place a rack or overturned shallow bowl in the pot. Bring to a simmer. Grease a 2-quart heatproof bowl with a tight-fitting lid and set it aside.
2. Whisk together the flour, bread crumbs, sugar, baking powder, salt, and spices in a large mixing bowl. Rub in the butter until the mixture resembles coarse meal with some larger pieces of butter remaining. Toss in the raisins and currants or cranberries. Pour in the milk and fold it in until the mixture is uniformly moistened. Turn out the mixture into the prepared dish and press the top down with a spatula.
3. Cover the dish with the lid, making sure it is tightly sealed. Place it in the pot; the water should come halfway up the sides of the dish. Steam for 3 hours. Add water to replenish as necessary. Remove the pudding, remove the lid, and invert it onto a plate. Serve warm with warm custard.

Serves 8

To make fresh bread crumbs, process 6 to 8 slices fresh bread in a food processor or blender. There is no need to remove the crusts.

No-Bake Chocolate-Bottom Pumpkin Tart

Harry, Ron, and Hermione can hardly wait for the pumpkin tart to be cleared away so they can rush over to Hagrid and congratulate him on his new position as Care of Magical Creatures teacher. Now that his name has finally been cleared, thanks to our dauntless trio, Hagrid is a qualified wizard and can fulfill his life-long dream to teach (see *Harry Potter and the Prisoner of Azkaban*, Chapter 5).

Most people associate pumpkin with pie, but the tart is a close relative. The only difference is that tarts are shallower than pies with straight rather than flared sides and use a richer dough than standard pie crusts.

Tart Dough

1 cup all-purpose flour

⅛ teaspoon salt

3 tablespoons granulated sugar

¾ stick (6 tablespoons) cold butter or margarine, cut into pieces

1 large egg yolk

2 tablespoons heavy cream

1 teaspoon vanilla

Chocolate Bottom

½ cup heavy cream

4 ounces bittersweet chocolate, chopped

Pumpkin Filling

1½ cups canned pumpkin, not pumpkin pie filling

½ cup granulated sugar

½ teaspoon ground cinnamon

⅛ teaspoon ground allspice

⅛ teaspoon ground cloves

⅛ teaspoon ground nutmeg

½ cup heavy cream

2 large eggs

1 tablespoon cornstarch

1½ ounces bittersweet chocolate, melted, for drizzling, optional

No-Bake Chocolate-Bottom Pumpkin Tart

(continued)

1. To make the dough, place the flour, salt, and sugar in the bowl of a food processor and pulse a few times to combine. Scatter the butter pieces over the flour and pulse about 15 times until the mixture resembles coarse yellow meal. Transfer the mixture to a large mixing bowl.

2. Whisk together the egg yolk, cream, and vanilla and pour over the flour mixture. Toss with a rubber spatula until the dough begins to stick together. Knead very briefly to form a cohesive mass and form into a disk. Wrap in plastic wrap and refrigerate 2 hours or up to 3 days.

3. Preheat the oven to 425°F. On a generously floured surface, roll out the disk (make sure you flour the top of the disk as well) to an 11-inch circle. Tart dough is hard to roll out, but this is a very forgiving dough, especially if you use margarine in place of the butter. Simply gather up the torn dough, re-flour the work surface, briefly knead the dough into a ball, and roll it out again. Fit the dough into a 9-inch tart pan. If the dough breaks, you can patch it by gluing extra scraps with a bit of water. Prick the bottom of the shell with a fork, line with aluminum foil, and fill with beans or pie weights. Bake for 20 minutes or until the dough is dry and set. Remove the foil and weights, reduce the heat to 350°F, and bake another 7 to 10 minutes until the crust is golden brown. Remove from the oven to cool.

4. To make the chocolate bottom, place the cream and chocolate in a microwave-safe bowl and microwave on high for 2 minutes, stopping to stir every 30 seconds. Stir until smooth and pour into the bottom of the tart shell. Cool until set.

5. To make the filling, combine the pumpkin, sugar, cinnamon, allspice, cloves, nutmeg, and heavy cream in a medium saucepan and cook, stirring frequently, until hot but not bubbling. Whisk the eggs with the cornstarch and add to the pan. Continue cooking, stirring constantly, until thickened and bubbling. Remove from the heat. Cool to room temperature.

6. Pour the cooled filling into the tart shell and smooth the top with a rubber spatula. If desired, drizzle melted chocolate on top. Refrigerate until firm.

Serves 8

Creamy, Dreamy Chocolate Gateau

The best foods are always served at the Hogwarts feasts, especially the start-of-term feasts, and the one in Harry's sixth year at Hogwarts is no exception. While Harry goes for his usual treacle tart, Ron reaches for the chocolate gateau (see *Harry Potter and the Half-Blood Prince*, Chapter 8).

Gateau is the French word for "cake," but there is a difference. Most Britons don't know this, but in England "gateau" refers to a cake in which the filling is the main point, and the cake is just a structure to support it. The cake layers would be some sort of unremarkable sponge cake. To make an especially decadent gateau, this recipe uses rich chocolate layers *plus* a rich filling, so you get the best of both worlds.

1 recipe Rich Chocolate Cake, baked, cooled, and split into 3 layers (recipe follows)
1 recipe Chocolate Pastry Cream from Chocolate Éclairs, prepared and cooled
1 recipe Chocolate Glaze from Chocolate Éclairs, prepared and cooled until thick enough to spread

Chocolate Whipped Cream

1 cup heavy cream
¼ cup confectioners' sugar
1 teaspoon vanilla extract
2 ounces bittersweet chocolate, melted
½ chopped, toasted pecans, for topping

1. Combine the heavy cream, sugar, and vanilla in a large mixing bowl and beat until stiff peaks form. Whisk ¼ of the whipped cream into the melted chocolate to lighten it, then fold the rest of the whipped cream into the melted chocolate.

2. To assemble the gateau, place 1 cake layer on a cardboard round or platter. Spread ½ of the chocolate whipped cream over the cake layer, then ½ of the chocolate pastry cream over the whipped cream. Repeat with another cake layer. Top with the last cake layer. Spread the glaze over the top layer and sprinkle the chopped pecans on top.

Creamy, Dreamy Chocolate Gateau

(continued)

Rich Chocolate Cake

1 cup boiling water

¾ cup unsweetened cocoa powder

1½ teaspoons instant coffee

1¼ cups all-purpose flour

1½ teaspoons baking powder

½ teaspoon salt

1½ sticks (12 tablespoons) butter, at room temperature

1½ cups granulated sugar

½ cup packed dark brown sugar

3 large eggs, at room temperature

1½ teaspoons pure vanilla extract

1. Preheat the oven to 350°F. Grease and flour a 9-inch round cake pan and line the bottom with parchment paper.
2. Whisk together the boiling water, cocoa powder, and instant coffee in a small bowl until smooth; set aside. In a separate bowl, whisk together the flour, baking powder, and salt, and set aside.
3. Using an electric mixer, beat the butter, granulated sugar, and brown sugar until light and fluffy, scraping down the sides of the bowl as needed, about 5 minutes. Add the eggs 1 at a time, beating after each until incorporated and scraping down the sides as needed. Add the vanilla extract and beat until combined. Add the hot cocoa mixture and beat until combined, scraping down the sides as needed.
4. Add the flour mixture and stir on the slowest speed until combined. Finish by scraping the bottom of the bowl with a spatula and folding all the batter together. Pour the batter into the prepared pan and bake for about 45 minutes, until the cakes feel firm and a toothpick inserted in the center comes out with a few crumbs attached. Be careful, as this cakes overbakes easily. Cool the cake in the pan for 10 minutes, then invert onto a wire rack and cool completely.

Serves 16

The easiest way to split the cake is to place it on a cake turner if you have one. Mark the cake into thirds either by eyeballing it or by placing toothpicks where you wish to cut. Begin slicing at the mark, using a large non-serrated knife such as a chef's knife and turning the cake as you slice it. Carefully lift off each cake layer and place it on a piece of plastic wrap or parchment paper.

Custard Tart

Professor Snape would dearly love to see Harry expelled after crashing Mr. Weasley's flying car into the Whomping Willow. But that punishment, Dumbledore reminds him, is for Professor McGonagall to decide. How to distract Snape, then? Dumbledore takes him by the arm and mentions a custard tart being served at the feast before sweeping him away (see *Harry Potter and the Chamber of Secrets*, Chapter 5).

The most important use for custard pies and tarts in the early 1900s was for throwing into people's faces in silent movies. This was considered for some reason extremely funny. Custard is very, very, very delicious, and the medievals liked it so much that they mixed anything and everything into it, from fruit and bread crumbs to ground meat and sage. For our purposes, however, a plain custard will suffice, thank you very much.

Tart Crust

1¼ cups all-purpose flour

¼ cup granulated sugar

¼ teaspoon salt

1 stick (8 tablespoons) cold butter, cut into small pieces

1 large egg yolk

2 tablespoons heavy cream

1 teaspoon pure vanilla extract

Custard

1 cup whole milk

½ cup heavy cream

3 large egg yolks

¼ cup granulated sugar

2 teaspoons cornstarch

1 tablespoon butter

1 teaspoon pure vanilla extract

Custard Tart

(continued)

1. For the crust, place the flour, sugar, and salt in the bowl of a food processor and pulse to combine. Scatter the pieces of butter over the flour mixture. Pulse until the mixture resembles coarse yellow meal without any white powdery bits remaining, about 15 pulses. Transfer the mixture to a large mixing bowl. Beat the egg yolk with the cream and vanilla and pour it into the flour-butter mixture. Toss with a spatula until the dough clumps together. If the dough is dry add 1 more tablespoon heavy cream (better too wet than too dry). Form into a disk, wrap in plastic wrap, and chill at least 2 hours or up to 3 days.

2. Preheat the oven to 425°F. Remove the dough from the refrigerator and roll it out on a floured surface to an 11-inch circle. (If it is too stiff for rolling out, let it first rest on the counter for 10 minutes.) Fold it into quarters, brushing off excess flour with a pastry brush after each fold, and then unfold it into a 9-inch tart pan with removable bottom. Ease the sides gently into the pan and press the dough gently against the sides. Use the rolling pin to roll the overhang off of the pan.

3. Freeze the tart shell for 10 minutes. Line the pan with aluminum foil and fill with pie weights. Bake until the dough is dry and set, about 20 minutes. Remove the foil and pie weights, reduce the heat to 350°F, and continue baking until the crust is golden, another 8 minutes.

4. Prepare the custard while the crust is baking. Heat the milk and cream in a small saucepan until hot but not simmering (do not boil). In the meantime, whisk the yolks, sugar, and cornstarch until smooth. Temper the yolk mixture by slowly pouring in ½ cup of the hot milk mixture while whisking vigorously. Pour the yolk mixture into the saucepan and continue to cook over medium-high heat, stirring constantly, until the wooden spoon scrapes up thickened bits of custard. Do not let the mixture simmer or boil. Remove from the heat and stir in the butter and vanilla.

5. Raise the oven temperature to 375°F. Pour the hot filling into the hot crust and bake until the custard puffs up and is still jiggly when you move the pan, about 15 minutes. Remove the tart from the oven and set on a wire rack to cool. The custard will set up as it cools. Cool completely before serving.

Serves 8

Blancmange

Ron would like to get another look at the stunning French veela girl who had asked for the bouillabaisse. He moves the blancmange, a French dish, in full view of her table, hoping to tempt her to come over and get some, but she pays no attention. Nice try, though (see *Harry Potter and the Goblet of Fire*, Chapter 16).

How does a molded dish of chicken mixed with ground almonds, rice, and sugar sound? This original medieval dish of *blanc manger* (white food) appealed to the nobility. The more modern version is made of milk flavored with ground almonds and thickened with gelatin, and it's so rubbery that you can bounce it off your walls, although your mom might not appreciate it if you try that. But there is no accounting for taste.

3 cups whole milk, divided
2 envelopes unflavored gelatin
1 cup heavy cream
½ cup granulated sugar
1 cup ground almonds
¼ teaspoon almond extract

Strawberry Sauce

1 pint strawberries
2 tablespoons granulated sugar

1. Grease 8 tartlet molds or a muffin pan and set aside. Put ½ cup of the milk in a bowl and sprinkle gelatin over it. Set aside.
2. Heat the remaining milk and the cream, sugar, and almonds in a small saucepan until hot but not simmering. Pour the mixture through a sieve and discard the almonds. Stir in the gelatin-milk mixture until gelatin is dissolved (if necessary, place over medium heat and stir until gelatin is dissolved; do not simmer or let boil). Stir in the almond extract.
3. Fill the molds to the very top and refrigerate until firm, about 2 hours. Place a plate over the mold and invert to unmold. If you're having trouble unmolding, wrap a hot towel around the mold for a few seconds. Serve with Strawberry Sauce.
4. To make the Strawberry Sauce, place the strawberries and sugar in a blender or food processor and pulse until completely blended.

Serves 8

Jam Tarts

At the Gryffindor party celebrating Harry's victory in the first task, Hermione wisely passes on the jam tarts Fred offers her. It's not a good idea to accept anything from the mischief-loving Weasley twins, as Neville finds out a moment later (see *Harry Potter and the Goblet of Fire*, Chapter 21).

There are several theories about how the word "jam" evolved, but the theory from the 1736 *Dictionarium Britannicum* is the sweetest: it comes from the French *j'aime*, which means "I love." Once sugar was cheap enough for jam to be affordable, it became a staple in England, finding its way into tarts and onto toast. Jam tarts are easy to make, and kids love them.

Tart Crust

2 cups all-purpose flour
⅓ cup granulated sugar
½ teaspoon salt
2 sticks cold butter or margarine, cut into chunks

1 cold large egg yolk
1 teaspoon pure vanilla extract
3 tablespoons ice water

Filling

½ cup any flavor jam

1. For the crust, place the flour, sugar, and salt in the bowl of a food processor and pulse to combine. Scatter the pieces of butter or margarine over the flour mixture. Pulse until the mixture resembles coarse yellow meal without any white powdery bits remaining, about 20 pulses. Transfer the mixture to a large mixing bowl. Beat the egg yolk with the vanilla and water and pour it into the flour-butter mixture. Toss with a spatula until the dough clumps together. If the dough is dry add 1 more tablespoon water (better too wet than too dry). Form into a disk, wrap in plastic wrap, and chill at least 2 hours or up to 3 days.

2. Preheat the oven to 425°F. Roll out the dough ⅛-inch thick. Stamp out circles of dough with a 4-inch round cutter. Fit the circles of dough into tartlet pans and arrange the pans on a baking sheet, or use a muffin pan.

3. Place 1 tablespoon of jam in each tart. The jam should just cover the bottom of the tart. If you put in too much, the jam will bubble over, and you will never be able to get the tarts out in one piece.

4. Decorate the tarts with cutouts from the leftover dough or make crosses with two strips of dough. Bake the tarts for 20 to 25 minutes, until golden. Cool completely before removing the tarts from the pans.

Makes 8 tarts

Custard Creams

Be very careful of anything the Weasley twins offer you to eat. Neville has just eaten a custard cream, seemingly harmless and probably quite tasty, but it turns him into a canary (see *Harry Potter and the Goblet of Fire*, Chapter 21).

If you've been wondering what in the world custard creams are, the mystery has been solved. They are nothing more than sandwich cookies, typically flavored with custard powder, which is similar to vanilla pudding mix.

Cookie Dough

2¼ cups all-purpose flour

½ cup vanilla pudding mix (1 packet, not instant)

1½ teaspoons baking powder

¼ teaspoon salt

1 stick (8 tablespoons) butter, at room temperature

1 cup confectioners' sugar

1 large egg, at room temperature

1 teaspoon pure vanilla extract

¼ cup whole milk, at room temperature

Filling

1¼ cups confectioners' sugar

¼ stick (2 tablespoons) butter, at room temperature

½ teaspoon pure vanilla extract

Bowl of sugar, for flattening cookies

Custard Creams

(continued)

1. Set the oven racks to the upper and lower positions, preheat the oven to 350°F, and line two cookie sheets with parchment paper. Whisk together the flour, vanilla pudding mix, baking powder, and salt in a mixing bowl and set aside.

2. In a separate bowl, cream the butter and confectioners' sugar with an electric mixer until light and fluffy, scraping down the sides of the bowl as needed, about 5 minutes. Add the egg and vanilla and beat until combined. Add the flour mixture and stir until the mixture is crumbly. Add the milk and stir until the mixture forms a dough. Break off small pieces, roll into balls (about 1 inch), and place them on the cookie sheets 1½ inches apart.

3. Oil the bottom of a glass and dip it into the bowl of sugar to coat. Press the glass down on the balls of dough, dipping it in the sugar between each cookie. Bake for 16 minutes, until the cookies are just beginning to brown a bit at the edges, rotating the cookie sheets and switching shelves halfway through baking. Cool on the cookie sheets for 5 minutes, then transfer to a wire rack to cool completely.

4. Beat the filling ingredients together until creamy. If the mixture is too dry, add milk 1 tablespoon at a time until it becomes spreadable. Sandwich the cooled cookies with about 1 teaspoon of the filling.

Makes 2 dozen

Chewy Ginger Biscuits

Ooh, Harry is in such trouble. He loses his temper with Professor Umbridge, and with a lot of fanfare and drama, she sends him to Professor McGonagall. Harry enters her office expecting to be scolded and punished, but to his surprise she offers him a newt-shaped ginger cookie (see *Harry Potter and the Order of the Phoenix*, Chapter 12).

The Oxford Companion to Food describes every cookie variety under the entry "cookies." But ginger biscuits are so important, they merit an entry all to themselves—not even chocolate chip cookies are granted that honor. As in this recipe, the biscuits are typically made with treacle and brown sugar. Also called ginger nuts, they are related to gingerbread, which in medieval times was molded into fancy shapes, called "fairings," and sold at fairs.

3 cups all-purpose flour
½ teaspoon baking soda
¼ teaspoon salt
1 tablespoon ground ginger
2 sticks butter, at room temperature
½ cup packed dark brown sugar
½ cup granulated sugar
1 large egg
1 large egg white
¾ cup golden syrup or light corn syrup
½ cup sugar for rolling the cookies

1. Set the oven racks to the upper and lower middle positions, preheat the oven to 375°F, and line two cookie sheets with parchment paper. In a large mixing bowl, whisk together the flour, baking soda, salt, and ginger.

2. In a separate bowl, beat the butter and the sugars with an electric mixer until light and fluffy, scraping down the sides of the bowl as necessary, about 5 minutes. Add the egg, egg white, and golden syrup and beat until combined. Add the flour mixture and stir on the lowest speed until combined. Scrape the bottom with a rubber spatula to make sure it is fully combined.

3. Scoop out balls of dough with a cookie scoop or tablespoon. Form into 1½-inch balls and roll in the sugar. Place the balls 2 inches apart on the prepared cookie sheets. Bake for 10 minutes, rotating the pans and switching shelves halfway through baking. Slide the parchment paper onto wire racks to cool; do not remove the cookies individually until they cool. Repeat until all the dough is used up.

Makes 3½ dozen cookies

Be very careful not to overbake these cookies or they will be hard instead of soft and chewy. The cookies will be very soft when you take them out of the oven; they will set up as they cool.

Meringues

You can almost see the front-page headline: KILLED BY A MERINGUE. Neville recounts at the first Hogwarts feast how his uncle dropped him out of the window when his wife offered him a meringue. Meringues are good, but come on, they're not that good. Luckily, Neville's magic abilities—his family was so relieved because they thought he was a Squib—saved him from crashing to his death (see *Harry Potter and the Sorcerer's Stone*, Chapter 7).

Have you ever wondered how people discovered that if you beat egg whites with a whisk, they turn into foam? In the 1500s, the Europeans discovered that happened when they beat egg whites with whisks made of twigs. They ate it raw, with cream, but a century later were already making meringue cookies.

2 large egg whites, at room temperature
⅛ teaspoon salt
⅛ teaspoon cream of tartar
½ teaspoon pure vanilla extract
½ cup granulated sugar

1. Preheat the oven to 225°F and line two baking sheets with parchment paper. Place the egg whites, salt, cream of tartar, and vanilla in a large mixing bowl and beat until soft mounds begin to form. Gradually add the sugar and beat until stiff but still glossy. If the meringue mixture is dry and cottony or has a curdled look, it's overbeaten, and you'll have to start over.

2. Fill a pastry bag fitted with a plain or star tip and pipe 1-inch kisses or rosettes ½ inch apart on the cookie sheets. For a more rustic look, plop down teaspoonfuls instead of piping. Bake for 1 hour, rotating the pans and switching shelves halfway through baking. Leave the meringues in the oven another hour to dry out. Discard any leftover meringue mixture; it will not keep until the first batch is done.

Makes about 80 meringues

Chapter Nine

Holiday Fare

Draco Malfoy taunts Harry Potter about having no proper family to return to for the Christmas holidays, but Harry isn't bothered at all. He can't think of a place he'd rather stay than Hogwarts. He's perfectly happy to be anywhere but with the Dursleys, who regard him as the most embarrassing thing that has ever happened to them. And nothing beats the decorations in the Great Hall, where fir trees are covered with everlasting snow and real, live fairies flit among the branches. Also, the Dursleys would never provide a glorious feast for Christmas dinner such as the ones produced by the Hogwarts house-elves.

Harry enjoys the other holidays as well. Halloween is fun, with real bats swooping around the Great Hall, and so is Easter, when he gets Easter eggs from Mrs. Weasley filled with homemade toffee.

English Muffins

It's so much fun to roast food over a fire, it hardly matters if it's s'mores or English muffins. During the Christmas holidays Harry and Ron sit in front of the fireplace in the cozy Gryffindor common room roasting everything from marshmallows to muffins (see *Harry Potter and the Sorcerer's Stone*, Chapter 12).

Oh, do you know the muffin man? In Victorian times you could count on finding him at teatime ringing his bell and selling English muffins, which didn't look like the blueberry or chocolate chip muffins we're used to having as a breakfast treat. The hard-working Welsh invented this food over a thousand years ago, but it didn't become a fad with the leisurely upper classes until the 1800s. The "prupuh" way to eat this yeasted bread is to break it open with the tines of a fork to reveal the rough texture inside. Then toast it and slather it with butter and jam.

½ cup whole milk
½ stick (4 tablespoons) butter
1 cup warm water
1 tablespoon (1 packet) active dry yeast
1 tablespoon granulated sugar
4 cups all-purpose flour
1 teaspoon salt

1. Heat the milk and butter in a small saucepan over low heat until the butter is melted. Set it aside to cool. Combine the water, yeast, and sugar in a small bowl and let it stand until the yeast dissolves and the mixture puffs up.
2. Measure the flour and salt into a large mixing bowl. Add the milk and yeast mixtures and stir to combine. Knead the dough until it cleans the sides of the bowl and is smooth and elastic, about 10 minutes. Transfer the dough to an oiled bowl, turning to coat the dough on all sides. Cover it with plastic wrap and set it in a warm place until the dough doubles in bulk, about 1½ to 2 hours.
3. On a lightly floured surface, roll out the dough ½-inch thick. Stamp out circles with a 3-inch cookie cutter or the rim of a glass. Lightly spray a large skillet with cooking spray. Cook the muffins over medium-low heat for 10 to 15 minutes on each side, or until light brown on each side.
4. Serve immediately while hot or break them open after they cool and toast them.

Makes about 1½ dozen muffins

Pumpkin Delights

On Harry's first Halloween at Hogwarts, he awakes to the "smell of baking pumpkin," which could mean anything. Therefore, included are two recipes, one for pumpkin pie and the other for pumpkin bread. Either one is a delicious way to spend your Halloween (see *Harry Potter and the Sorcerer's Stone*, Chapter 10).

The place: Plymouth, Massachusetts; the time period: Thanksgiving 1621; the scene: a feast of roast turkey with cranberry sauce and pumpkin pie enjoyed by white settlers and Native Americans alike. If that's how you've been imagining the first Thanksgiving, sorry to ruin your pretty picture. The earliest pumpkin "pies" the settlers would have eaten would have been pumpkin cooked with other ingredients in the hollowed-out shell. Pumpkin pie appears much later in America, although, surprisingly, French and English cookbooks from the 1600s contain recipes for this beloved pie.

Pumpkin Pie

Pie Crust

1¼ cups all-purpose flour

2 tablespoons granulated sugar

¼ teaspoon salt

1 stick (8 tablespoons) cold butter, cut into small pieces

4–6 tablespoons ice water

Filling

2 cups canned pumpkin, not pumpkin pie filling

1 cup granulated sugar

1 cup heavy cream

1 teaspoon ground cinnamon

¼ teaspoon ground nutmeg

⅛ teaspoon ground cloves

⅛ teaspoon ground allspice

¼ teaspoon salt

3 large eggs

Pumpkin Delights

1. For the crust, place the flour, sugar, and salt in the bowl of a food processor and pulse to combine. Scatter the pieces of butter over the flour mixture. Pulse until the mixture resembles coarse yellow meal without any white powdery bits remaining, about 15 pulses. Transfer the mixture to a large mixing bowl. Sprinkle 4 tablespoons water over the mixture and toss with a rubber spatula until the dough sticks together. Add more water 1 tablespoon at a time if the dough is dry (better too wet than too dry). Form the dough into a disk, wrap in plastic wrap, and chill at least 2 hours or up to 3 days.

2. Preheat the oven to 425°F. Remove the dough from the refrigerator and roll it out on a floured surface to a 12-inch circle. Fold the dough into quarters, brushing off excess flour with a pastry brush after each fold, and unfold it in a 9-inch pie pan, easing the sides down into the pan. Trim the overhang to within 1 inch of the rim with a sharp knife or kitchen scissors. Fold the overhang under and crimp with a fork or your fingers. Freeze for 20 minutes.

3. Remove the pie shell from the freezer, line with aluminum foil, fill with pie weights, and bake for 25 minutes until the dough is dry and set. Remove the foil and weights, reduce the temperature to 375°F, and continue to bake another 10 minutes, until the shell begins to brown. Prepare the filling during these 10 minutes.

4. To prepare the filling, combine the pumpkin, sugar, heavy cream, spices, and salt in a small saucepan and cook over medium heat, stirring constantly, until hot to the touch. Whisk in the eggs one at a time and continue to cook, stirring constantly, until the filling is very hot but not simmering. Do not let it boil. If the pie shell isn't ready by the time the filling is done, remove the filling from the heat.

5. Pour the filling into the crust (if the crust is still in the oven, it's easier to remove the pan from the oven than to try to pour the filling into the crust while the pan is on the oven rack) and continue to bake until it puffs up around the edges and doesn't look wet, about 30 minutes. The filling will be jiggly when you remove it from the oven; it will set up as it cools. Serve at room temperature with whipped cream.

Serves 8

You can make the crust a day in advance, and also freeze it for up to 2 months if it is well wrapped in plastic.

Pumpkin Delights

(continued)

Pumpkin bread is a type of quick bread. Any baked goods made with chemical leaveners such as baking powder are called quick breads, so even pancakes are a type of quick bread.

Pumpkin Bread

1½ cups all-purpose flour
¼ teaspoon salt
1 teaspoon baking powder
1 teaspoon cinnamon
¼ teaspoon ground nutmeg
⅛ teaspoon ground cloves
1 stick (8 tablespoons) butter, at room temperature

1 cup granulated sugar
2 large eggs, at room temperature
¾ cup canned pumpkin, not pumpkin pie filling
⅓ cup whole milk
Confectioners' sugar, for dusting

1. Preheat the oven to 350°F. Grease and flour an 8½" × 4½" loaf pan. Whisk together the flour, salt, baking powder, cinnamon, nutmeg, and cloves and set aside.

2. In a separate bowl, beat the butter and sugar with an electric mixer until light and fluffy, scraping down the sides of the bowl as needed, about 4 minutes. Add the eggs one at a time, beating after each until incorporated. Add the pumpkin and beat until combined. Add the milk and again beat until combined. Add the flour mixture and mix on the lowest speed until combined. Scrape and fold with a rubber spatula to finish.

3. Scrape the batter into the prepared pan and bake for 1 hour, rotating halfway through baking, until the top is golden and the loaf is well risen and feels firm when pressed lightly in the center. Remove from the oven and cool in the pan. To serve, remove the loaf from the pan, dust with confectioners' sugar, and cut into thick slices.

Makes 1 loaf

Classic Roast Turkey

At his first Christmas dinner at Hogwarts, Harry has never seen so many roast turkeys—a hundred of them, served with gravy and cranberry sauce (see *Harry Potter and the Sorcerer's Stone*, Chapter 12).

Peacocks and swans appeared regularly on the royal table in merry old England. They looked impressive, but tasted awful because of their tough, stringy meat. That's why, when the turkey was introduced to Europe in the 1500s, it quickly replaced the peacocks and swans. King Henry VIII (that's the one with the six wives) was the first to eat turkey as part of the Christmas feast.

3 onions, peeled and cut into quarters
1 head of garlic, separated into cloves and peeled
6 carrots, peeled and cut into 2-inch chunks
6 celery ribs, cut into 2-inch chunks
Several sprigs thyme

1 cup water
1 turkey, 12–14 pounds, giblets and neck removed (can be used to make turkey stock for gravy)
Olive oil or melted butter or margarine
Salt and pepper

1. Preheat the oven to 400°F. Scatter the onions, garlic, carrots, celery, and thyme in the bottom of a large roasting pan. Pour in the water. If you have a roasting rack, grease it and place it in the roasting pan.

2. Rinse the turkey and pat it dry with paper towels. Place it on top of the vegetables in the roasting pan breast-side down, or on the rack, if using. Brush the back with the olive oil or melted butter and sprinkle it with the salt and pepper.

3. Roast the turkey for 45 minutes. Using oven mitts or towels, flip the turkey breast-side up. Pat the breast dry; then brush more oil or butter over the breast and sprinkle with salt and pepper. Roast for another 1 to 1½ hours, until the thickest part of the thigh registers 170°F on a meat thermometer. Transfer the turkey to a carving board and let it rest 20 to 30 minutes before carving.

Serves 10–12

To make turkey stock for gravy, place the turkey giblets and neck in a small saucepan along with 1 carrot, 1 celery, ½ onion cut into chunks, 1 peeled garlic clove, and a few sprigs of dill. Cover with water and bring to a boil, then simmer for 1 hour. Strain the stock through a sieve and use a fat separator to remove the fat.

Homemade Marshmallows

Harry and Ron toasted marshmallows, but they didn't make them. However, don't put it past the kitchen house-elves, who are excellent cooks, to make batches of this spongy confection in the Hogwarts kitchens and send them up to be available as snacks (see *Harry Potter and the Sorcerer's Stone,* Chapter 12).

Marshmallows used to be made from the marsh mallow plant. The roots have an extract that's mucilaginous, a word that sounds like what it means. Today we use gelatin (or commercially, gum arabic), but the name has stuck. Over 4,000 years ago the Egyptians also developed a treat made from the mallow plant, which grew in the marshes of Egypt.

½ cup confectioners' sugar, divided, plus more as needed

1 cup water, divided

3 tablespoons (3 envelopes) unflavored gelatin

2 cups granulated sugar

1¼ cups light corn syrup

¼ teaspoon salt

1 tablespoon pure vanilla extract

Homemade Marshmallows

(continued)

1. Spray a 9" × 13" pan with cooking spray and line with parchment paper to come up the two narrow ends for easy removal. Thickly coat the parchment paper with ¼ cup of the confectioners' sugar, using a sieve to dust the sugar over the paper.

2. Place ½ cup of the water and the gelatin in a large mixing bowl to soften. Combine the sugar, corn syrup, salt, and the remaining ½ cup water in a medium saucepan. Bring to a boil, stirring constantly. If sugar crystals form on the sides of the pan, wash down the sides with a pastry brush dipped in hot water. Clip a candy thermometer to the saucepan and cook over medium-high heat, stirring occasionally, to 238°F.

3. With the mixer on low speed, slowly pour half the sugar syrup into the softened gelatin. Increase the speed to medium and slowly pour in the rest of the syrup. Increase the speed to high and beat 10 to 15 minutes until thick and creamy. Beat in the vanilla.

4. Scrape the batter into the prepared pan and spread it to the edges. Smooth the top with a rubber spatula. The mixture will be sticky and hard to spread, but do the best you can. Thickly coat the top with the remaining ¼ cup confectioners' sugar, using a sieve to dust the sugar over the top. Leave the pan to set and dry out, uncovered, overnight.

5. To cut the marshmallows, pull out the marshmallow sheet by the overhanging parchment and place it on a cutting board. Using a chef's knife or a large, non-serrated knife, press down with one motion to make a single cut through the center. It's going to be sticky. Make 8 even cuts along the length and then along the width to form rectangles. Dip the cut sides into the confectioners' sugar to prevent sticking.

Makes 64 pieces

To store the marshmallows, lay them in a single layer in an airtight container, covering each layer with plastic wrap or parchment paper. The nice thing about homemade marshmallows is that you can flavor them any way you want. Try replacing the vanilla with 1 teaspoon almond extract or ½ teaspoon mint extract. You can also add a few drops of food coloring to tint it to any shade. For a really delicious treat, you can toast shredded coconut, grind it in the food processor, and use it in place of the confectioners' sugar, or you can use ground toasted nuts.

Easiest Cranberry Sauce

Along with the one hundred roast turkeys, cranberry sauce is served at Harry's first Christmas dinner at Hogwarts (see *Harry Potter and the Sorcerer's Stone,* Chapter 12).

Fenwort, marshwort, moss berries . . . they sound like they belong in a witch's brew, but in fact, those are all medieval words for cranberries. When cranberries are fresh, they bounce, so in the olden days people sorted cranberries by rolling them down the stairs: whatever bounced to the bottom got sold; whatever stayed on the stairs was discarded.

1 12-ounce package of cranberries, fresh or frozen
1 cup water
1 cup granulated sugar
Generous pinch salt

1. Combine the cranberries, water, sugar, and salt in a small saucepan. Bring to a boil.
2. Reduce the heat and simmer until the cranberries burst open, about 10 minutes.
3. Cool the sauce completely before refrigerating.

Makes about 2 cups

Christmas Pudding for Kids

Anxiety about drinking the illegal Polyjuice Potion does not interfere with Harry and Ron's appetites. They have three helpings of Christmas pudding before Herm-ione hustles them away to pluck hair off the heads of the two thugs that the potion will change them into (see *Harry Potter and the Chamber of Secrets*, Chapter 12).

In medieval times, the Roman Catholic Church decreed that Christmas pudding should contain thirteen ingredients to symbolize Christ and his twelve apostles and that everyone in the family should get a turn to stir it from east to west to represent the Magis' journey. Traditional Christmas pudding is made with brandy, but this recipe leaves it out.

1½ cups all-purpose flour
1 cup fresh bread crumbs
1 cup packed dark brown sugar
1½ teaspoons ground cinnamon
1 teaspoon ground ginger
½ teaspoon ground nutmeg
½ teaspoon ground cloves
½ teaspoon salt
2 sticks cold butter, cut into pieces

1 cup dried currants or cranberries
1 cup dark raisins
1 cup golden raisins
4 large eggs
¼ cup marmalade
Grated zest and juice of 1 orange
Grated zest and juice of 1 lemon
¾ cup apple juice

1. Fill a large, wide pot halfway with water, place an overturned shallow bowl in the pot, and bring to a simmer. Grease and flour a 2½-quart bowl with a tight-fitting lid and set aside.

2. Whisk together the flour, bread crumbs, brown sugar, spices, and salt in a large mixing bowl. Scatter the pieces of butter over the flour mixture and rub it in with your fingers until it reaches the consistency of wet sand. Add the currants or cranberries, dark raisins, and golden raisins, and toss to combine.

3. In a separate bowl beat the eggs, marmalade, grated zest and juice of orange and lemon, and apple juice until well combined. Pour the egg mixture into the flour mixture and stir to combine. Pour the batter into the prepared bowl and snap the lid tightly in place. Place the pudding in the pot, making sure the water comes halfway up the sides. Cover the pot and steam for 6 hours, adding water to the pot as necessary.

4. Remove the pudding from the pot and allow it to cool. Unmold the pudding onto a serving platter and serve warm with custard or cream.

Serves 8

To flambé the pudding, as in the Harry Potter books, drizzle brandy over it and ignite with a long match.

Christmas Cake for Grownups

On Harry's first Christmas at Hogwarts, he attends the biggest Christmas dinner he's ever seen, followed by a light supper of sandwiches and tea cakes, such as Christmas cake (see *Harry Potter and the Sorcerer's Stone*, Chapter 12).

This rich fruitcake, also called plum cake (in the Middle Ages "plum" referred to dried fruit, and this usage has survived today in such foods as plum cake or plum pudding), is very popular at Christmas. The tradition to cover it with marzipan and then royal icing started in the late 1700s. Royal icing is made with uncooked egg whites, so if you're concerned about food-borne illness, hold off on the icing.

Cake

½ cup dark raisins
½ cup golden raisins
½ cup dried currants or cranberries
½ cup chopped dried dates
½ cup chopped dried apricots
1 cup brandy
3 cups all-purpose flour
½ cup ground walnuts
1 teaspoon baking powder
½ teaspoon salt
2 teaspoons ground cinnamon
½ teaspoon ground nutmeg
¼ teaspoon ground cloves
¼ teaspoon ground allspice
1½ sticks (12 tablespoons) butter, at room temperature
1½ cups packed dark brown sugar
4 large eggs, at room temperature
Grated zest and juice of 1 lemon
Grated zest and juice of 1 lime
Grated zest and juice of 2 oranges
½ cup marmalade
1 cup chopped walnuts
¼ cup brandy, to finish
½ cup currant jelly, melted
2 pounds marzipan
Royal Icing (recipe follows)

Royal Icing

3 large egg whites
¼ teaspoon cream of tartar
5 cups confectioners' sugar, sifted
2 teaspoons pure vanilla extract

Christmas Cake for Grownups

(continued)

1. For the cake, place the dried fruit in a bowl and pour the brandy over it. Let it soak overnight. Drain the fruit, reserving the brandy.

2. Preheat the oven to 275°F. Grease and flour a 9-inch spring form pan and line the bottom and sides with parchment paper. The sides will be a bit tricky, but you can do it. Whisk together the flour, ground walnuts, baking powder, salt, and spices in a large mixing bowl.

3. Beat the butter and sugar in a separate bowl using an electric mixer until light and fluffy, scraping down the sides of the bowl as needed, about 4 minutes. Add the eggs one at a time, beating after each until incorporated. Add the zest and juice of the lemon, lime, and oranges along with the marmalade and reserved brandy and beat until combined. Don't worry if the mixture looks curdled.

4. Add the flour mixture and mix on the lowest speed until combined. Add the soaked dried fruits and chopped walnuts and mix until combined. Scrape and fold with a rubber spatula to finish.

5. Scrape the batter into the prepared pan and bake for 2½ hours. A toothpick inserted in the center should come out clean. Cool completely in the pan.

6. Release the latch on the springform pan to remove the cake. Invert the cake and remove the bottom. Poke holes in the bottom of the cake with a skewer and spoon the ¼ cup brandy over the bottom. Wrap the cake well in plastic wrap and store upside down. The cake will stay fresh for several months. If you want the cake to keep for longer (or even years—no kidding), then once a month unwrap the cake and spoon ¼ cup brandy over the bottom. Rewrap it well and store it upside down.

7. When you are ready to assemble the cake, place it right-side up on a cardboard round or platter. Brush the top and sides of the cake with the melted jelly. Roll out the marzipan on a work surface dusted with confectioners' sugar to a 14-inch circle. Drape the marzipan over the cake, press it in place, and trim off the bottom with a sharp knife. Eat the trimmings while you work.

8. To make the Royal Icing, beat the egg whites with the cream of tartar until soft mounds form. Reduce the speed to medium and gradually add the confectioners' sugar. Add the vanilla and beat on high speed until stiff. Use an icing spatula to thickly cover the top and sides of cake. Make peaks and swirls with the icing spatula or the back of a teaspoon. Allow the icing to set before serving; it will harden. Do not refrigerate the cake—the condensation will ruin the Royal Icing. Once the cake has set, even after it has been cut, it can be stored at room temperature wrapped in plastic wrap.

Serves 16 hungry people for tea or 32 stuffed people for dessert

Most recipes for fruitcakes advise maturing the cakes for a few months to allow the flavors to ripen. This cake, however, also tastes delicious fresh. To make this cake for kids, replace the brandy with apple juice and serve within 24 hours, or wrap well in plastic wrap and freeze, unfrosted. Defrost before coating it with marzipan and icing.

Christmas Trifle

Despite eating four helpings of trifle at Christmas tea, Crabbe and Goyle have no problem polishing off the chocolate cakes Hermione had set up as a trap (see *Harry Potter and the Chamber of Secrets*, Chapter 12).

Christmas trifle is a natural outgrowth of Christmas cake or pudding. Take some of the leftover slices from Christmas dinner, throw 'em in a bowl, top 'em with custard and whipped cream, and voilà! You have something fabulous to serve for Christmas tea.

1½ cups whole milk

2 tablespoons cornstarch

⅓ cup packed dark brown sugar

Pinch salt

3 large egg yolks

¼ stick (2 tablespoons) butter

¼ teaspoon rum extract or ½ teaspoon pure vanilla extract

Leftover slices of Christmas pudding or Christmas cake

¼ cup marmalade

1 cup heavy cream

¼ cup confectioners' sugar

1 teaspoon pure vanilla extract

Ground nutmeg or cinnamon, for dusting

1. Combine the milk, cornstarch, brown sugar, and salt in a medium saucepan and stir to dissolve the cornstarch. Cook over medium-high heat, stirring constantly, until hot but not bubbling. Pour ½ cup of the hot mixture into the egg yolks while whisking constantly, then pour the mixture into the saucepan while stirring. Continue to cook, stirring constantly, until the mixture is thick and bubbling. Remove from the heat and add the butter and rum or vanilla extract. Stir to combine, then pour through a sieve, using a rubber spatula to push the mixture through. Cover the surface directly with plastic wrap to prevent a skin from forming, and cool to room temperature. Refrigerate until cold or up to 3 days.

2. Crumble a few slices of the Christmas cake or pudding into the bottom of a 9-inch serving dish, preferably clear glass, that is 2½ to 3 inches deep. The crumbled cake or pudding should come about 1½ inches up the sides. Spread the marmalade as well as you can over the cake or pudding; it will be sticky. Then spread the brown sugar custard over the marmalade, cover with plastic wrap, and refrigerate until ready to serve or up to 3 days.

3. Before serving, combine the heavy cream, sugar, and vanilla in a bowl and beat until stiff peaks form. Spread or pipe the whipped cream over the trifle and dust with ground nutmeg or cinnamon.

Serves 8 to 10

Stewed Tripe and Onions

Professor Trelawney was crystal-ball gazing and she saw herself join-
ing the Christmas feast. Imagine that! So here she is at the table, and Professor McGonagall, though she has little patience for the old fraud, offers
her some tripe (see *Harry Potter and the Prisoner of Azkaban*, Chapter 11).

£ike Haggis (Chapter 7) and Black Pudding (Chapter 7), tripe isn't for everyone. The honeycomb variety specified in this recipe is the second stomach compartment (there are four of them) of the animal. If you're brave enough, give this recipe a try.

1½ pounds dressed honeycomb tripe
  (beef, goat, or sheep)
3 cups sliced yellow onions
2 cups whole milk
1 pinch ground nutmeg

½ teaspoon dried thyme
1 bay leaf
2 tablespoons butter
2 tablespoons flour
¼ cup minced fresh flat-leaf parsley

1. Place the tripe in a large pot and cover with cold water. Bring to a boil, remove, drain, and rinse with cold water. Cut the tripe into bite-size pieces and return to the pot along with the onions, milk, nutmeg, thyme, and bay leaf. Bring to a boil, cover, reduce to a simmer, and simmer for 2 hours.

2. Strain the tripe and reserve the liquid. You should have 2 cups of liquid; if necessary, add enough milk to make 2 cups.

3. Wipe the pot. Melt the butter in the pot over medium-high heat. Add the tripe and stir to coat. Add the flour and stir to coat. Add the reserved liquid and continue stirring until the mixture comes to a boil. Reduce the heat and simmer for 15 minutes.

4. Transfer to a bowl and garnish with parsley.

Serves 4

Eggnog for Kids

At Harry's second Christmas at Hogwarts, Hagrid is greatly helped by the eggnog. With every cup he consumes, he's able to sing carols progressively louder (see *Harry Potter and the Chamber of Secrets*, Chapter 12).

Noggin now means "head," but that has nothing to do with eggnog, except maybe that the alcohol in the adult version goes straight to your head. Rather, the word "eggnog" comes from the archaic definition of "noggin," which is "mug." It's easy to see, then, how "eggs in a noggin" evolved into "eggnog."

6 large eggs
¾ cup granulated sugar
3½ cups whole milk
2 cups heavy cream, divided

2 teaspoons pure vanilla extract, divided
⅓ cup confectioners' sugar
Ground nutmeg for serving

1. Whisk the eggs with the granulated sugar in a medium saucepan until frothy. Whisk in the milk and 1 cup of the heavy cream and cook over medium-high heat, whisking constantly, until the mixture reaches 160°F or is very hot but not bubbling. Remove from the heat and stir in 1 teaspoon of the vanilla. Pour through a sieve. Cover the surface directly with plastic wrap to prevent a skin from forming, and cool to room temperature. Refrigerate until cold.

2. Beat the remaining cup of heavy cream with the remaining teaspoon of vanilla and the confectioners' sugar until stiff peaks form. Pour the chilled eggnog into mugs or glasses. Top with a dollop of whipped cream and sprinkle with the nutmeg.

Serves 6

Goulash

At the Yule ball, diners get to choose their food from menus, which include foreign foods to accommodate the visitors from Durmstrang and Beauxbatons. Harry chooses goulash, a Hungarian dish. Perhaps he was curious . . . or maybe Aunt Petunia made a delicious goulash all the time and he just loved it (see *Harry Potter and the Goblet of Fire*, Chapter 23).

Did you know that in Hungarian, *goulash* means "cowboy," or "cowboy's soup," and the dish that we call goulash is called *paprikash* in Hungarian? When the Hungarians discovered paprika in the 1820s they loved it so much that they pretty much stopped using other spices, and visitors to that country loved Hungarian goulash so much they added it to their cuisines as well.

3 tablespoons vegetable oil (divided use)
2 pounds chuck roast, trimmed and cut into 1-inch pieces
1 onion, finely chopped
2 ribs celery, finely chopped
3 tablespoons all-purpose flour
2 14-ounce cans chicken broth
1 10-ounce package mushrooms, chopped
3 tablespoons paprika
3 tablespoons tomato paste
1 sweet red pepper, seeded and chopped
½ cup sour cream
Egg noodles, for serving

1. Heat 1 tablespoon of the oil in a Dutch oven or wide pot. Sear the meat in batches over high heat on both sides until crusty brown, about 4 minutes per side. Transfer the batches to a large plate. Heat the remaining 2 tablespoons oil and add the onions and celery, cooking over medium-high heat until softened, scraping up the fond (browned bits), about 5 minutes. Add the flour and toss to combine. Pour in the chicken broth while stirring constantly. Cook, stirring constantly, until thickened and bubbling.

2. Add the mushrooms, paprika, tomato paste, and the browned meat along with its accumulated juices. Bring the stew to a simmer and continue to simmer for 1½ hours. Add the red pepper and cook another ½ hour. Remove from the heat.

3. Whisk the sour cream with a ½ cup of the cooking liquid, then stir it into the goulash. Serve the goulash over buttered egg noodles.

Serves 8

Chapter Ten

Treats in the Village

Ah, Hogsmeade! The only entirely wizarding village in all of Great Britain and the highlight of the year for third-year students at Hogwarts . . . but it's a problem for our hero. You need a permission slip signed by a parent or guardian in order to be allowed into Hogsmeade, and Uncle Vernon is never going to sign it.

Harry thinks he solved his problem by striking a deal with his uncle, but then he loses his temper in a really bad way and has to flee. Scratch that. So he asks the Minister of Magic, Cornelius Fudge, to sign his permission slip, but the Minister won't do it, either. He tries to explain the situation to Professor McGonagall, but she's very strict: no permission slip, no Hogsmeade. So it's a very dejected Harry who heads to the Gryffindor common room while everyone else leaves for Hogsmeade.

Like many misfortunes in life, this turns out to be a blessing in disguise. Fred and George, in a rare show of generosity and sympathy, give Harry one of their most precious possessions, the Marauder's Map, which will show Harry a secret way into Hogsmeade. The map plays a very important role many, many times throughout Harry's adventures, right up until his final confrontation with Voldemort.

Treats in the Village *cont'd*

Harry gets the map and he gets to visit Hogsmeade, and is it ever worth it to break the rules to come see this place. There's nothing like Honeydukes in the Muggle world. Not only does it sell fine confections like toffees and chocolates and fudges, but it also carries a line of magical sweets. Unfortunately, this cookbook cannot replicate the magic of Honeydukes. The Bonbons don't explode, the Sherbet Pouches don't cause you to levitate, the Acid Drops will not burn a hole in your tongue, and the Sugar Mice won't squeak in your stomach. But don't be disappointed, because the sweets that follow taste magically good. And the chocolates really will protect you from despair should you be visited by a dementor (see *Harry Potter and the Prisoner of Azkaban*).

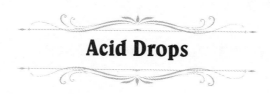

Acid Drops

Ron reminisces about Acid Pops, remembering how the one Fred gave him when he was little burned a hole in his tongue. He wonders if he should try getting Fred back by buying him a Cockroach Cluster and telling him it's peanuts (see *Harry Potter and the Prisoner of Azkaban,* Chapter 10).

Acid drops, short for "acidulated drops," are a popular candy in England. The acid is added to make the candy sour. You can make them into pops by sticking lollipop sticks into the drops while they're still hot or pouring them into oiled heatproof lollipop molds. Be careful not to use chocolate molds, because they will melt when you pour in the hot candy.

¼ cup water
1 cup granulated sugar
½ cup light corn syrup

¼ teaspoon cream of tartar
1 teaspoon citric acid (see note)

1. Line two baking sheets with parchment paper and set aside. Combine the water, sugar, corn syrup, and cream of tartar in a small saucepan. Cook over medium heat, stirring constantly, until the sugar is dissolved and the mixture begins to bubble. Wash down the sides of the pan with a pastry brush dipped in hot water if sugar crystals have formed on the sides. Clip a candy thermometer to the pan and continue cooking over medium heat, stirring occasionally, until the mixture reaches 300°F.

2. Remove the pan from the heat. Sprinkle the citric acid over the sugar syrup and stir to combine. When the bubbling has subsided, use an oiled teaspoon to drop teaspoonfuls of the sugar syrup onto the prepared sheets 2 inches apart to allow room for spreading.

3. To store candies, wrap them in sheets of parchment paper, making sure the candies don't touch, as they will stick together.

Makes about 40 candies

Citric acid is available in fairly small quantities on the Internet.

Honeydukes Treats

Harry sneaks into Honeydukes through the cellar, and boy, what a sweetshop! The mouthwatering candies that line the shelves are a sweets-lover's fantasy. The following recipes represent the nougat, coconut ice, sugar mice, peppermint creams, sherbet balls, chocolates, and bonbons that Harry saw (see *Harry Potter and the Prisoner of Azkaban*, Chapter 10).

"Nougat" comes from the Latin word *nux*, which means "nut." The most famous type of nougat, the soft, chewy, white kind with nuts, is sometimes called Montélimar, after the French town where it originated.

This recipe is for more experienced cooks. It's better to have some experience with boiling sugar in other applications before attempting this recipe. As with all recipes that call for boiling sugar, this recipe should not be made by children. Also, you will need a stand mixer with a 5-quart bowl and whisk attachment to make this recipe.

Nougat

Rice or wafer paper, for lining the pan and the top of the nougat (you can order it online)

2 cups granulated sugar

¾ cup light corn syrup

¼ cup honey

1 cup water

4 large egg whites, at room temperature

¼ teaspoon salt

¼ teaspoon cream of tartar

1 tablespoon pure vanilla extract

1 cup whole toasted pistachio nuts

1 cup toasted blanched slivered almonds

Honeydukes Treats

(continued)

1. Spray a 9" × 13" pan with cooking spray and line it with the rice or wafer paper. You may need to cut the paper to fit or use two sheets. Combine the sugar, corn syrup, honey, and water in a medium saucepan. Place the egg whites, salt, and cream of tartar in the 5-quart bowl of a standing mixer fitted with the whisk attachment and begin beating on medium speed. Place the saucepan on the heat and cook, stirring constantly, until the mixture is dissolved. Bring the mixture to a boil, wash down the sides of the pot with a pastry brush dipped in hot water if necessary, and clip on a candy thermometer.

2. Here's the first tricky part. Try to time the egg whites reaching soft mounds and the sugar syrup reaching 240°F at the same time. When this happens, increase the mixer speed to medium-high. Dip a 1-cup heatproof measuring cup into the sugar syrup, and then, with the mixer still running, pour the syrup slowly into the egg whites against the side of the bowl (if you pour the sugar syrup into the center of the mixer bowl, the mixture will fly against the sides and harden instead of incorporating into the egg whites). Beat the egg whites until they are stiff and glossy while continuing to cook the remaining sugar syrup, stirring to prevent scorching.

3. Here's the second tricky part. Try to time the egg whites reaching the stiff, glossy stage with the sugar syrup reaching 300°F. As soon as that temperature is reached, turn the mixer to medium-high and slowly pour in the sugar syrup against the side of the bowl. Add the vanilla and beat until combined. Add the nuts and fold in by hand. Immediately pour the mixture into the prepared pan. It sets up quickly, so the hotter it is, the easier it will be to spread it in the pan. Smooth the top with a rubber spatula and press down rice or wafer paper over the top.

4. Let the mixture cool and set overnight. Use a serrated knife to cut 8 sections along the width and 8 sections along the length to make 64 rectangles. The nougat is hard to cut and remove from the pan and won't look as neat and professional as the one at Honeydukes, but it tastes absolutely stupendous. Cover the pan tightly with plastic wrap and store at room temperature for up to 3 weeks.

Makes 64 pieces

Even though it's difficult to find wafer paper, it's really the only thing that works. Nougat is very soft and sticky; unlike marshmallows, it absorbs cornstarch or confectioners' sugar, so if you used those it would still stick to the pan, and you would have to use copious amounts of grease to allow you to remove the nougat. Doing that, of course, would ruin the candy.

Honeydukes Treats

(continued)

Coconut Ice

2 cups granulated sugar

2 cups whole milk

2 tablespoons golden syrup or light corn syrup

¼ stick (2 tablespoons) butter

¼ cup heavy cream

¼ teaspoon salt

1 teaspoon pure vanilla extract

1 cup ground desiccated coconut (shredded sweetened coconut may be substituted)

Few drops red food coloring

Coconut ice is not ice at all, though it is made with coconut, so it's not a complete misnomer. This candy really is coconut fudge. In America it's called coconut candy or coconut praline. The traditional way to make this is to pour half the mixture into the pan, then tint the rest pink and pour that on top. It looks real pretty when you slice it.

1. Grease an 8-inch square pan. Line it with parchment paper, allowing the paper to come up two of the sides. This will make it easy to remove the fudge and slice it.

2. Combine the sugar, milk, golden syrup or corn syrup, butter, heavy cream, and salt in a large saucepan. (As you cook, the mixture will expand like crazy, so be sure the pot is large enough. A 4-quart pot is a good size, but you'll still need to watch it.) Cook over medium heat, stirring constantly, until the butter is melted and the ingredients are combined. Wash down the sides of the pan with a pastry brush dipped in hot water to get rid of sugar crystals. Just a few crystals on the sides can cause the fudge to recrystallize.

3. Clip a candy thermometer to the side of the pot and continue cooking, stirring frequently, until the mixture reaches 238°F. This whole process may take more than 30 minutes, so be patient. Don't worry if it looks curdled; it will smooth out as it thickens during the beating process.

4. Remove the pan from the heat and wait until the mixture cools to 125°F. Remove the thermometer, add the vanilla and coconut, and beat or stir vigorously with a wooden spoon until the mixture loses its gloss and is very thick, about 10 to 15 minutes. You might want to enlist a friend to help with the beating—you can take turns.

Scrape half the mixture into the prepared pan and smooth the top. If necessary, you can use a piece of plastic wrap and the palm of your hand to do this. Add the food coloring to the remaining half and mix until the color is evenly distributed. Spread it over the first layer. If this seems too complicated, tint the whole lot pink instead of making layers, or don't add the color at all.

5. Cool completely before cutting into 1-inch squares (8 cuts in one direction and 8 cuts in the other). Store in an airtight container. The fudge keeps for several weeks.

Makes 64 pieces

If the mixture gets too hot, the fudge will seize up into a hard, grainy clump when you try to stir it. If it doesn't get hot enough, the fudge will not thicken and will remain a gloopy glump. You can then try to save it by putting it back in the pot with some water (don't worry; the water will evaporate) and reheating it to the correct temperature.

Honeydukes Treats

(continued)

Making little animals such as mice or pigs out of an easy-to-make fondant is a popular activity for British kids. (Real fondant is a much bigger deal to make.)

Sugar Mice

¾ stick (6 tablespoons) butter, at
  room temperature
¼ cup light corn syrup

½ teaspoon pure vanilla extract
3 cups confectioners' sugar, sifted

1. Combine the butter, corn syrup, and vanilla and beat until thoroughly combined. Add the confectioners' sugar slowly on the slowest speed until it forms a dough-like consistency. Add more confectioners' sugar, 1 tablespoon at a time, if the mixture is sticky. Wrap the fondant in plastic wrap and refrigerate until ready to use. It will keep for several months in the refrigerator.
2. To make the sugar mice, pinch off a small piece of fondant and roll into a ½-inch ball. Roll the ball into an oval and pinch one end for the nose and two ends to make pointed ears. You can make two indentations for eyes with a toothpick. Pinch off another piece of dough to form a 1½-inch ball and shape into an oval for the body. Attach the body to the head. You can stick a piece of licorice into the back for the tail. If the fondant gets too soft to work with, put it back in the refrigerator to firm up again.
3. Repeat until all the fondant is used up. Line up the mice on parchment paper and leave out overnight to dry.

Makes about 20 Sugar Mice

Honeydukes Treats

(continued)

Peppermint creams are pieces of peppermint-flavored fondant coated with chocolate. Fondant was invented in the mid-1800s, and this is probably one of its most popular uses. For easy peppermint creams that kids can make and that also taste delicious, see the note that follows.

For easier peppermint creams, use the easy fondant recipe from the Sugar Mice recipe, substituting ¼ teaspoon peppermint extract for the vanilla. Form the fondant into 1½-inch balls and flatten them before placing them on the parchment. You can dip the creams in the melted chocolate right away rather than letting them harden first.

Peppermint Creams

3 cups granulated sugar
¼ teaspoon cream of tartar
1 cup water

¼ teaspoon peppermint extract
10 ounces bittersweet chocolate,
    chopped

1. Place the sugar, cream of tartar, and water in a medium saucepan and clip a candy thermometer to the side of the saucepan. Cook over medium heat without stirring until the mixture reaches 240°F. Pour the hot syrup onto a rimmed baking sheet and cool to 125°F.

2. Use a rubber spatula to scrape and fold the fondant until it turns white, thick, and crumbly, about 10 minutes. Knead until smooth, a few seconds. Wrap in plastic wrap and let it rest overnight.

3. Warm the fondant in the microwave, stirring every 30 seconds for about 2 minutes, until liquidy. Stir in the peppermint extract and cover the surface with plastic wrap. Cool the mixture until lukewarm.

4. Use oiled hands to roll pieces of fondant into 1½-inch balls, oiling hands between rolling as needed. Keep the fondant covered with the plastic wrap as you work, as it dries out quickly. Place the balls on a sheet of parchment paper and leave room for spreading—they will flatten as they cool further. Set aside the cream centers for a few hours to harden.

5. Melt the chocolate. Using two forks, or your hands if you don't mind getting them dirty, dip the cream centers into the chocolate, turn to coat, lift out, and let the excess chocolate drip back into the bowl. Set the candies back onto the parchment paper to harden. Once the chocolate is set, store the peppermint creams in a single layer between sheets of parchment in an airtight container at room temperature for several days.

Makes about 2 pounds (30 pieces)

(continued)

Fizzy Sherbet Pouches

½ cup granulated sugar

½ teaspoon citric acid (see note)

1½ teaspoons baking powder

Rice or wafer paper, cut into 2 dozen 2-inch squares, for making the pouches

> *£evitating sherbet balls! Wow, that would be some treat. In England, balls made of rice paper are filled with a sherbet powder (a sweet powder that fizzes in your mouth). In the Harry Potter books, the fizz is strong enough to lift you off of the ground. Unfortunately, when you make them at home you'll have to imagine you're levitating.*

1. Combine the sugar, citric acid, and baking powder in the bowl of a food processor. Process until combined and the sugar forms finer grains, about 1 minute.

2. Set out 12 of the rice or wafer paper squares. Place a small amount (about ⅛ teaspoon) of the sugar mixture into the middle of each square. Moisten the remaining squares around the edges with water (don't get them too wet, or they will disintegrate) and carefully attach them to the squares that are topped with the sugar. Pinch the edges to seal and lay them out on a sheet of parchment paper to dry. Reserve the remaining powder for another use, such as for dipping lollipops. Or cut out more squares and make more pouches—you can make up to 200 of them with this amount of sugar mixture.

Makes 1 dozen pouches

Citric acid is available in fairly small quantities on the Internet.

Honeydukes Treats

(continued)

Dark Chocolate Truffles

12 ounces bittersweet chocolate, chopped

¾ cup heavy cream

10 ounces bittersweet chocolate, melted

Unsweetened cocoa powder for dusting, optional

To represent the chocolates at Honeydukes, two basic truffle recipes are provided. For most people, the black truffle, a type of mushroom, is too expensive and rare to eat—it has been a delicacy since Roman times. So, toward the end of the 1800s, the chocolate truffle was invented. The classic method for making truffles includes rolling them in cocoa powder so they resemble freshly dug truffles. They look very pretty, but not everyone likes the bitter taste of the cocoa powder, which is why it's an optional ingredient.

1. Place the chopped chocolate and heavy cream in a microwave-safe bowl and microwave for 2 minutes, stopping to stir every 30 seconds, until melted and smooth.
2. Cool the chocolate mixture at room temperature until it stiffens. Pinch off pieces and roll them into 1½-inch balls. Lay the balls on a piece of parchment paper. This is messy work; you may want to stop and rinse your hands from time to time, as the melted chocolate on your palms will make it difficult to roll the balls.
3. Make sure the balls are very stiff before dipping them. You can place the balls in the refrigerator to speed things up. Using two forks, lift the balls one at a time, dip into the melted chocolate, roll to coat, lift out, and allow the excess chocolate to drip back into the bowl before laying the balls back on the parchment.
4. When the chocolate coating has set, peel the balls off the parchment paper and roll them in the cocoa powder, if using. Store in an airtight container. To speed things up, you can put the coated truffles in the refrigerator for 10 minutes, but no longer than that. The condensation can ruin the chocolate.

Makes 2 dozen truffles

Honeydukes Treats

(continued)

White chocolate is not really chocolate. It's made of milk solids, sugar, and flavorings, but it does contain cocoa butter (the fat pressed out of the chocolate mass during processing), which allows it to use the name "chocolate."

White Chocolate Truffles

14 ounces white chocolate, chopped
½ cup heavy cream
10 ounces white chocolate, melted

1. Place the chopped white chocolate and heavy cream in a microwave-safe bowl and microwave for 2 minutes, stopping to stir every 30 seconds, until melted and smooth. Do not overheat the mixture.
2. Cool the mixture at room temperature until it stiffens. Pinch off pieces and roll them into 1½-inch balls. Lay the balls on a piece of parchment paper. This is messy work; you may want to stop and rinse your hands from time to time, as the melted candy on your palms will make it difficult to roll the balls.
3. Make sure the balls are very stiff before dipping them. You can place the balls in the refrigerator to speed things up. Using two forks, lift the balls one at a time, dip into the melted white chocolate, roll to coat, lift out, and allow the excess coating to drip back into the bowl before laying the balls back on the parchment. Allow the coating to set before serving. To speed things up, you can put the truffles in the refrigerator for 10 minutes, but no longer than that. The condensation can ruin them. Store in an airtight container.

Makes 2 dozen truffles

When melting the white chocolate for the coating, be careful not to overheat the chocolate or it will be ruined. Chop the white chocolate and microwave it for 2 minutes, stopping to stir every 30 seconds. If it feels very warm, but you can still see pieces of chocolate, just keep stirring. It may take a good few minutes.

228 The Unofficial Harry Potter Cookbook

Honeydukes Treats

(continued)

These sophisticated candies, soft and melt-in-your-mouth, are for adults to make, as sugar boiling is part of the process. Perfect for gifts, if you can resist eating them before you pack them.

*Bonbons is a French word that literally means "goodies" (*bon *means "good"). In the old days, gentlemen would present their ladies with fancy boxes filled with bonbons. You can place the bonbons in tiny foil holders and put them in fancy boxes to give away as gifts, too.*

If you have any bonbons left over the next day, which is unlikely, you can store them in an airtight container at cool room temperature for weeks.

Date-Walnut-Coconut Bonbons for Grownups to Make

2 cups whole milk

1 cup granulated sugar

1 cup packed dark brown sugar

2 tablespoons golden syrup or light corn syrup

¼ teaspoon salt

1 teaspoon pure vanilla extract

½ cup chopped dates

½ cup finely chopped toasted walnuts

½ cup ground desiccated coconut (you can substitute shredded coconut after grinding it in a food processor)

1. Combine the milk, sugars, golden syrup or corn syrup, and salt in a large saucepan. (As you cook, the mixture will expand like crazy, so be sure the pot is large enough. A 4-quart pot is a good size, but you'll still need to watch it.) Cook over medium heat, stirring constantly, until the sugar is dissolved and the mixture begins to bubble. Wash down the sides of the pan with a pastry brush dipped in hot water to get rid of sugar crystals. Just a few crystals on the sides can cause the candy to recrystallize.

2. Clip a candy thermometer to the side of the pot and continue cooking, stirring frequently, until the mixture reaches 242°F. This whole process may take more than 30 minutes, so be patient. Don't worry if it looks curdled; it will smooth out as it thickens during the beating process.

3. Remove the pan from the heat and add the vanilla, dates, and walnuts. Beat or stir vigorously with a wooden spoon until the mixture loses its gloss and is very thick, about 20 minutes.

4. Press a piece of plastic wrap directly on the surface to prevent a dry crust from forming, and let the mixture cool until it is stiff enough to form into balls. Place the coconut into a bowl. Pinch off pieces of the mixture and roll them into 1- to 1½-inch balls and roll them in the coconut. The balls will be very sticky and soft, so they may flatten a bit when you set them down. Don't worry about getting them perfect. Store in an airtight container. The bonbons will keep for several weeks at room temperature.

Makes about 30 bonbons

(continued)

1-2-3 Chocolate Peanut Butter Crunch Bonbons for Kids

These are called "1-2-3" because you'll be done before you finish counting to three. Also, they are so irresistible that they'll be gone in the same amount of time.

1½ cups confectioners' sugar
1½ cups creamy peanut butter
1 teaspoon pure vanilla extract
1 cup crisp rice cereal
10 ounces milk chocolate, melted, for coating

1. Combine the confectioners' sugar, peanut butter, and vanilla in the large bowl of an electric mixer. Mix on low speed until the mixture begins to come together. Beat on high speed until it reaches a dough-like consistency, with no crumbs. If it's too sticky, add a bit more confectioners' sugar; if it's too dry, add milk, 1 tablespoon at a time. (It's better to avoid adding the milk, as the rice cereal will begin to lose its crunch after several hours due to the added moisture.) Add the rice cereal and mix until combined.

2. Form the mixture into 1½-inch balls and line them up on parchment paper. Using two forks, dip the balls one at a time into the melted chocolate, turn to coat, and then lift out, allowing the excess chocolate to drip back into the bowl. Place the coated candies back onto the parchment paper. Try to wait until the chocolate has set before you eat them. To speed things up, you can put the bonbons in the refrigerator for 10 minutes, but no longer than that. The condensation can ruin the chocolate.

Makes about 30 bonbons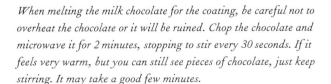

When melting the milk chocolate for the coating, be careful not to overheat the chocolate or it will be ruined. Chop the chocolate and microwave it for 2 minutes, stopping to stir every 30 seconds. If it feels very warm, but you can still see pieces of chocolate, just keep stirring. It may take a good few minutes.

Sources

Author's note: While I used the sources below for my research, any errors in historical fact are my own.

Books

America's Test Kitchen. *The America's Test Kitchen Family Cookbook*. Brookline, MA: America's Test Kitchen, 2006.

Aresty, Esther B. *The Delectable Past*. New York: Simon and Schuster, 1964.

Ayto, John. *An A–Z of Food and Drink*. Oxford: Oxford University Press, 2002.

Broomfield, Andrea. *Food and Cooking in Victorian England: A History*. Westport, CT: Praeger Publishers, 2007.

Davidson, Alan. *The Oxford Companion to Food*. Oxford; New York: Oxford University Press, 2006.

Day, Martha. *Complete Baking*. London: Anness Publishing Ltd., 1999.

Friberg, Bo. *The Professional Pastry Chef*, 4th ed. New York: John Wiley and Sons, Inc., 2002.

Garmey, Jane. *Great British Cooking: A Well-Kept Secret*. New York: HarperCollins Publishers, 1992.

Jones, David. *Candy Making for Dummies*. Hoboken, NJ: Wiley Publishing, Inc., 2005.

Rowling, J. K. *Harry Potter and the Chamber of Secrets*. New York: Arthur A. Levine Books, 1999.

Rowling, J. K. *Harry Potter and the Deathly Hallows*. New York: Arthur A. Levine Books, 2007.

Rowling, J. K. *Harry Potter and the Goblet of Fire*. New York: Arthur A. Levine Books, 2000.

Rowling, J. K. *Harry Potter and the Half-Blood Prince*. New York: Arthur A. Levine Books, 2005.

Rowling, J. K. *Harry Potter and the Order of the Phoenix*. New York: Arthur A. Levine Books, 2003.

Rowling, J. K. *Harry Potter and the Prisoner of Azkaban*. New York: Arthur A. Levine Books, 1999.

Rowling, J. K. *Harry Potter and the Sorcerer's Stone*. New York: Arthur A. Levine Books, 1998.

Spencer, Colin. *British Food: An Extraordinary Thousand Years of History*. New York: Columbia University Press, 2002.

Turner, Brian. *Brian Turner's Favourite British Recipes*. London: Headline Book Publishing, 2005.

Walden, Hilaire. *Traditional British Cooking: The Best of British Cooking: A Definitive Collection*. London: Southwater, 2004.

Websites

www.asf.ca/about_salmon.php?type=cultural
www.bakingforbritain.blogspot.com
www.bbc.co.uk/food/recipes
www.boddingtonsberries.co.uk
www.britannia.com/cooking/recipes
www.browfarm.co.uk
www.carrotmuseum.co.uk/history.html
www.classbrain.com
www.cookitsimply.com
www.cooksillustrated.com
www.cornell.edu
www.denbydale.com
www.flyingswan.com.au/nougat.html-history
www.foodreference.com
www.foodtimeline.org
www.greatbritishkitchen.co.uk
www.greenchronicle.com
www.indepthinfo.com/carrots/history.htm
www.irish-genealogy-toolkit.com/Irish-stew-recipe.html
www.ndwheat.com
www.pbm.com/~lindahl/foc/8cury11.txt
http://samuraiknitter.blogspot.com/search?q=brussels+sprouts
www.thecooksguide.com
www.thefoody.com
www.uktv.co.uk/food
www.urbanext.illinois.edu
www.videojug.com/tag/pie-recipes
www.webmd.com/diet
www.whatscookingamerica.net
www.wikipedia.com

Index

About the Author

Dinah Bucholz's favorite pastime is producing fine desserts and sharing them with her family and neighbors, who take it in turns to be exasperated and appreciative. Mrs. Bucholz has a degree in English and even taught English for a brief period, but teaching was just not her thing. She prefers to cook and write.

Mrs. Bucholz lives in Philadelphia with her husband and five children.